Approaches to Teaching Behn's *Oroonoko*

Approaches to Teaching World Literature

For a complete listing of titles, see the last pages of this book

Approaches to Teaching Behn's *Oroonoko*

Edited by

Cynthia Richards

and

Mary Ann O'Donnell

The Modern Language Association of America
New York 2014

Library of Congress Cataloging-in-Publication Data
Approaches to Teaching Behn's Oroonoko / edited by Cynthia Richards and Mary Ann O'Donnell.
pages cm.— (Approaches to Teaching World Literature ; 127)
Includes bibliographical references and index.
ISBN 978-1-60329-127-9 (cloth : alk. paper)—
ISBN 978-1-60329-128-6 (pbk. : alk. paper)—
ISBN 978-1-60329-171-2 (EPUB)—
ISBN 978-1-60329-172-9 (Kindle)
1. Behn, Aphra, 1640–1689. Oroonoko. 2. Behn, Aphra, 1640–1689—Study and teaching.
I. Richards, Cynthia, editor of compilation. II. O'Donnell, Mary Ann, editor of compilation.
PR3317.O73A67 2013
823'.4—dc23 2013032448

Approaches to Teaching World Literature 127
ISSN 1059-1133

Cover illustration for the paperback and electronic editions: Pietro Tacca's model for a statue from the monument of Ferdinand I de' Medici in Livorno: full-length, seated figure of a slave with his hands bound behind his back and wearing a drapery around his loins. Photograph © Hickey & Robertson, Houston / The Menil Foundation

Published by The Modern Language Association of America
26 Broadway, New York, New York 10004-1789
www.mla.org

For my family.
—CR

For Bernard Dhuicq, Maureen Duffy, Sharon Valiant, pioneers all.
—O'D

CONTENTS

PREFACE

Once merely a footnote in Restoration and eighteenth-century studies and rarely taught, *Oroonoko; or, The Royal Slave* (1688), by Aphra Behn, has now become essential reading for scholars and a classroom favorite—and our survey respondents confirm its popularity. This work can be found in all the expected venues: general surveys, Restoration and eighteenth-century literature courses, early British literature courses, women writers' courses, and courses on the rise of the novel. But it also appears in somewhat less expected places—in courses on Renaissance writers, postcolonial literature, American literature, drama, the slave narrative, and autobiography. Many instructors use it as an exercise in the ethos of reading itself; it can introduce the discipline of reading to the newly declared English major or to the undergraduate just curious about how this discipline works. In seminars on race and empire, where it is frequently placed, it is employed as a cautionary tale, used not only to give the specifics of slavery in the West Indies in the late seventeenth century but also to unsettle students' certainty about the meaning and practice of slavery in general and to challenge associated concepts such as race and freedom. With settings in West Africa and Surinam, the novel's placement in courses in the travel narrative has become a natural fit, the transatlantic context edging out the English as the geographic venue where it most belongs. Given its varied content, *Oroonoko* proves particularly amenable to thematic courses, finding a place in such standard topics courses as Love and Death as well as more customized courses such as Concepts of Male and Female or New World Utopias. A *Google* search extends the possibilities: "*Oroonoko* and syllabus" delivers over twenty thousand hits, strong evidence of the appeal of this text in curricula for tenth-grade high school classes, graduate seminars, and more than a few history courses.

As this range suggests, *Oroonoko*'s popularity in the classroom arises in part from its deceptive simplicity. It is a short text—sixty pages in the Norton Critical Edition—with themes of immediate interest to the novice reader. It tells the story of a captured African prince enslaved in the English colony of Surinam and details his failed insurrection against the white plantation owners and his subsequent horrific death. Before his capture and execution, Oroonoko speaks eloquently about liberty, in a speech unprecedented at a time when England's fortunes were beginning to rely on the forced transportation of Africans to sugar plantations in the New World. Yet *Oroonoko* is not an abolitionist text, despite the narrator's obvious sympathy for Oroonoko and students' even more obvious desire to read it in this way.

The narrator finds Oroonoko's enslavement contemptible, but for her it is primarily his status as prince and his loss of freedom by treachery rather than by conquest that make it so. Behn begins the African phase of Oroonoko's story with his military daring and classical education, and what drives her protest of his condition throughout the novel is his superiority, physically and morally, both in birth and deed, to all around, slavers and slaves alike. Love further complicates the story. Although Oroonoko rebels against his enslavement, he is motivated less by indignation at a practice of slavery divorced from the honor of war than by Imoinda's sighing and weeping over their fate as slaves ([Lipking] 51): it is his great love for his wife and unborn child that spurs him to rebel. Indeed, love leads to one of the novel's most troubling events: the pregnant Imoinda's death at Oroonoko's hands once the insurrection fails. Add to these layers of plot the novel's narration by a white woman, whom students generally want to identify as Behn herself and who seems to profit from his death, and the novel quickly reaches a level of complexity remarkable for what at first seems a simple tale of protest.

Oroonoko's Place in the Canon

Rarely has a text escalated in significance as dramatically as *Oroonoko*. Until the 1970s, *Oroonoko* generated only moderate interest, with that interest fueled by a brief resurgence in attention to Behn's career in the early twentieth century, triggered by Montague Summers's collected edition (*Works* [1915]). Even then, the novel was generally read in the context of her larger body of work and was not published separately. Interest in the novel often took second billing to interest in Behn's unusual life: her time as a spy for Charles II, the rumors of her imprisonment for debt and later for slurring Monmouth publicly, and the reports of her bawdy lifestyle, including hints of a romantic liaison with Oroonoko propagated in a posthumous biographical notice prefacing the 1696 first collected edition of her works (*Histories*). Thus, critical focus tended to center on the truth claims of *Oroonoko* rather than on its story. The logic went that if Behn's life was suspect, so was the veracity of her account of Surinam and of her spying for the king, with some critics even doubting that she had ever been in Surinam or had acted as a spy despite the compelling case for her firsthand knowledge of Surinam made in 1934 by Harrison Platt and the documentation of her spying mission by William Cameron in 1961.

More popular through the eighteenth century was Thomas Southerne's revision of the novel for the stage, also titled *Oroonoko*, along with its various readaptations (see Iwanisziw, Oroonoko). The dramatized versions of *Oroonoko* as well as Shakespeare's *Othello* were the most performed plays of the eighteenth century, appearing on the stage at least once a year for a hundred years (Nussbaum 157). This fame, however, did not translate into Behn's own, for as the eighteenth century grew more sexually conservative and politically liberal, her reputation waned, and the play did little to remedy that. Southerne's version bore no more resemblance to Behn's narrative than it did to *Othello*: Southerne eliminated the account of Oroonoko's life in Coramantien and made his love interest not an African but a white slave. Southerne's Oroonoko is more traditionally heroic: he takes his own life, like Othello, instead of being executed by the white plantation owners. By the end of the eighteenth century and through its near constant reinscription for the stage, Behn's complex prose narrative had become a more straightforward tragedy, one that nominally protested the effects of slavery while diminishing Behn's original portrait of this "Royal Slave." In the popular understanding, little remained of the story that marked it as Behn's and distinguished it as a novel.

Not until 1973, when Norton published *Oroonoko* with an introduction by Lore Metzger, did the text exist in an affordable teaching edition. Metzger's introduction changed the context for understanding Behn's work, linking it with the recovery of women's writing and declaring it fundamental to that tradition. Although Metzger never mentions Virginia Woolf's much quoted mandate that all women should "let flowers fall upon the tomb of Aphra Behn . . . for it was she who earned them the right to speak their minds" (*Room* 66), she does use Woolf to introduce her project of revisiting this text as one notable for its craft as much as for its message. By 1986, when Maureen Duffy published her edition of *Oroonoko*, Behn's story began to be noticed for its "fresh and energetic" style (Oroonoko *and Other Stories* 13). Duffy sees Behn's writing as free of any "taint of racism" and lauds Behn's credentials as "the first authoritative female narrative voice in English secular literature" (11, 13). To this day, Behn's value as a writer continues to be difficult to disengage from her value as a woman writer—a question that Jane Spencer's essay in this volume addresses.

Oroonoko's rapid ascent in the canon resulted not only from its being the product of an authoritative "female pen" but also from the way the novel readily applied to the intersection of the triple axes of race, class, and gender so dominant in literary studies since the 1980s. Ironically, it was one of the less adulatory of the essays addressing this intersection that sealed the text's canonicity, Laura Brown's "The Romance of Empire: *Oroonoko* and the Trade in Slaves," in the influential anthology *The New Eighteenth Century* (1987). Writing at a time when "*Oroonoko* has almost entered the canon" (41), largely because of its extraordinary female narrator-writer, Brown focused instead on the narrator's historical limitations as representative of a colonizing perspective from which even this extraordinary woman could not escape. "In this reading of *Oroonoko* . . . the figure of the woman in the imperialist narrative . . . provides the point of contact through which the violence of colonial history . . . can be represented" (43). Instead of celebrating Behn's craft—her fusion of romance and realism in this novel—Brown pointed to the novel's "failures of discursive coherence" (61), the fissures in the text produced by Behn's conflicting loyalties both to the colonizers and to the colonized.

Thus valorized, *Oroonoko* appeared in 1993 in the sixth edition of *The Norton Anthology of English Literature* (Abrams et al.), the only unabridged prose text by a woman in the volume and one of only fourteen entries by a woman. Since then, it has achieved nothing less than hypercanonicity. Since 1973, when Metzger introduced the Norton *Oroonoko*, close to two dozen editions have been published, over half those after 1985. It is currently anthologized in Blackwell's *British Literature, 1640–1789* (DeMaria), *The Longman Anthology of British Literature* (Damrosch et al.), and *The Norton Anthology of Literature by Women* (Gilbert and Gubar), and in 2001 it was included in the Norton Major Author series (Greenblatt and Abrams). Six editions of *Oroonoko* since 1985 are teaching editions, the two most popular being Joanna Lipking's Norton Critical Edition (1997) and Catherine Gallagher's Bedford Critical Edition (2000). Additional evidence of its popularity is its translations into French, Dutch, Spanish, Catalan, German, and Japanese, among other languages.

Oroonoko's hybrid form and unique history have continued to make the work a useful teaching text even as literary criticism has drifted away from the emphasis on race, class, and gender. Its colonial setting has made it a rich source for new historical and cultural readings. As Srinivas Aravamudan notes, "A book on colonialism and eighteenth-century literature cannot begin without invoking *Oroonoko*" (29). Recent approaches have focused on the figure of Imoinda, one of the few representations of a black woman in the long eighteenth century, and on the myth of Oroonoko, with readers moving freely from the novel to its various theatrical adaptations and their history on the stage (Nussbaum). *Oroonoko* is once again alive on the stage, both literally and figuratively, with both the Royal Shakespeare Company and the Theater for a New Audience in New York City staging productions of *Aphra Behn's* Oroonoko, an adaptation by the Nigerian-born playwright 'Biyi Bandele (in 1999 and 2008, respectively), and with the reintroduction of Thomas Southerne's *Oroonoko* into standard anthologies of Restoration plays. Thus, recent scholarship tends to be comparative: critics compare the novel with one of its many theatrical adaptations or with Behn's *Widdow Ranter*, which is also set in the New World, in the Virginia Colony, and features a doomed English captain, Nathaniel Bacon, whose heroism resembles that of her African prince. *Oroonoko* has emerged once again as a trope independent of its originating text, as Susan B. Iwanisziw's collection *Troping* Oroonoko *from Behn to Bandele* (2004) attests. Derek Hughes makes *Oroonoko* one of the principal works in his 2007 anthology of readings on race for the classroom, *Versions of Blackness: Key Texts on Slavery from the Seventeenth Century*. This collection positions *Oroonoko* as well as Henry Neville's *Isle of Pines*, Behn's *Abdelazer*, and Southerne's *Oroonoko* in sixteenth- and seventeenth-century contexts and "attitudes toward slavery, colonization, black Africans, and Native Americans" that "might have influenced them" (vii). It functions both as a learned exposition on the significance of Behn's literary forays into the arena of race and empire and as a corrective to the application of late-eighteenth-century and contemporary attitudes toward race to these late-seventeenth-century works.

But history is not repeating itself: Oroonoko's dramatized story has not superseded Behn's novel. Recent articles on *Oroonoko* place emphasis again on Behn's craft, positioning the text in literary conventions of the time and now without the qualifier of relating that text to a women's literary tradition.

Issues in Teaching *Oroonoko*

It has become a cliché in teaching to say that there is no right way to read a text, but in the case of *Oroonoko*, this adage is particularly apt. The novel contains not just one story but many, and instructors in the classroom need to address this multiplicity in the novel and avoid privileging any one critical approach to the novel's various themes and issues. Yet for all its appeal, the text continually challenges the instructor as to how best to frame this narrative. The choices of defining contexts are innumerable, and what is at stake in that choice is high.

Is *Oroonoko* the crowning achievement of the first professional woman writer in England, or is it a colonizing narrative that turns its eponymous hero into a pet, as Aravamudan suggests? Is it one of the last novels of the first English novelist, as some have argued, or is it the swan song of the classic romance plot as it is rescripted for a new transatlantic age? Is it in part an autobiography written by one of the century's most remarkable women, or is it an elaborate lie that ultimately reveals its author's artistic and even moral shortcomings? Even framing these questions can prove contentious; for example, although the work is frequently taught in courses on the history of the novel, some critics do not consider it a novel. And when we have so few records of the author's life, how can we even begin to speculate that this work functions autobiographically? Given the complexity of teaching *Oroonoko* and the range of courses in which it can be taught, it is essential to have a thorough materials section providing guideposts for teaching this text. To this end, we include a brief chronology of Behn's life and work with key historical dates of the transatlantic slave trade. Many of the respondents to our questionnaire also noted the usefulness of visual aids, with instructors adding that they often select an edition of the text based on its providing access to these materials. We therefore give references to printed and online maps of Surinam, West Africa, and the routes used during the slave trade, along with illustrations of the treatment of slaves in the West Indies. The amount of scholarship on *Oroonoko* is extensive, making it essential that the volume sift some of these materials for both the student reader and the teacher. In short, the "Materials" section seeks to ease the pedagogical challenges of this text while the organization of the "Approaches" section makes those challenges its underlying theme.

Our contributors—American, Austrian, British, Canadian, and hailing from liberal arts colleges, major research institutions, and state universities—represent a diversity appropriate to this text. Among them are foremost Behn scholars and leading experts in areas related to her novel, such as the slave narrative or Caribbean literature. But many are new scholars—another kind of diversity valuable in conveying the rewarding complexities of *Oroonoko* in the classroom. This volume will not resolve the question of how best to frame this narrative. It will not simplify *Oroonoko*'s meaning, but it will demonstrate how extraordinarily rewarding its complexities are when staged in the classroom.

Part One

MATERIALS

All volumes in the MLA series Approaches to Teaching World Literature develop from a questionnaire sent to teachers and scholars asking for descriptions of courses that use the text in question; the editions used; contextual material for both students and teachers; Internet, electronic, and audiovisual resources used; other literary texts used; and classroom emphases, cruxes, and challenges.

Although we knew that *Oroonoko* was taught widely at the university level, we were still surprised at the variety of courses using the text. In selecting the materials that students of *Oroonoko* should use, we have attempted to match the range of critical approaches and lenses used in those courses. Since it is usually the instructor who guides the student in research and since the materials we have chosen are clear, cogent, and accessible at all levels, we have decided not to separate out materials for instructors from materials for students.

Basic Resources

Students should learn to use, and not just for studying *Oroonoko*, the *Oxford English Dictionary* and the *Oxford Dictionary of National Biography*, both available online at most college and university libraries. A useful guide to online materials and databases for Restoration literature in general is *Literary Research and the British Renaissance and Early Modern Period*, edited by Jennifer Bowers and Peggy Keeran.

Editions

The Works of Aphra Behn, edited by Janet Todd, in seven volumes, is the standard edition. *Oroonoko*, in the third volume, has excellent explanatory notes. All seven volumes are available online and may be purchased by libraries through InteLex (www.nlx.com); they are fully searchable.

Joanna Lipking's Norton Critical Edition of *Oroonoko* is the edition reported by our respondents as the most generally used in the classroom when an anthology is not the chosen text. Because it is scrupulous in following Behn's text while providing sensible emendations that are clearly marked, this is the edition quoted in this volume. For all references to Behn's other works, we use Todd's *Works*.

Classroom Texts

Most of our respondents prefer the old-spelling editions of *Oroonoko*, which also replicate the use of italics for quotations, but some instructors find that their students are better served by a modernized edition. Solid old-spelling texts with intelligent annotation and supporting material are provided by Lipking's Norton Critical Edition, Catherine Gallagher's Bedford Cultural Edition, and Derek Hughes's *Versions of Blackness*. Gallagher's edition reproduces Todd's text (*Works*) and concentrates in the supporting materials on the triangular trade in the late-seventeenth and eighteenth centuries; Hughes's edition attends more closely to the materials of Behn's time. That his carefully vetted text is accompanied by editions of Neville's *Isle of Pines*, Behn's *Abdelazer*, and Thomas Southerne's *Oroonoko* makes his book useful in a course stressing seventeenth-century literature, cultural history, slavery, or attitudes toward race and gender. Lipking, following the Norton Critical Edition format, offers excerpts from contemporary documents on slavery and Surinam, as does Gallagher's Bedford edition, but Lipking's edition also provides excerpts from six influential critical studies.

Among the modernized English editions is Todd's Penguin Classics edition, which has a student-friendly introduction. Her other modernized edition, in Oroonoko, The Rover, *and Other Works*, also with a good introduction, supplies some of Behn's poetry, along with *The Widdow Ranter*. Paul Salzman's World's Classics edition, Oroonoko *and Other Writings*, has a useful introduction and provides five additional short works of fiction and a representative selection of poems. Our respondents found these collections useful when they wished to include other works by Behn.

The anthologies most frequently used by respondents to our questionnaire are *The Norton Anthology of English Literature* (Greenblatt and Abrams) and *The Norton Anthology of Literature by Women* (Gilbert and Gubar), both of which use a modernized version prepared by Lipking; *The Broadview Anthology of British Literature* (Black et al.), which uses a modernized version with reference to Todd's *Works*; and *The Longman Anthology of British Literature* (Damrosch et al.), which also uses a modernized, but unspecified, edition. Our respondents valued these anthologies for their supporting cultural essays and for their useful Web sites, especially Norton's.

Students might find useful an audio recording of *Oroonoko*, read by Elizabeth Klett, available free for download at *LibriVox* and through *iTunes*.

Online Editions

A reliable online text, a transcription of the 1688 first edition, is in the *Chadwyck-Healey Literature Collections: Early English Prose Fiction*. The *Early English Books Online* (*EEBO*) collection provides the digitized images of the original edition as well as of subsequent editions. Less reliable online editions can be found in *Project Gutenberg*, which uses the superseded and sometimes flawed six-volume edition by Montague Summers, and in the *E-Server Fiction* collection, which also presents the Summers text, with additional errors introduced.

Concordances

The fully searchable text of Todd's edition through *Intelex* and the online editions can be used like a concordance, but an online concordance to a modernized *Oroonoko* has been prepared by Mitsuharu Matsuoka on *The Victorian Literary Studies Archive*.

Bibliographies

The standard bibliography of primary and secondary sources for Behn is Mary Ann O'Donnell's second edition, which is close to comprehensive through 2002 (*Aphra Behn*). To keep up with criticism, the annual MLA, Modern Humanities Research Association, and *The Year's Work in English Studies* bibliographies are essential; especially useful for their commentaries and reviews are the journals *Restoration*, *Scriblerian*, and the summer issue of *Studies in English Literature*.

Biographies

The fullest biography to date is Janet Todd's *Secret Life of Aphra Behn*, although it is better on Behn's times and on critical approaches than on framing Behn's life story, much of which remains elusive. Older biographies, by George Woodcock, by Maureen Duffy, and by Angeline Goreau, are still useful. A good short biography is O'Donnell's "Aphra Behn: The Documentary Record," in *The Cambridge Companion to Aphra Behn*, and the chronology that precedes it ("Chronology"). Another good short biography of Behn is Todd's entry in the *Oxford Dictionary of National Biography* ("Behn"). Generally, students should be discouraged from consulting online biographies, with the exception of *Orlando*, as most to date contain inaccuracies.

Monographs

Although a bit outdated, Frederick Link's volume in the Twayne series presents a good overview of Behn's works. Susan Wiseman's volume in the Writers and Their Works series provides a compact introduction to Behn and her works that is especially useful to students. William Cameron's *New Light on Aphra Behn* proves an invaluable study of her spying mission in the mid-1660s, transcribing all the known documents from the Public Record Office and allowing access to the raw voice of a young and troubled Aphra Behn on her spying mission. Cameron also provides a chapter on Behn in Surinam that examines most of the documentary evidence available. Other books devoted to Behn focus on her drama (D. Hughes, *Theatre*; Aughterson; Kreis-Schinck), her poetry (Stapleton), or her literary reputation (Todd, *Critical Fortunes*; Spencer, *Aphra Behn's Afterlife*).

Collected Essays

The only collection dedicated to *Oroonoko* criticism to date is Susan Iwanisziw's *Troping* Oroonoko, comprising five new essays and three reprints. There are several useful collections devoted to Behn's work, all having at least one solid essay on *Oroonoko*. The most popular of these is Hughes and Todd's *Cambridge Companion to Aphra Behn*, a collection of essays that serve both scholar and student. Essays on *Oroonoko* appear in collections edited by Hutner; Todd (*Aphra Behn Studies* and *Aphra Behn*, a New Casebooks volume); O'Donnell, Dhuicq, and Leduc; O'Donnell and Dhuicq; and Lamarra and Dhuicq. These last three collections record proceedings of the Aphra Behn Europe symposia.

Book Chapters and Articles

Essays by Jane Spencer and Lipking present starting places for students and teachers alike. The chapter on *Oroonoko* in Spencer's *Aphra Behn's Afterlife* manages in forty-two pages to supply solid analysis, a survey of key criticisms, and an exploration of later manifestations of the Oroonoko myth. Lipking's "Confusing Matters" captures the main issues that need to be considered when approaching *Oroonoko*—Africa, genre, slavery, and contemporary documents, among others. Germaine Greer's always provocative takes on Behn can best be sampled in a general survey of her life and works in Susanne Woods and Margaret P. Hannay's *Teaching Tudor and Stuart Women Writers*.

Jacqueline Pearson's two-part study of gender and narrative remains essential reading on Behn's narrative techniques and use of language, especially pronouns, in *Oroonoko*. Also focusing on the vexing role of the narrator, Robert Chibka examines trust, betrayal, and truth claims in an article frequently cited by our respondents ("'Oh!'"). Ros Ballaster addresses issues of spectacle and eroticism in *Oroonoko* and examines authority and empowerment in an essay that is accessible also for students ("'Devil'"). In "New Hystericism," she discusses the intersections of feminist and historicist criticism in an essay that can profitably be read, as one of our respondents has noted, against Spencer's section on Behn in *The Rise of the Woman Novelist* and against Laura Brown's "Romance of Empire."

Brown's often reprinted "Romance of Empire" is one of the most referenced essays by our respondents and by our contributors, whether to further develop Brown's analyses of race, gender, politics, slavery, the Europeanization of the hero, and the stance of the narrator—or to take issue with these same analyses. Reading Brown's work in conversation with the work of others is worth the exercise. Other frequently cited essays are Catherine Gallagher's "Who Was That Masked Woman?" and "The Author-Monarch and the Royal Slave: *Oroonoko* and the Blackness of Representation." The first seeks to show that Behn "introduced to the world the professional woman writer as a newfangled whore" (14); the second seeks to relate Oroonoko's skin color to the blackness of print. Margaret Ferguson's "Juggling the Categories of Race, Class, and Gender" focuses on the narrator's use of personal pronouns but then moves on to issues of the narrator's fear and desire related to her Royal Slave's sexuality. Susan Andrade's "White Skin, Black Masks" raises issues of imperialism. Although these essays by Brown, Gallagher, Ferguson, and Andrade are influential studies of *Oroonoko*, they must be read with Hughes's "Race, Gender, and Scholarly Practice," as Hughes deconstructs the focus of these essays and several others on race, sexual rivalry, and miscegenation.

Discussions of Race and Slavery

Race and slavery form twin axes for students and teachers alike as they address the many vexing issues in *Oroonoko*. The best single introduction to the slave trade in Behn's time is Lipking's "The New World of Slavery." Seventeenth-century concepts of race are discussed in several of the essays in this Approaches volume, especially Hughes's. See also his enlightening introduction to *Versions of Blackness* (vii–xxviii). Students will find in Gallagher's introduction to her edition materials on the triangular trade, the literary tradition, and concepts of kingship (Introduction); Gallagher also provides accessible headnotes to the chapters and individual readings. Respondents praise Roxann Wheeler's work, especially *The Complexion of Race*, for helping students grasp the development of racial consciousness in the seventeenth and early eighteenth centuries, and they recommend Nicholas Hudson's "From 'Nation' to 'Race'" as a companion piece. While Kim Hall's *Things of Darkness* does not directly address *Oroonoko*, it reprints twenty-six Renaissance and early modern poems on blackness that can be used in context with *Oroonoko*. The best sources for further study of race and slavery can be found in the bibliographies of Hughes's *Versions* and Wheeler's works and the materials excerpted in Hughes's *Versions* and Lipking's Norton Critical Edition.

A number of reliable Web sites are related to the British slave trade. Brycchan Carey's *Slavery, Abolition, and Emancipation* contains, among a wide variety of resources, a time line of the British slave trade from 1400 to the beginning of the twentieth century (www.brycchancarey.com/slavery/). The Web site of the International Slavery Museum in Liverpool provides documents on the trade triangle, European traders, slave ships, a bibliography, and additional links (www.liverpoolmuseums.org.uk/ism/slavery/). The National Archives' *Caribbean Histories Revealed* has images, documents, and a downloadable map (www.nationalarchives.gov.uk/caribbeanhistory/). Although James Handler and Michael L. Tuite's Web site on the Atlantic slave trade focuses predominantly on North America, the site is regularly updated and provides a number of useful images and maps related to Caribbean and South American slavery (hitchcock .itc.virginia.edu/slavery/index.php).

Historical Approaches

Many instructors approach *Oroonoko* through historical analysis, especially in relation to Behn's political support for the Stuart kings Charles II and his brother, James II. An early study of Behn's use of the crises of James II's reign can be found in George Guffey's "Aphra Behn's *Oroonoko*," which also examines contemporary accounts of Surinam and Africa. Richard Kroll expands Guffey's thesis that Behn used *Oroonoko* to solicit sympathy for James II. His "'Tales of Love and Gallantry': The Politics of *Oroonoko*" is must reading for any instructor seeking to grasp the political chaos of 1688. Kroll reads *Oroonoko* as an open warning to James II that he risks the same fate that befell his father, Charles I, deposition and execution. Brown's "The Romance of Empire" also explores the connection between *Oroonoko* and Charles I.

Kroll's essay signals a new trend in Behn criticism in its placement of Behn in a classical tradition. She probably did not know Latin yet published a paraphrased translation of Ovid, wrote appreciative poems for editions of Lucretius and Juvenal, and in her poetical miscellanies published translations from Greek and Latin poets rendered by a coterie of university fellows. Several studies pursue the classical influences in *Oroonoko*. David Hoegberg's "Caesar's Toils" attends to Oroonoko's relation to Achilles, Hercules, and Caesar, and O'Donnell's "Myth and Mythmaking" expands on Hoegberg's essay to discuss Behn's use of Apollodorus, especially in *Oroonoko*.

The Oxford Dictionary of National Biography is a major online source for tracking historical figures of the period, even though some of those referred to in *Oroonoko*—for instance, Trefry and Byam—do not have entries (although Byam is noted in his father's entry). The BBC's *British History in Depth* (www.bbc.co.uk/history/british) presents modules on all aspects of British history, but especially useful are the modules "Civil War and Revolution (1603–1714)," "Empire and Sea Power (1714–1837)," and "Abolition of the Slave Trade." An interactive time line is also provided on the site.

Comparative Approaches

For those interested in a comparative approach using subsequent dramatic versions, Iwanisziw's anthology Oroonoko*: Adaptations and Offshoots* provides texts from Southerne's to 'Biyi Bandele's (but not Behn's) with short commentary. Hughes's *Versions of Blackness* is also a valuable comparative text. A student-friendly article comparing Behn's and Southerne's texts is Laura Rosenthal's "Owning Oroonoko." Other juxtapositions of Behn's and Southerne's versions can be found in this Approaches volume, particularly in the essays by Scott J. Juengel; Joyce Green MacDonald; Jane Milling and Cynthia Richards; and to some extent Jessica Munns. Munns also reads Behn's *Oroonoko* against Bandele's, a reading supplemented by Elizabeth Kowaleski-Wallace in her *The British Slave Trade and Public Memory*. However, Munns's and Kowaleski-Wallace's approaches should be read with Anne F. Widmayer's demurral, which finds that Bandele's work "overwhelms and overwrites" Behn's text, muting its moral ambiguity (193). Gary Gautier's "Slavery and the Fashioning of Race" expands the examination of racial differences to study class differences not just in *Oroonoko* but also in *Robinson Crusoe* and Olaudah Equiano's *Interesting*

Narrative, providing provocative comparisons. Anyone using Equiano's work with *Oroonoko* should consult Vincent Carretta's biography of Equiano and his edition of *The Interesting Narrative*.

Surinam

Surinam itself offers an avenue of study. Even though John Gabriel Stedman wrote about Surinam a century after Behn published *Oroonoko*, his *Narrative of a Five Years' Expedition against the Revolted Negroes of Surinam* provides enough similarities to make it a profitable comparison. The early editions of this work were bowdlerized by a proslavery editor, so the recommended reading text is the 1988 edition, edited by Richard Price and Sally Price. Both the original and the new editions contain engravings of Stedman's artwork illustrating scenes that are likely close to what Behn herself may have seen. Most notable are sixteen plates signed by William Blake, including depictions of tortured slaves. Another point of access can be made by pairing Behn and *Oroonoko* with the life and work of Maria Sibylla Merian, the artist and natural philosopher who studied and illustrated the flora, insects, and fauna of the Dutch-held colony of Surinam in the late 1690s. Sharon Valiant's groundbreaking article on Merian is invaluable. Also useful is Natalie Zemon Davis's chapter on Merian in her *Women on the Margins*. Other recommended studies of Surinam and the Caribbean slave trade are by Hilary Beckles and Verene Shepherd and by Michael Craton.

Other Approaches

Oroonoko can also be studied in terms of genre, of women's studies, of class stratification, of colonialism and postcolonialism, of Caribbean and transatlantic or circumatlantic studies. Among the criticisms most highly valued by the respondents to our questionnaire is Srinivas Aravamudan's "Petting Oroonoko," which helps position the narrator in terms of the Restoration penchant for pets and provides a surprisingly different way to read the narrator. Felicity Nussbaum, in her *The Limits of the Human*, pushes the commonplace of race and gender to include the anomalous, seen as a deviation of either biological or social construct, and uses that to probe issues of white women, black men, and women of color—including Imoinda. While attending to *The Widdow Ranter*, Richard Frohock moves the discussion to class and natural hierarchy ("Violence").

Colonial and postcolonial approaches appear in a number of articles—Aravamudan's and Brown's, for example. A valuable article for students and teachers is Albert J. Rivero's "*Oroonoko* and the 'Blank Spaces' of Colonial Fictions," an article hard to categorize as it lays a foundation of comparative colonialism with Joseph Conrad's *Heart of Darkness*, raises the relation between Behn's work and travel literature (including *The Odyssey*), sees the novel as a "work of mourning" (447), all while providing a close textual analysis of the complications of the story. Using *The Tempest* as a point of comparison, Stephanie Athey and Daniel Cooper Alarcón also have explored issues of colonial constructions of race and gender and the commodification of human beings, as does Andrade.

Any discussion of genre should start with Michael McKeon's *Origins of the English Novel*, but one of our respondents urges that his approach be read against Spencer's *Rise of the Woman Novelist*. Whether *Oroonoko* is the first American novel has been addressed by William Spengemann, whose "Earliest American Novel" is widely cited and has proved important in opening up British Atlantic studies. Frohock, in *Heroes of Empire*, studies the impact of the discovery of the New World, its assimilation into the literary consciousness of English authors, and the presentation of the heroic figure in narratives of the New World. In addition to *The Widdow Ranter*, he examines Behn's rarely discussed poem on Albemarle's appointment as governor of Jamaica.

Maps and Illustrations

Both Gallagher's and Lipking's editions include maps and illustrations that can enhance the teaching of *Oroonoko*. Both reproduce contemporary maps of Surinam from the John Carter Brown Library (http://jcb.lunaimaging.com/luna/servlet/JCBMAPS~/~/), maps of the slave trade, and a view of Fort Coramantine (Behn's Coramantien). Gallagher includes several sketches from the dramatic adaptations, and Lipking reproduces the famous mezzotint of Anne Bracegirdle in *The Indian Queen*, featuring a full feathered headdress such as Behn mentions in *Oroonoko*. A major collection of 189 maps along with charts, graphs, and informative section introductions related to all aspects of the slave trade, David Eltis and David Richardson's *Atlas of the Transatlantic Slave Trade* is the kind of reference anyone teaching *Oroonoko* wants available in the library. The near-contemporary maps of Surinam (or Guianas) reproduced by Lipking and Gallagher are available on the Web site of the John Carter Brown Library database *Archive of Early American Images*. These maps are enlargeable and can be printed. This site is invaluable in classroom presentations to show such places as Byam's Point and Parham Hill as well as some seventeenth-century representations of the indigenes. Nine useful maps from Eltis and Richardson's *Atlas of the Transatlantic Slave Trade* can be found in the *Voyages Database*, an important site for materials on all aspects of the slave trade, sponsored by Emory University (www.slavevoyages.org/tast/database/index.faces). Northwestern University's Melville J. Herskovits Library of African Studies provides maps and other materials related to Africa and the slave trade (www.northwestern.edu/african-studies/herskovits-library/index.html).

Additional Online Resources

Alan Liu's *Voice of the Shuttle* has extensive online materials on Behn, the Restoration, and slavery (http://vos.ucsb.edu/), and Jack Lynch's *Eighteenth-Century*

Resources, last updated in 2006, has some background material and useful links (http://andromeda.rutgers.edu/~jlynch/18th/). While most of our respondents have not used the Web much in teaching *Oroonoko* so far, those who do consider *Luminarium* a useful site to access poetry by Behn and her contemporaries (www.luminarium.org). Students can find relevant material posted on two subscription databases that might be available in the instructor's library: *Orlando* and *Women Writers Online*.

The site of the Aphra Behn Society, which covers a large range of women writers, is noted by our respondents as useful more for the instructor than for the student. In 2011, the Society site launched its journal, *Aphra Behn Online: Interactive Journal for Women in the Arts, 1640–1830*, an annual forum on women in the arts between 1640 and 1830, edited by Laura Runge and focusing on scholarly articles, pedagogy, reviews, and Web publications (www.aphrabehn.org/ABO/).

Finally, *Invitation to a Funeral* is a site that students might enjoy. Although posted to promote a novel of the same name featuring Behn, the site invites students to review the cast of historical characters, with generally accurate brief information, and to sample the food, sights, and sounds of London (www.okima.com).

As research on Behn continues apace, it will prove easier to keep track of print media than Web sites. Publications on Behn are reviewed in such venues as *Restoration*, *Scriblerian*, and *Studies in English Literature*, but Web materials are generally elusive and not critiqued. It appears that a review of Web sites that cover Behn will be a feature of the new *Aphra Behn Online*. That will help a great deal.

Chronology

1562 England begins trading in slaves as Sir John Hawkins takes a shipload of African captives to Hispaniola.

1596 Sir Walter Raleigh's *Discoverie of the Large, Rich and Bewtiful Empyre of Guiana* is published.

1607 The colony of Jamestown, Virginia, is settled.

1614 Bermuda comes under the British Crown. Slaves arrive within the next five years.

1625 James I dies and is succeeded by his son, Charles I. England takes control of Barbados. Sugar becomes a main crop over the next twenty-five years.

1631 Charles I gives a group of merchants a patent to trade with Guinea.

1640 It is generally accepted that 14 December is the date of Behn's birth as Eaffrey or Aphra, daughter of Bartholomew Johnson, a barber, and Elizabeth Denham Johnson, a wet nurse, in Harbledown, Canterbury.

1642 Theaters are closed; the Civil War breaks out.

1647 John Wilmot, later earl of Rochester, is born.

1649 Charles I is executed 30 January, and the Commonwealth period begins.

1653 Oliver Cromwell is named lord protector. Margaret Cavendish's *Poems and Fancies* and *Philosophicall Fancies* are published.

1655 England takes control of Jamaica. Lord Willoughby issues a prospectus to develop his colony, Surinam.

1658 Oliver Cromwell dies. His son Richard assumes the role of protector 3 September.

1660 Charles II returns to London from France on his thirtieth birthday, 29 May. King's Men (established by Thomas Killigrew) and Duke's Men (established by William Davenant) are given patents to open theaters. Women appear on stage. Thomas Southerne is born.

1661 Charles II is crowned 23 April.

1662 Charles II marries Catherine of Braganza, a Catholic. The Royal Society of London for Improving Natural Knowledge is founded. Cavendish's *Playes* is published.

1663 It is probably in this year that Behn goes to Surinam, which is under the governorship of Lord Willoughby of Parham.

1664 The Second Anglo-Dutch War starts. Dryden and Sir Robert Howard's *The Indian Queen* is produced. The feathers that Behn says she brought back from Surinam were probably not used for this production but for a later revival of it. By March, she probably leaves Surinam and begins to write *The Young King*. If she ever married, she probably married in this year. Katherine Philips ("The Matchless Orinda") dies.

1665 The Great Plague spreads to London; theaters close on 5 June for sixteen months.

1666 The plague abates thanks in part to brutal frosts of the winter of 1665–66. The Great Fire rages through London 2–6 September. If there was a Mr. Behn, he probably died in the plague at this time. Behn spies for the Crown against the Dutch. In September, she warns Whitehall of a Dutch naval plan to attack the Thames. In debt, she borrows £150 to return to England, around December. Cavendish's *The Description of a New World, Called the Blazing World* is published.

1667 Behn returns to London deeply in debt, probably in early January. She tries to recoup personal losses incurred in the service of the Crown. In a surprise attack, the Dutch sail into the Thames and then up the Medway to destroy a number of British ships. This is the attack Behn had warned Whitehall of, but her warning was ignored. The Treaty of Breda ends war with the Dutch and gives them Surinam in exchange for the Dutch holdings of New Amsterdam (New York and environs), 21 July. Milton publishes the first version of *Paradise Lost* (10 books).

The authorized edition of Katherine Philips's *Poems* and the folio edition of her *Works* are published. Cavendish publishes the biography of her husband, the duke of Newcastle.

1668 Behn petitions the Court to prevent her imprisonment for debt. There is no evidence that she was ever in debtor's prison.

1670 Behn's first play, *The Forc'd Marriage*, is produced.

1671 Behn's *The Amorous Prince* is produced.

1672 The Third Anglo-Dutch War begins; it ends in 1674. The Royal African Company is given the patent to control the English slave trade; its monopoly is ended in 1698.

1673 Behn's *The Dutch Lover* is produced but is not successful. James, duke of York (later James II), marries as his second wife a Catholic, Mary of Modena. As a result of York's open Catholicism, the Test Act is passed to exclude Catholics and nonconformists from all aspects of public affairs. The Royal African Company opens up slave trade with the West Indies. Cavendish, duchess of Newcastle, dies.

1674 The Third Anglo-Dutch War ends. Milton's *Paradise Lost* is published (12 books). Milton dies.

1675 Christopher Wren prepares to restore Saint Paul's Cathedral, which had been destroyed in the Great Fire.

1676 Nathaniel Bacon leads a rebellion against the colonial government of Virginia and attacks Native American settlements. He dies, probably of dysentery. Bacon's Rebellion later forms the central event of Behn's *The Widdow Ranter*. Her *Abdelazer* and *The Town-Fopp* are produced.

1677 William of Orange marries his cousin Mary, daughter of James, duke of York (later James II), and of the late Ann Hyde, duchess of York. Behn's *The Rover* is produced.

1678 Titus Oates precipitates the Popish plot by alleging that Catholics are scheming to seize control of the country. Behn's *Sir Patient Fancy* is produced.

1679 The Exclusion Crisis attempts to keep the Catholic brother of Charles II, James, duke of York, from the succession and leads to James's exile. The Licensing Act is not renewed; plays no longer have to be approved for presentation. Behn's *The Feign'd Curtizans* and *The Young King* are produced.

1680 John Wilmot, earl of Rochester, dies. His *Poems* is published in an unauthorized edition and includes several poems by Behn.

1681 The earl of Shaftesbury attempts to secure the Protestant succession through Charles II's illegitimate son James, duke of Monmouth. Shaftesbury is arrested for treason, but the charge is dismissed. Monmouth is arrested and released. Dryden publishes *Absalom and Achitophel*, which satirizes Shaftesbury's actions. Behn's *The Second Part of* The Rover, *The False Count*, and *The Roundheads* are produced.

1682 The United Company is formed from the Duke's Men and the King's Men. Behn's *The City-Heiress* is produced. The prologue and epilogue to her *Romulus and Hersilia* result in a warrant for her arrest, although there is no evidence that the warrant was executed. The elopement of Lady Henrietta Berkeley and her brother-in-law, Ford, Lord Grey of Werke, forms the basis of Behn's *Love-Letters between a Noble-Man and His Sister*.

1683 The Rye House Plot to assassinate Charles II is uncovered.

1684 Behn's *Poems upon Several Occasions* is published. Part 1 of *Love-Letters between a Noble-Man and His Sister* is published.

1685 Charles II dies 6 February, and the theaters close for ten weeks. James II is crowned 23 April. Monmouth's Rebellion is put down at Sedgemoor. Monmouth is executed 15 July. Part 2 of Behn's *Love-Letters between a Noble-Man and His Sister* is published.

1686 Behn's *The Luckey Chance* is produced.

1687 Behn's *The Emperor of the Moon* is produced. Her *To the Most Illustrious Prince Christopher Duke of Albemarle on His Voyage to His Government of Jamaica* is published. Part 3 of her *Love-Letters between a Noble-Man and His Sister* is published.

1688 The birth of a son in June, James Francis Edward (later the Old Pretender), to James II sets off a succession crisis. Because the new male heir to the throne is Catholic, James II's Protestant daughter Mary, wife to William of Orange, also a Protestant, is removed from the immediate royal succession, and James II finds himself under intensified attack over religion. In the Glorious or Bloodless Revolution, William of Orange (who as nephew of Charles II and James II has a claim to the throne) is invited by a group of English nobles to take the throne and so invades England in November. James II flees to France. Behn's *The Fair Jilt*, *Oroonoko*, and *Agnes de Castro* are published separately and reissued in *Three Histories*.

1689 William and Mary are crowned 11 April. Behn dies 16 April and is buried in the East Cloister of Westminster Abbey. Her play *The Widdow Ranter* is produced; Dryden writes the prologue and epilogue for it.

1690 Locke's *Essay concerning Human Understanding* and *Two Treatises on Government* are published.

1694 Queen Mary dies. Southerne's *The Fatal Marriage*, his adaptation of Behn's *The History of the Nun*, is produced. Mary Astell publishes *A Serious Proposal to the Ladies*.

1695 Southerne's stage adaptation of Behn's *Oroonoko* is produced. Catharine Trotter's dramatization *Agnes de Castro* is presented at Drury Lane.

1696 Southerne's *Oroonoko* is published. *An Essay in Defense of the Female Sex*, attributed to Judith Drake, is published. Behn's *The Younger Brother* is produced and later published with the earliest biographical notice of Behn.

1698 The monopoly on the slave trade held by the Royal African Company is ended.

1700 Dryden dies.

1701 James II dies in exile.

1702 King William dies and is succeeded by Mary's sister Anne, the second daughter of James II.

1714 Queen Anne dies, leaving no surviving children; thus ends the Stuart reign. George I, elector of Hanover, becomes king.

1746 Southerne dies.

1759 Hawkesworth's adaptation of Southerne's *Oroonoko* is presented with David Garrick as Oroonoko and Susannah Cibber as Imoinda. It is also published.

1760 Francis Gentleman's adaptation of Southerne's *Oroonoko* is published in Glasgow, dedicated to James Boswell. Another adaptation of Southerne's *Oroonoko* is published anonymously.

1772 Lord Mansfield's ruling in the Somerset slave case is used to free slaves in England.

1787 The Society for the Abolition of the Slave Trade is founded.

1788 *The Prince of Angola*, John Ferriar's redaction of Hawkesworth's *Oroonoko*, is published.

1789 Equiano publishes his biography.

1796 Stedman's illustrated account of his assignment in Surinam to put down a slave rebellion (1772–73) is published, an important abolitionist work. William Blake provides some of the illustrations.

1797 Equiano dies.

1807 Parliament's Slave Trade Act abolishes transatlantic slave trading throughout the empire.

1833 With the Slavery Abolition Act, Parliament emancipates all slaves in all British colonies from 1834 on.

1999 'Biyi Bandele's greatly revised version of Hawkesworth's adaptation of Behn's *Oroonoko* is produced and published.

Part Two

APPROACHES

Introduction

Remarkably, for all the complexity of teaching *Oroonoko*, little has been written on how to approach the novel in the classroom. It is not that scholars fail to recognize the difficulties of teaching this text; rather, the enthusiasm with which it has been embraced and the speed with which it has risen to prominence have left little space and time for pedagogical reflection. Consider, then, this volume as that much-needed collective pause—the volume serving as both a primer on teaching *Oroonoko* and a venue for reflecting on the politics of discussing a text that can never be fully divorced from its historical and cultural contexts or the fluid interpretative practices of today's classrooms. Both James Grantham Turner and Erik Bond, in this volume, point to the pedagogical bonanza of a text so amenable to a variety of interpretative practices. *Oroonoko* can build the confidence of the student as interpreter in the introductory literature course (Turner) and instill caution in the instructor preparing to teach rather than dictate those interpretative skills (Bond).

Yet to expect reflection to stop production of still more ways of reading *Oroonoko* would be unrealistic. In the opening essay, Srinivas Aravamudan identifies over twenty generic frames for reading the work while at the same time eloquently simplifying it as a meditation on kind, with all the attendant meanings of *kind*, including the fundamental manifestation, humankind. Teaching *Oroonoko* necessarily produces new ways of looking at it, and this volume identifies approaches to the text yet to appear in scholarly form. For example, Sharon Alker and Holly Faith Nelson remind us of the prevalence of war in this text, and Laura Rosenthal points to the strong presence in it of a cosmopolitanism that embraces an emerging ethos of global citizenship.

Oroonoko gives rise to so many questions in the classroom. For example, is the story primarily Behn's own? As many critics have argued, this novel seems key to her life story and evinces a personal vulnerability rarely seen in her other works. It offers details about her time in Surinam, reflects on the Tory and Whig politics of her period, and hints at her fears of her approaching death. Behn uses a narrator who speaks in the first person and who openly claims that Oroonoko's fame relies on the power of her "Female Pen" (36)—a point that some have noted implicates Behn in his trade by suggesting that her female pen, like her narrator's, will profit from his enslavement and death. In blunter terms, Behn sells Oroonoko once again. The narrator can seem so close to Behn that for students it may prove hard to detect any difference at all between them. Yet instructors cannot present the text as simple autobiography; there is too much self-conscious craft in it. As she readied *Oroonoko* for publication in mid-1688 in England, just months before James II's flight to France and just months before her death, Behn returned to a time and space, Surinam in the 1660s, that was inaccessible to her, as the colony had been traded to the Dutch at the end of the Second Anglo-Dutch War. The text, then, is retrospective, a self-conscious reflection from a distance on that time, its politics, and even the narrator herself. Thus, instructors must gingerly address the question of Behn's voice in the text or they will risk ignoring what is truly radical in this work: Behn's crafting of an unprecedented history of an African slave and the troubling silences that pepper the text and that suggest the author's colonizing complicity in Oroonoko's fate.

Certainly, instructors must acknowledge the centrality of Oroonoko's story. As many have argued, the significance of the novel lies in the attention it draws to the long-lasting effects of colonialism on the representation of the other in literary history. Hence the more cleanly we can extract Oroonoko's story from the prevailing ideologies that influenced Behn's representation—the imminent Glorious Revolution and Behn's royalist sympathies, the incipient racism of her period, the brutal economic realities of a new mercantile state, and an overly simplistic equation of the female condition with that of the enslaved African—the more illuminating Oroonoko's story will become. Yet, even filtered from these influences, Oroonoko remains a complicated hero in the classroom. At times he is the traditional epic hero, fighting battles in Africa, struggling with tigers and numb eels in Surinam, yet at the moment we expect action from him, he exhibits "passive valor" instead (50). In this volume, both Shawn Lisa Maurer and Laura Runge address the complexity of his heroism; Maurer views him as a "transitional figure" for a new model of masculinity, while Runge links his unreliable heroism with the already compromised heroes of Milton and Dryden. Oroonoko's story proves entangled with Behn's political, cultural, and literary sensibilities and the politics of a Christian nation for which martyrdom was a potent political and religious symbol.

Even Imoinda, a seemingly minor character, could rightfully claim priority in the classroom. Students may view her as the character who acts most consistently in the story—even more heroically than Oroonoko, as Jane Milling and Cynthia Richards point out in their essay. It is she who fights alongside Oroonoko in the short-lived rebellion, she who first encourages the insurrection, and she who can survive intact both the predations of the old African king and the threats of sexual violation as a slave in Surinam. Imoinda is the one character whom neither Behn nor the white plantation owners can appropriate, and hers is the last name Behn mentions. Despite her slave name of Clemene, Imoinda retains her African name after enslavement, even when Oroonoko is reestablished as Caesar, as Bill Overton details in his essay in this volume. But if instructors highlight Imoinda's story, do they make *Oroonoko* more conservative than its author intended? Imoinda dies happily at the hands of her husband, accepting an estimate of her value antithetical to the early feminism we associate with Behn's writing. Yet not to tell her story risks effacing a rare narrative account of an African woman.

How do we do justice to the complexity of this novel while at the same time providing clearly defined categories that aid in its instruction? How do we engage students at their level while pushing them toward a more sophisticated understanding? For students, the novel seems immediately an abolitionist text, one that promises a sympathetic account of a royal slave and the hope of a thorough denunciation of a historical racism still difficult to acknowledge, much less accept. Yet from Behn's opening description of Surinam and her cool presentation of the economics that led to the use of transported Africans for the grueling labor of sugar harvesting, students sense that the novel will not deliver on that promise. The succeeding account of Oroonoko in Africa and of his thwarted love for Imoinda further confuses them. Is this work a romance novel or a slave narrative, and can Oroonoko be viewed as a hero of emancipation if he is himself a trafficker in slaves? Arguably, Behn intended her opening as a stabilizing point of reference for her audience, revealing Oroonoko's princely status and claims to honor both in matters of state and in matters of love, but for students today his rank and claims can just as readily create a moral morass.

Even more important than such concerns can be the quick and unexpected evidence of what our students take to be racism: Behn's description of the physical perfection of Oroonoko, a perfection that arises from his similarity to European notions of beauty and his difference from African ones. This description alone can elicit denunciations of the text and stymie further conversation in the classroom. This volume contains several essays that address this concern. Ana de Freitas Boe examines it in detail. How do we explain the complex politics and cultural codes that make Oroonoko's rank and education matter more to Behn than his race, without ignoring the way the representation of race in the text compromises her vision?

The introduction of the second section of the novel and what students typically take to be the real novel—Oroonoko's experience as a slave in Surinam—usually shifts the focus. Students interested in the romance plot will be surprised to see it transform into a realistic, political narrative. Yet in general the second section of the novel appears closer to what they expect, and Behn's description of the insurrection and Oroonoko's passionate protest of his enslavement confirms their hope that the novel is an early attack on slavery. But even in this section of the novel, students can feel cheated. Oroonoko is not the hero they want him to be. He harshly criticizes his fellow slaves when they lose courage and surrender to the plantation owners, he does not follow through on his plans to attack his oppressors after killing Imoinda, and he seems too easily diverted by the narrator's stories and schemes. Some students even suggest that he is upstaged by Imoinda, who never veers from a more traditional heroic role. They are unsure to whom their sympathy belongs, and the instructor can be at a loss to balance the novelistic demands of emotional identification with Behn's innovative and fluid technique.

The ending of the novel usually resolves that dilemma. Oroonoko's stoicism in the face of death marks him as heroic. But students may still be angry at Behn, protesting that she goes too far to gain their sympathy for the hero. Even for those inured to the gore of violent video games and horror movies, Behn's detailed recitation of Oroonoko's dismemberment can appear excessive. The novel gives students more than they wanted to know about the cruelties of slavery. As a result, the novel can seem defined solely by its most graphic moment.

Approaches to teaching *Oroonoko* are, then, as diverse as is this text and are complicated by its perplexing hybridity. Thus, although standard rubrics have been chosen for this volume—formal and thematic contexts, pedagogical contexts, comparative contexts, and authorial contexts—most of its essays answer to more than one of these categories and could be positioned under a different rubric. Issues of slavery are addressed in a paper on economics, of Tory politics in a paper on paracolonialism, of the influence of Milton and Dryden in a paper on heroism. Race and gender, not surprisingly, are the most diffuse and most common issues for framing the text. Two essays, namely Derek Hughes's and Vincent Carretta's, address race, and Laura Stevens's specifically addresses gender, but the significance of race and gender permeates the volume. And even in these cases, these essays are not exclusively about race and gender but acknowledge other qualifying factors, both geographic and historical. Difference in class is addressed in nearly all the essays; in Karen Gevirtz's, however, it becomes, surprisingly, one way in which American students can relate to the novel. Recognizing that Behn's novel is difficult to pin down, we have preferred to allow the variety of essays to interrogate the work itself and then one another to allow for the widest possible range of intersecting and sometimes conflicting approaches, since this best represents the essence of the classroom encounter between students and text, between teacher and students, between this text and related texts.

Because this volume strives to make the complexity of Behn's text manageable in the classroom, we begin by addressing the formal and thematic uncertainties. We ask, with Aravamudan, "What kind of story is this?" Employing a strategy that both complicates the answer to this question and eloquently simplifies it, Aravamudan has students "make a list of the many kinds of story implied" from which a discussion of interpretative practices and contexts will naturally follow. From understanding different kinds of stories, students can move to understanding the classifications of different kinds of human beings in the story, and the ethical implications of what constitutes our kindred. Keith Botelho places *Oroonoko*'s classificatory exercises in the context "of a larger discursive network" intent on distinguishing fact from fiction in the late-seventeenth-century growth of the news industry and the establishment in 1662 of the Royal Society, the first learned scientific society in England. Just as Oroonoko learns to be less credulous as the novel progresses, so can students learn to read with suspicion the narrator's claims that she is telling the truth. Rose Zimbardo also uses the Royal Society as a starting point for understanding the language of the novel, arguing that *Oroonoko* can "demonstrate to students a key transition in poetic mimesis," the movement from the Renaissance "discourse of patterning" to the "discourse of modernism," the language that the Royal Society endorsed. Bill Overton's essay makes the language of *Oroonoko* its focus, arguing explicitly what is implicit in the other essays in this section, that a "detailed study of its language" allows students "to find things out for themselves."

At the end of our section "Formal and Thematic Contexts," Shawn Lisa Maurer takes up the question of what kind of hero Oroonoko is, using the classification systems available to Behn. For Maurer, Oroonoko represents both the traditional notion of the heroic, with its emphasis on birth, courage, aggression, and revenge, and the notion of feminized passive valor that was emerging at the end of the seventeenth century. Yet this text "falls fatally between the cracks of two overlapping and contradictory systems of heroic virtue."

Although this volume examines first the debates regarding the genre and form of *Oroonoko*, the "Cultural Contexts" section is likely to function as the natural starting point for most instructors. The first essays in this section deliberately invoke the three contexts so instrumental in the book's emergence in the canon: race, class, and gender. Yet none of these essays focuses solely on one of these contexts. Hughes details the structure of his fourth-year seminar on racial difference, which uses his *Versions of Blackness*. His course moves students through excerpts of major sixteenth- and seventeenth-century accounts of the New World, *Isle of Pines*, *Abdelazer*, *Oroonoko*. It goes back to *Othello*, *The Tempest* (both the original and its Restoration revision by Dryden and Davenant), and *The Indian Emperor*, then forward to Thomas Southerne's and 'Biyi Bandele's dramatic versions. Focusing on seventeenth-century representations of race, however, has the interesting effect of deemphasizing race as an absolute signifier of physical difference. Gevirtz also uses an account of the New World to illuminate *Oroonoko*: the PBS historical reenactment series *Colonial House*, which serves to defamiliarize students' conceptions of the economics of slavery while providing the familiar genre of the reality series to access those differences. Stevens discusses the forces of commodification in the New World and in particular how women functioned as "authors, objects, and metaphors" in the traffic of transatlantic expansion.

The significance of *Oroonoko*'s transatlantic context continues even into the essay that most fully elucidates Behn's involvement in the Tory and Whig conflicts of the late seventeenth century. Laura Doyle's essay positions *Oroonoko* in the tradition of history writing in England that followed upon the heels of the "revolutionary upheavals" of the seventeenth century. The point for Doyle is how the novel's "Anglo-Atlantic female narrator enters English history at the collision point of these stories in the colony of Surinam." Alker and Nelson deepen our reading of *Oroonoko* as a text that responds to many of those same upheavals in the seventeenth century and, more broadly, war: as they explain, "War and its effects are repeatedly, almost obsessively, etched on nearly every page of *Oroonoko*." The authors provide practical strategies for guiding students to discover the truth of this assertion for themselves.

The final essay in this section moves the reader farther afield but closer to *Oroonoko*'s terrain. Thomas Krise argues that "the novel's African and Caribbean characters" are more than "exotic props in a drama" about English conflict at home and imperialism abroad; they are identifiable "representatives of traditions that created the Caribbean culture of today." The novel functions then not just as a parable for English politics or even a primer for newly emerging Anglo-Atlantic politics but also as an originating document of a new Caribbean culture.

"Pedagogical Contexts" foregrounds the broad range of literature courses in which *Oroonoko* is taught, from introductory courses to seminars for advanced English majors. It also takes into account the kind of institution in which *Oroonoko* is taught and how that influences student response. Leslie Richardson takes as her primary theme the challenge of teaching British literature at a historically black college or university (HBCU) "whose core curriculum focuses on the legacy of the transatlantic slave trade" and not the contested achievements of the Enlightenment. At her predominantly female and science-oriented HBCU, *Oroonoko*'s subject matter is not enough to make it "meaningful," and she points to the parallels between Oroonoko's lack of self-ownership in Surinam and the status of the married woman in the late seventeenth century. For Erik Bond, the high number of Muslim students in his institution in Detroit is only one of several local conditions making him cognizant of the provisionality of interpretation. Teaching teachers, he transforms *Oroonoko* into a case study for interpretation itself and asks his students to engage directly in the ethics of distilling any one meaning from such a rich and "messy" text.

The volume includes two models for teaching *Oroonoko* in a British survey course. Because Behn's novel is a transitional text, on the cusp of important ideological, thematic, and linguistic changes, it may be taught either at the beginning or the end of the course. Ana de Freitas Boe positions the narrator's description of Oroonoko's beauty in the tradition of the blazon in the sonnet and helps students see what makes this description remarkable. Ashley Cross makes a strong case for *Oroonoko*'s suitability as the lead text in the second half of a survey, "as a model for the kind of contextualized close reading" she promotes in the course to "challenge . . . students' commonplaces about women writers," while mapping for students the survey's "new literary, psychic, and geographic territory."

No volume on teaching *Oroonoko* would be complete without addressing its place in a travel narrative course. Margarete Rubik not only compares Behn's narrative with other travelogues by women but also complicates its relation to standard anthropological discourse. James Grantham Turner addresses the relation of this text to an established discourse of the New World and its many wonders—including the size of its snakes—but he does so in the context of making the argument for *Oroonoko*'s suitability as a "training text for readers at all levels." By "making the smallest details speak, letting the larger ideological tensions and imaginative contradictions echo from their fissures," instructors can use *Oroonoko* in any literature classroom geared toward producing a sophisticated reader.

From our questionnaires, it is clear that *Oroonoko* is rarely taught in isolation and is paired instead with a broad range of texts. The "Comparative Contexts" section speaks to both the significance of these pairings and their variety. Laura Rosenthal looks backward and forward, connecting *Oroonoko* to an emerging sense of world citizenship and situating it in earlier seventeenth-century texts that foreground other worlds, such as *Paradise Lost*, *The Blazing World*, and *The New Atlantis*. Reading these texts serially, students notice in *Oroonoko* a "whole world of mobility" and a hero at odds not only with the plantation economy of Surinam but also with the traditional society of Coramantien. Laura Runge considers how Oroonoko compares with heroic figures in the work of Milton and Dryden. Focusing on *Paradise Lost* and *Absalom and Achitophel*, she draws attention to the shared status of Satan, Absalom, and Oroonoko as leaders of failed insurrections. The next three essays focus on *Oroonoko*'s relation to the theater, a popular frame for the study of *Oroonoko*. Joyce Green MacDonald reads the work in the context of Behn's *Abdelazer*, Shakespeare's *Othello*, and Southerne's adaptation of *Oroonoko*. By reading these works together, students learn to see the historicity of early modern dialogues regarding race and masculinity but also to appreciate how *Oroonoko* departs from those historical norms. Scott Juengel also compares Behn's *Oroonoko* with Southerne's adaptation but focuses on the differences in how these two works stage the death of Oroonoko. Juengel tackles directly the "grisly end" of *Oroonoko* that can so unsettle students. By comparing it with the treatment of Oroonoko's suffering in Southerne's more sentimental adaptation, Juengel helps students recognize Behn's refusal to look away from the brutalities of slavery. Jessica Munns compares Behn's novel with Bandele's version, which increasingly rivals Southerne's as a comparative teaching text. Her review draws particular attention to the scenes in Africa in both works and explores the difference in tone in these scenes, especially how Imoinda changes the way we view the effects of slavery in Surinam. Vincent Carretta compares *Oroonoko* with one of its most frequent pedagogical partners, *The Interesting Narrative of Olaudah Equiano*. Many instructors may wish to begin their reading with this essay because it provides a tight framework for comparing these two works as well as a thorough account of the evolving structure and definition of slavery from the late seventeenth to the late eighteenth century. Carretta lets students discover for themselves that terms such as "race, identity, status, slavery, and abolition" are not "synchronically stable." His method cleverly allows students to correct their own naïveté regarding these concepts.

The final section, "Authorial Contexts," returns us to what first earned *Oroonoko* a place in the canon and what has remained most stable in the assessment of this text: Behn's extraordinary career as the first professional English woman writer and this novel's status as her crowning achievement. This final section elucidates that standing, drawing attention in its final entry, by Jane Spencer, to the reception of Behn's work during her lifetime and the continuing questions about her significance as a woman writer in our own. In highlighting Behn's career as a poet, novelist, and playwright, Jane Spencer draws attention to the many genres in which Behn wrote and shows how each can serve as a frame for teaching *Oroonoko*. In our questionnaires, *The Widdow Ranter* emerged as the most frequent authorial context for the work. Jane Milling and Cynthia Richards pair *Oroonoko* with *The Widdow Ranter* and an upper-level literature class in an American liberal arts college with a first-year drama course at a British university to show how these two texts continue to spark vigorous debate on national identity. Their essay details the specific outcome of this cross-cultural exchange and notes the parallels between the contested heroes of both works, the importance of generic expectation, the opposition between American and English identity, and the nascent heroism of the New World woman. Emily Hodgson Anderson explores the connections between Behn's final experiment in fiction and earlier ones, such as *The Fair Jilt* and *The History of the Nun*, in the incorporation of *Oroonoko* into a course on the history of the novel. When these texts are taught together, students can learn to recognize that novelty itself is a theme in Behn's novels.

Respondents to our questionnaire also indicated that *Oroonoko* is routinely taught alongside Behn's poetry. Roberta Martin examines "The Disappointment" and seventeenth-century "humoral imbalance" in *Oroonoko*, providing an ingenious comparison between the fainting male body in Behn's poem and the dying one in *Oroonoko*, and between twenty-first-century notions of the body and late-seventeenth-century ones.

We give Spencer the final word in this volume, in an essay that examines just that: what will be the "final word" on Behn's significance? Spencer, in turn, reads this volume itself as "one indication of how far Aphra Behn has traveled since the 1970s." Yet equally important in her essay is how Behn wished to be read during her own time, and Spencer reminds us of how much Behn looked back to the past for her image of the writer, how she remained true to her Royalist allegiances—and how surprised she would be to find her literary period redubbed at one university "the age of Aphra Behn."

In other words, Spencer gives Behn the final word.

FORMAL AND THEMATIC CONTEXTS

What Kind of Story Is This?

Srinivas Aravamudan

Consider the four kinds of *kind* in these passages from *Oroonoko*:

> A Poet is a Painter in his way; he draws to the Life, but in another kind; we draw the Nobler part, the Soul and Mind; the Pictures of the Pen shall out-last those of the Pencil, and even Worlds themselves. (5)

> Though, as *Oroonoko* afterwards said, he had little Reason to credit the Words of a *Backearary*, yet he knew not why; but he saw a kind of Sincerity, and awful Truth in the face of *Trefry*. . . . (35)

> *Trefry* was infinitely pleas'd with this Novel, and found this *Clemene* was the Fair Mistress of whom *Caesar* had before spoke; and was not a little satisfied, that Heaven was so kind to the *Prince*, as to sweeten his Misfortunes by so lucky an Accident. . . . (40)

> The Trees appearing all like Nosegays adorn'd with Flowers of different kinds; some are all White, some Purple, some Scarlet, some Blue, some Yellow; bearing, at the same time, Ripe Fruit and Blooming Young, or producing every Day new. (43)

In the last two decades, Behn's novel has been elevated from the status of literary enigma and designated a canonical origin of the genre. Many editions and full-scale critical attention have transformed informational deficit into scholarly surfeit. Students approaching *Oroonoko* for the first time can be encouraged to find tools for their exploration in the first few pages of the text, cues for them to recognize the interpretive scaffolding as well as the contextual frameworks that they will confront in the classroom and in the accompanying critical readings. The most general question to begin with might therefore be: what kind of story is this?

In this essay, I use that question to frame three crucial pedagogical goals for the teaching of *Oroonoko*. First, I alert students to register the complexity of genres, whether this work is taught in a history-of-the-novel context, in an early-women-writers setting, in a special topics slavery-and-abolition seminar, or in a standard survey course. Students learn quickly when they realize that genre questions are paramount for understanding truth claims made both in a text and about a text. Second, focusing on sophisticated decision making about the kind of story *Oroonoko* is (or whether it is indeed just one story) helps the novice evaluate as well as pigeonhole competing claims made about the text, even as it provides the conceptual hooks on which to hang the bewildering number of critical essays and contextual notes that supplement the text's many available editions. Third, I turn this pedagogical plan away from a classificatory exercise to one that has students ask whether a disruptive story about kind and kindred, as well as about kindness and unkindness, can be classified at all. What kind of story—and what kind of interpretation—will allow the emergence of other questions about kin, kindred, and kindness, and about genre, gender, and genus?

Kinds of Story

The autobiographical aspects of *Oroonoko* are both compelling and ambiguous. First-person narration is combined with avowals of honesty and protestations against artifice. The first four words of the story are "I do not pretend . . ." (8). Students might be asked to make a list of the many kinds of story implied in the first few pages—what genre theorists term the "rules of recognition" that tell readers which reading protocols to use. A discussion exercise could involve asking each student to state possible genre categories that various moments in *Oroonoko* exemplify, and then to sketch attributes of that genre. The instructor could improvisationally expand on these attributes and tie them back to the opening pages. If students are reticent, the instructor might do a show-and-tell based on the list below. The goal of this discussion is to acknowledge the usefulness of labeling even while recognizing that classificatory exercises stabilize meanings of texts by creating expectations early in the reading process. The interaction of genre, theme, and trope will help the instructor work the classroom. Is a genre formed around a storytelling technique? Is the story the kind that features a certain theme? a certain trope? a particular treatment? In the following list of genres and subgenres, the point is not to suggest that all genres are equally useful for analyzing a text but to make students aware that genre diversity expands a text's interpretive horizon:

autobiography: "I do not pretend . . ." (8)
travel narrative: "Those on that *Continent* where I was," or Behn's trip to Surinam (10)
tall tale: Is her novel historically accurate or the "Adventures of a feign'd *Hero*" (8)?
mirabilia: "various Excellencies, such as Art cannot imitate," wonders (9)
biography: "the Story of this *Gallant Slave*" (8)
testimony: "I was my self an Eye-Witness to a great part" (8)
slave narrative: story received from "the Mouth of the chief Actor in this History" (8)
history: "the History of this *Royal Slave*" (8)
hagiography: "the Character of this great Man" (8)
colonial propaganda: "the manner of bringing [Slaves] to these new *Colonies*" (8)
ethnography: description of the natives of Surinam (8–11)
early novel: "True History" on the title page (3)
primitivist myth, noble savage subgenre: the theme of native naïveté (8–11)
epic: the Homeric parallels to Oroonoko's heroic exploits throughout the novel
classical romance: comparison of Oroonoko and Imoinda with Mars and Venus (14)
transcontinental tale: featuring Europe, Africa, Asia—the triangular trade may come up anachronistically but can be anticipated
oriental tale: will be recognized as characteristic of the Coramantien section
tragedy: will come up in relation to Oroonoko's hubris and cruel death
medieval courtship tale: Coramantien episodes featuring Oroonoko and Imoinda
civil war narrative: "frightful Spectacles of a mangl'd King" at the end of the story (65)

Kinds of Interpretation

For the next exercise, during another class session, the instructor orchestrates a discussion of how powerful interpretations of the text take generic cues to conclusions that totalize. By going through some of the historical background and criticism in any scholarly edition used, the instructor can demonstrate how certain themes, tropes, and even entire approaches connect with rules of recognition. Asking what kind of story *Oroonoko* is leads logically to the question of which interpretation one might be looking for. Intention and reception dialectically structure the text; both sides of the picture are needed. What was Behn thinking? What forms influenced her? Why did she write the story as she did? These questions matter as much as the reasons why we take up this story today, in the context of the historical aftermath of transatlantic slavery and of race relations in the New World; they matter as much as the modern awareness of economics, gender, and sexuality that we bring to Behn's work. The novel's "Female Pen" (36) raises feminist questions about gendered authority and agency in the literary sphere, even while the Middle Passage is rendered as historical fact and reimagined fiction. To read historically and to read anachronistically are not opposing but dialectical moves: readers confront preexisting facts and interpretations that they then contest and decenter but also reappropriate. Meaning is made through a readerly negotiation of textual givens.

Attending to the tragic, allegorical, biographical, and historical elements in the story that connect with Behn's life can lead to an interpretation of *Oroonoko* as a coded lament over the execution of Charles I, as Laura Brown suggests. Yet picking up on the gendered silences and historical contexts of slavery, plantation culture, and marronage can lead to a powerful reading of the narrative as encoding resistance against a slave economy through self-inflicted violence and suicide, as Charlotte Sussman argues. Robert Chibka discusses the dizzying nature of the contradictory truth claims and silences that can prompt speculation about the early novel, the epistemological nature of truth and falsity, and the way that fiction arises precisely in the zone of uncertainty generated between these two poles.[1] Slavery, orientalism, civil war, colonialism, and intergenerational and intercultural love triangles are important themes. Students should also be made aware of the intersectionality of frames and the way the many interpretations of *Oroonoko* are a direct consequence of framing devices in the text, while the articulation of new contexts creates a discursive spiraling of themes to address new situations.

Stories about Kind(ness)

It is a commonplace that the institution of slavery denies the humanity of the slave. But *Oroonoko* is a good text to teach students that they need to denaturalize their expectations concerning the human, a construct that is profoundly cultural, philosophical, and historical and therefore subject to considerable variation. *Oroonoko* was written at a moment when new discourses on species were being initiated in Europe, in the context of the colonial encounter in the Americas as well as of the development of oceanic trade routes around the world. The species discourse in Behn's text ranges from curiosity about and interest in exotic birds and insects, electric eels and man-eating tigers, to concerns about human groups and cultural systems as defined through processes such as ornamentation and mutilation. It is fascinating that *Oroonoko* provides at least two contested definitions of humanity. Is truth telling (or keeping one's word) a definition of humanity? If so, almost no one is genuinely human. *Oroonoko* is full of episodes of betrayal: the English governor does not keep his promise to return to visit the indigenes in Surinam; the ship's captain does not keep his repeated promises to Oroonoko, when he kidnaps him, makes him eat and drink, and sells him down the river. These betrayals are repeated in Oroonoko's friendship with Trefry and with the unnamed female narrator. We need to problematize any equation of the author with the narrator and of the 1688 narrator with her recollected self of 1663. *Oroonoko* is a text that benefits from careful separation of the story world from the discourse world, of diegesis from nondiegesis. Oroonoko's promises to the slaves he leads into rebellion are as rhetorical and vacuous as those made by any demagogue. Perhaps lying is a better definition of humanness, as some evolutionary anthropologists now argue. In any case, the text has its readers confront human beings as creatures who make promises to one another and betray one another—and the circumstances and consequences of both promise and betrayal are revealed in the narrative only through the passage of time. Although some promises are made in good faith but cannot be kept later, in Behn's work the focus is on the promise made in bad faith, where betrayal becomes not so much tragic as cynical and the innocence and gullibility of some are paired with the cunning and wickedness of others. But *Oroonoko* does not take place in a completely cynical universe, which would lead to detachment and misanthropy; there is occasional generosity and compassion, mixed with apology and excuses.

The question of the status of his progeny begins to obsess Oroonoko when Imoinda is pregnant with "his" child, and he becomes intractable (in the terminology of slavery), rebelling against his role as pet of the narrator and her company (Aravamudan). He is an honorary king and superior to most Africans and Europeans in his circle, but his child may not have the freedoms that were temporarily withdrawn from him and yet are not completely out of reach. A further complication is the ambiguous character of Imoinda, whom Oroonoko reclaims as his sexual property and who welcomes the suicide pact with him when she is pregnant. Is the baby definitely Oroonoko's? Paternity is always a matter of opinion, especially under the sexual brutality of slavery (Spillers). Let's not forget too quickly Trefry's sexual interest in Imoinda before Oroonoko reclaims her. Because Oroonoko himself bought and sold slaves, he knows that the freedom of human beings is uncertain and Imoinda's child may be enslaved at birth. He cannot accept that possibility.

The notion of kindred obtains across gender and genus. What kind of child will Oroonoko and Imoinda parent? What will the status of that child be in a culture where there are at least three kinds of quasi-racialized people (Europeans, Africans, Amerindians) who intersect yet share no common definition of humanity? This metaphysical and anthropological uncertainty points to rebellion. Some English colonists conflate Oroonoko and his kindred with all those of his color; others want to treat him differently but according to his rank. The kindred question is a classificatory exercise, to choose an ethnocultural and indeed biological order. The text offers three genealogies: first, of the English Civil War; second, of the Coramantien monarchy; and third, of the Amerindian indigene. The reproduction of a slave (Imoinda's pregnancy) interrupts the cultural encounter among the three groups in a manner that causes violence. The question of biological kind appears to challenge all generic classifications. In this regard, *Oroonoko* connects Renaissance discovery, travel, and colonial endeavor. Our transnational and global age is posing the question of species classification anew, with the challenges posed by transgenic technologies.

The meaning of biological kindred is framed through a discourse of kindness. This meaning will be denied yet reaffirmed through its denial—denied through the colonists' refusal to liberate Oroonoko or to fulfill the various broken promises made to him yet reaffirmed through the martyrdom that turns him into a kind of secular saint even though he must die to achieve this elevation. Christian notions of kindness as well as an anachronistic sense of Enlightenment abolitionism frequently associated with this text are the results of a double operation: kindness denied through action and kindness reaffirmed through recollection. The animal instincts of reproduction create monsters out of the classificatory system that sees *Oroonoko* as an animal story rather than a human story. Behn's work is about pets, the infrahuman, the partially human, and the not yet recognized as human (Aravamudan). The animal-oriented narrative involves a sliding scale from exotic birds and beasts to creatures who speak and fight and perform incredible exploits and expect truthfulness. The Christlike martyrdom becomes a beast fable, parable, or allegory. Oroonoko is totemic, infrahuman, and superhuman at once. He "gave up the Ghost, without a Groan, or a Reproach," making him a "Great Man," and a "Glorious Name," even though cut "in Quarters" to become the "frightful Spectacles of a mangl'd King" (64–65).

Do our students—do we—really want to admit what kind of story *Oroonoko* is? It tells of creatures who refuse to allow other creatures to recognize their kindred, who see—and yet do not see—others as the same and of their own kind. It tells of pretending to be kind while being cruel. It tells how to make stories out of other people's deaths, about condoning the killing of others while spinning a tale, and it anticipates our repetition of that literary spinning as readers, unless we can resist the generic mechanisms that lead to the closure of the form and the closing of the pages of the physical book. *Oroonoko* is a story about the narrator's implicit jealousy of Imoinda, about the narrator's participation in the colonial project of diverting the protagonist from rebellion, and about her disappearance downriver at the moment when Oroonoko needs her most. Therefore it is an indirect autobiographical confession of complicity, taking the form of an obituary of a great man more than two decades after his death. It is exculpatory and self-incriminating at the same time. Where does that leave the readers: are they guilty or judgmental? entertained or sorry? outraged or seeking justice? in the narration or beyond it? This readerly complicity in an authorial crime is what makes *Oroonoko* truly disturbing. As the narrator says in Toni Morrison's *Beloved*, "This is not a story to pass on" (275). Given that stories such as *Oroonoko* and *Beloved* are indeed passed on despite narratorial qualms, what kind of cultural transmission do they enact and reenact? Communicating this paradox will ensure that the story survives even as the reader becomes its critic or dupe. *Oroonoko* reveals how much reading is an ethical act, and that ethics, to be responsive, has to interrogate thoroughly any unexamined assumptions about humankind.

In these comments I have not focused exclusively on instructional techniques but have also given teachers a general sense of the principles we need to keep in mind when teaching *Oroonoko*. Many of the essays in this volume connect principles with techniques in innovative ways, but at the beginning I wanted to suggest that *Oroonoko* is about reading, reflecting, and enacting a form of readerly self-awareness that is fundamental to experiencing the literary text as a rhetorical and aesthetic practice. Contexts are important, and information is crucial, but they can all become lifeless documentation if, as teachers of *Oroonoko* or of any literary text, we do not consider carefully how reading tracks from intention to reception to appropriation to re-creation.

Students need to recognize that there is something fruitful as well as abstruse about *Oroonoko* as a literary work, that its literariness is a separate matter from all the noble attempts that enshrine it as a historical document. There is a happy interdisciplinary critical consensus about the topics of race, gender, and sexuality, but there are many knowledge projects in a pluridisciplinary university. If historians read texts as documents, literary critics read them as rhetorical artifacts. Outcomes of disciplinary reading therefore vary considerably and will not always agree.

Oroonoko can survive, indeed thrive, under the weight of the referential critical apparatus that uses it to document slavery, the Middle Passage, and colonialism. But it will fare better if we unfold our pedagogy around the word that I treat as a pressure point in this exposition: *kind*. Of the four citations of kind from *Oroonoko* that I offered at the start of this essay, the first involves aesthetic genre (poetry vs. painting), the second features a variety of emotion (sincerity), the third references divine compassion, and the fourth classifies flowers. Kinds of representational media and kinds of sentiment are ultimately forced to yield pride of place to the genre or genus of stories about kind that challenge pre-established notions of who or what a human being might be.

The production of the text is linked to the failed reproduction of the slave who desires unenslaved status for his kindred; in fact, its success is a direct outcome of that failure. *Oroonoko* is the kind of story about humankind that should give us, and our students, pause.

NOTE

[1] Brown's, Sussman's, and Chibka's essays are excerpted, respectively, in Behn, *Oroonoko* [Lipking] 232–45, 246–56, 220–32.

Credibility and Truth in *Oroonoko*

Keith M. Botelho

> *"The end of Reason, is Truth; the end of Fancy, is Fiction."*
> —Margaret Cavendish, *The Description of a New World*

> "Knowledge and truth are never identical; there is no true knowledge and no known truth. Nevertheless, certain pieces of knowledge are indispensable for an account of the truth."
> —Walter Benjamin

Oroonoko begins and ends by reflecting on the slipperiness of truth. First, in the "Epistle Dedicatory" to Lord Maitland, Behn asserts that she is telling "a true Story," and of those "unconceivable Wonders" that she recounts in the pages that follow, she adds, "What I have mention'd I have taken care shou'd be Truth, let the Critical Reader judge as he pleases" (7). In the concluding pages of *Oroonoko*, when the "wild *Irish* Man," Banister, tells Caesar that "he shou'd Dye like a Dog, as he was" (64), Caesar is reported to reply that if Banister kept his word, he "wou'd declare, in the other World, that he was the only Man, of all the Whites, that ever he heard speak Truth" (64).

The examination of truth-telling practices in Behn's hybrid masterpiece has been well rehearsed by critics, from Michael McKeon's study of the "self-defensive efforts by authors of voyages both 'real' and 'imaginary'" (111) to Robert L. Chibka's exploration of truth, falsehood, and fiction in *Oroonoko* ("Truth") to Katharine M. Rogers's analysis of Behn's authenticity and accuracy. Yet the varied and often maddening claims to credibility and truth do not make Behn's text unique; rather, they reflect how the novel is part of a larger discursive network stretching before and beyond the century in which it was written. Teaching *Oroonoko* in the context of many other discourses gives texture to Behn's text, and such teaching can be successfully employed both at the general education level and in lower- and upper-division English courses.

I have taught *Oroonoko* at two large state universities in a variety of classes: Survey of British Literature to 1800, British Literature: Beginnings to 1660, World Literature, and an upper-level course on women writers from 1500 to 1700. I always aim to have my classes read aloud the "Epistle Dedicatory" as well as the novel's opening paragraphs in order to frame pertinent issues. Immediately students ask what makes this narrator (and any narrator) credible, and they often show critical savvy as readers in their willingness to question information or knowledge that is many times removed from its original source.

The narrator begins the novel with the claim that she does not intend to divert from "the Truth" of the hero's story: "I do not pretend, in giving you the History of this *Royal Slave*, to entertain my Reader with the Adventures of a feign'd *Hero*, whose Life and Fortunes Fancy may manage at the Poet's Pleasure; nor in relating the Truth, design to adorn it with any Accidents, but such as arriv'd in earnest to him." Nor, she assures the reader, will she engage in distorting the story, for there is "enough of Reality to support it, and to render it diverting, without the Addition of Invention." In fact, she seeks to authenticate her sources: "I was my self an Eye-Witness to a great part, of what you will find here set down; and what I cou'd not be Witness of, I receiv'd from the Mouth of the chief Actor in this History, the *Hero* himself, who gave us the whole Transactions of his Youth" (8).

Throughout their engagement with the text, students struggle with the question of how reliable a narrator can be who leaves gaps in the narrative, "[omitting] for Brevity's sake, a thousand little Accidents of [the hero's] Life" because they "might prove tedious and heavy to my Reader, in a World where he finds Diversions for every Minute, new and strange" (8). Whether or not she willfully lies, she does succumb to the period's practice of secondhand reporting to construct a number of details of the narrative. For instance, after Caesar and Clemene reunite, the narrator remarks that Trefry comes to Parham House "to give me an Account of what had hapned." She also seeks to hear this report from Caesar's "own Mouth," which is "confirm'd by his *French*-man" (40). Various accounts punctuate the final pages of the novel, as news is brought that Caesar fled to the woods and later that "*Caesar* was taken" (57). After returning from down the river to Parham with Colonel Martin, the narrator notes, "[W]hen we came, the First News we heard was, that the *Governor* was Dead of a Wound *Imoinda* had given him; but it was not so well" (58). It is interesting that she seems to cement her credibility by raising the possibility that the news is erroneous and so needs confirmation.

Students often notice that the narrator is absent during Caesar's dismemberment, having left with others on a three-day journey down the river because of her sickly state, and they wonder about the credibility of her mother and sister, who apparently gave her the details after the execution and "were by [Caesar] all the while" (64). The paradox of the early modern period, of course, is that unless one can verify the information independently, one must inevitably trust the source or the narrator of the events. As students wrestle with the thorny issue of credibility, they come to understand that secondhand truth claims are a staple in texts of the period. As Sir William Strachey writes in *A True Reportory of the Wreck and Redemption of Sir Thomas Gates* (1610), widely believed to be a source for Shakespeare's *The Tempest*, "Thus shall we make it appear, that Truth is the Daughter of Time, and that men ought not to deny everything which is not subject to their own sense" (181). Perceptive students will come to see a resemblance between themselves as readers dependent on a narrator's depiction of truth and Oroonoko as he at first fails to detect the lack of credibility of those around him.

Oroonoko's credulity (*credulity* is defined as "aptness to believe" in the 1678 edition of Edward Phillips's dictionary, *The New World of Words* [N2r]) is repeatedly taken advantage of in the course of the novel, for Oroonoko is one "whose Honour was such as he never had violated a Word in his Life himself, much less a solemn Asseveration" (32). We might say that in the seventeenth century, fidelity (*fidelity*, dating from the early sixteenth century, often meant a person's truthfulness, veracity, or conformity to truth or fact) marked people as being credible. Oroonoko trusts too easily, and the ease with which many in the novel distort the truth is paradigmatic of the issue of credibility in the period. Instances abound in the novel: the king employs a messenger to relay to Oroonoko that Imoinda is dead (27); Oroonoko is lulled into "Familiarity" with the commander of the English ship and later, when he is betrayed, is said to be "too generous, not to give Credit to his Words" (31, 33). Note that *generous* comes from the Latin *generosus*, meaning "of noble birth." Byam, the deputy governor who "pretended the most Friendship to *Caesar*" (54), fools Caesar and Trefry with his guarantee ("ratify'd by their Hands in Writing") that if Caesar surrenders, he will allow him to "*depart free*" from the land (56). Students should trace how Oroonoko grows increasingly incredulous during the course of the novel, though his realizations come too late. The narrator reports that he suspects his captors of falsehood as they continue to delay his and Clemene's liberty (41), and he soon learns that "there was no Faith in the White Men" and that, for his own safety, he must be careful "never to credit one Word they spoke" (56). Yet he notes that "he had little Reason to credit the Words of a *Backearary*, yet he knew not why; but he saw a kind of Sincerity, and awful Truth in the Face of *Trefry*" (35) while also putting his "intire Confidence" in the narrator (42). At once able and unable to detect truth, Oroonoko is representative of the seventeenth century's unstable relation to news and credibility.

In early modern travel narratives, truth is often clouded because of unverifiable claims. According to McKeon, the seventeenth century was "heir to an ancient and habitual association of travel narratives with tall tales and travelers with liars" (100). The narrative strategies in *Oroonoko* that take care to establish credibility with the audience (while presenting a story of liars and the credulous) are similarly present in two sixteenth-century examples. Alvar Núñez Cabeza de Vaca, in his *Chronicle of the Narváez Expedition*, employs conventional modesty and praise in his "Prologue to the Catholic Majesty," where he asserts his truth claim about his experiences and the "care and diligence" with which he set everything to memory in order to be of use to his country. He writes, "For this I have written with great surety so that even though one will read about many new things that many people will find hard to believe, they should be able to believe them without hesitation" (4). In the chronicle's final lines he writes, "[I]n testimony of that what I have stated in the foregoing narrative is true, I hereunto sign my name" (105). Similar attention to asserting one's narrative credibility is taken in Thomas More's *Utopia*. In More's second letter to his friend Peter Giles in the second edition of *Utopia* (1517), More, recalling how an acquaintance speculated about the truth content of the work, laments, "I see some people are so suspicious that what we naïve fellows have written down of Hythloday's account can hardly find any credence at all with these circumspect and sagacious persons. I'm afraid my personal reputation, as well as my authority as a historian, may be threatened by their skepticism" (590). He concludes that "these doubters" should seek out and consult Hythloday himself so that they can confirm what More has recorded. At the beginning of the work in his first letter to Giles, he writes, "Truth in fact is the only quality at which I should have aimed, or did aim, in writing this book" (521). While these truth claims certainly echo Behn's in *Oroonoko*, they also point to a history of doubt and a crisis of skepticism that became a cornerstone of a more literate seventeenth-century society.

Students are invariably intrigued when we situate the novel's examination of truth and credibility in the context of the burgeoning news industry and the early Royal Society. Resources such as *Early English Books Online* allow students to explore truth claims on the title pages of travel narratives, accounts of remarkable occurrences, and newspapers in the seventeenth century. Because there was more information in circulation than ever before and easier distribution and access to news from inside and outside England, the issue of credibility—of what and whom to believe—became a pressing concern in the period. News became a commodity, beginning in the 1620s with the circulation of corantos, letters or papers containing public news, and then in the 1640s with the proliferation of news books relating foreign and domestic events. According to Brendan Dooley, by the end of the seventeenth century, with its succession of wars and instability, the newspaper "had become the method *par excellence* for conveying political information" (9). In my survey courses I show students copies of the numerous title pages of newspapers published during the English Civil War—*The True Informer*, *Mercurius Civicus*, *Londons Intelligencer; or, Truth Impartially Related*, and *The Kingdomes Weekly Intelligencer: Sent Abroad to Prevent Misinformation*, to name a few—and we explore how news reports in the decades before the publication of Behn's text asserted the credibility and truth of their news. Given the increase of ambiguous and unauthorized information to contend with, numerous cultural, political, and literary discourses attempted to make sense of the changing face of communication as well as deal with the potential, both destructive and productive, inherent in reports.

Oroonoko was written in the shadow of the emergence of the new science and the establishment of the Royal Society of London, which received its charter in 1662 from King Charles II. Steven Shapin has shown how various English contexts, including those of natural history and natural philosophy, were "replete with justificatory gestures at testimonial sources as 'credible persons'" (241), although the culture at large believed that gentlemen were society's most reliable truth tellers. *Oroonoko* can usefully be taught in connection with the documents of the early Royal Society, particularly Thomas Sprat's *History of the Royal-Society* (1667). Sprat outlines how Royal Society members were to judge matters of fact as well as reach truth through experimentation and replication. He has much to say about dealing with false reports and relates how fellows of the Society engaged with reports from various sources: "[T]hey employ others to discourse with the Seamen, Travellers, Tradesmen, and Merchants, who are likely to give them the best light" (155 [V2r]). Students will find this statement troubling when they see that notions of truth are conditioned by many variables and that what is finally represented may not be accurate or credible. In Behn's novel, it is Oroonoko who makes the best (though it proves to be a naive) case for establishing credibility when he tells the English captain that he "was very sorry to hear that the *Captain* pretended to the Knowledge and Worship of any *Gods*, who had taught him no better Principles, than not to Credit as he would be Credited" (32).

Finally, students can examine how literary works in the century after the publication of *Oroonoko* continued to challenge the issues of truth and credibility. The last chapter of Swift's *Gulliver's Travels* begins with Gulliver's justification of his veracity and a general commentary on the nature of truth. Gulliver argues that because remote countries are seldom visited by Englishmen, it is essential that travelers reporting on their experiences inform accurately; thus he imposed on himself a maxim from which he would never swerve: to "*strictly adhere to truth*" ([Greenblatt and Abrams] 2459). By the end of a semester, students often find that such a statement is highly questionable. Gulliver seems to be reacting to the sort of secondhand reporting in which both he and the narrator of *Oroonoko* engage. He wants every traveler to take an oath before publishing a voyage that it was "absolutely true to the best of his knowledge," for the world is deceived by writers who impose the "grossest falsities on the unwary reader," and he laments "the credulity of mankind so impudently abused" (2459).

To explore *Oroonoko* through the abundant fictional and non-fictional cultural material on truth foregrounds how complicated and challenging appeals to credibility can be. Truth, many students conclude, is a cultural and social construct, and the practice of being attentive to the truth claims found in various contexts of Behn's time allows them to be that "Critical Reader" who, Behn notes, should judge as he pleases. Yet for the narrator of *Oroonoko*, it is ultimately her word, her credibility, that stands as the only truth.

Oroonoko: Romance to Novel

Rose Zimbardo

Oroonoko is a crucial text in any study of the aesthetics and discourse of the "Zero Point" journey from the Restoration to the eighteenth century (Zimbardo). As a literary text, the novel reveals two important changes that occurred in the movement from seventeenth- to eighteenth-century practice: its combination of the old "discourse of patterning" and the new analytico-referential "discourse of modernism" (Reiss 50) with its "naturalizing" of experience by creating interiority in character and realism in setting. Behn's novel can be used to demonstrate to students a key transition in poetic mimesis, marking the transformation of a closed classical form—the romance or the prose epic—into the first novel in English. To effect this change, Behn uses two distinctly different modes of discourse, which for clarity's sake may be called "high heroic" and "low realistic." It is precisely this use of language that makes *Oroonoko* an important landmark in the history of ideas, for it looks backward toward the Renaissance "discourse of patterning" and forward to the "discourse of modernism," the language that the "Natural Philosophers" of the Royal Society endorsed.

The editors of Southerne's play *Oroonoko* say of Behn's novel that the "combination of realistic action and *précieuse* style in Behn produces an effect that is grotesque" (Novak and Rodes xl). While these critics recognize that there are two different styles in Behn's novel, they unfortunately miss the significance of that difference. I would argue that Behn employs the two distinctly different modes of discourse purposely and to brilliant effect. She uses the high heroic style for the very purpose it served in Restoration heroic drama and *précieuse* prose romance—to elevate our minds to an appreciation of ideas of heroic greatness embodied by her protagonists, who, in this mode, are figures of majesty and virtue rather than characters in the usual sense. She uses the low realistic mode to serve the very purpose for which the novel was invented—that is, to admit us into a fictional world that, while exotic, is, above all, probable and to explore nuances of thought and feeling in characters, who, like us, have interiority and psychology. By means of the low realistic mode, we enter into the text where we not only imagine the setting into being but also share the unspoken inner lives of characters and thereby share their emotions and participate in their actions.

In telling Oroonoko's story, Behn uses the high style when her aim is to delineate the spiritual essence of her hero, "that real Greatness of Soul, those refin'd Notions of true Honour, that absolute Generosity, and that Softness, that was capable of the highest Passions of Love and Gallantry" (12). She uses low discourse, and indeed simulates reportage, to create the effect of an unadorned account of "reality" as human experience; she claims to be "Eye-Witness to a great part" of the story and what she did not witness, she says, she "receiv'd from the Mouth of the chief Actor in this History" (8). The two linguistic modes design the tension between Caesar, the slave, in all the realism of his condition, and Oroonoko, the prince, in all the heroic elevation demanded by the Idea of Majesty that he figures. The consequence is to make *Oroonoko* a hinge that registers the turn from Renaissance conceptions of mind and language to eighteenth-century Enlightenment conceptions of "human understanding" and material reality.

For the Middle Ages and the Renaissance, Word equals Idea and exists in the mind of God, in the incorporeal realm, and in the human mind. Word is the perfect image of thought and can be transmitted whole from mind to mind. As Theophilus Gale observed in *The Court of the Gentiles*: "*There are in speech certain Symbols or notices of the Soul's passions*. . . . Look as in the *mind,* there is a certain . . . *Character* or *Idea* of things; so likewise in *oration* or speech, there is a *Character* or *Idea* of the *Mind*" (52). Because words are perfect and complete signs, they are conduits for conveying pure Idea from mind to mind, from the storehouse of Truth to mind, from the Idea of Truth itself to mind.

Clearly, Behn deliberately employs a *précieuse* style to convey Ideas of Honor, Love, and Virtue. She uses the traditional language of romance when her aim is to shape, in Gale's terms, a "Character of the Mind," a figuration of the greatness that Oroonoko the Prince represents. For example, when Oroonoko first falls in love with Imoinda, Behn employs the classical romance formula (the hero bred to the wars from infancy is instantaneously struck with heroic love by the sight of Ideal Beauty) in high heroic language. Furthermore, the narrator uses this discourse not only to describe Oroonoko's state but to shape her own expression of Love as a heroic Idea:

> [A]s he knew no Vice, his Flame aim'd at nothing but Honour, if such a distinction may be made in Love; . . . as he had right Notions of Honour, so he made her such Propositions as were not only and barely such; but . . . he made her Vows, she shou'd be the only woman he wou'd possess while he liv'd; that no Age or Wrinkles shou'd incline him to change, for her Soul wou'd be always fine, and always young; and he shou'd have an eternal *Idea* in his mind of the Charms she now bore, and he shou'd look into his Heart for that *Idea*, when he cou'd find it no longer in her Face. (15)

This discourse could appear unaltered in any French romance of the early seventeenth century. The style is directly antithetical to Behn's low realistic style. In the high heroic style words have reference not to things but to abstract essences and ideas: "his Flame aim'd at nothing but Honour," and "her Soul" would exist as an "eternal *Idea* in his mind." We do not hear the characters speak nor do we see their physical appearances, actions, postures, or gestures. Here we are not in the world of experience but in the metaphysical world of pure mind and spirit. In this metaphysical world, Oroonoko is not a person we can visualize, as we can through the low realistic mode in such passages as "His

Face was not of that brown, rusty Black which most of that Nation are, but a perfect Ebony, or polish'd Jet" (13). He is rather a figure of heroic Majesty we are made to admire. Here Imoinda is not a character whose grief and fears we share, as she will be in the low novelistic mode; rather here she figures Ideal Beauty and Virtue.

Students can be shown this transition from Renaissance to late-Restoration and eighteenth-century thought, wherein the equivalency between "Character in the Mind" and "Character in Words" is fundamentally and forever broken. For John Locke, all knowledge derives from experience, and truth can be validated only by reference to—and reflection upon—experience, since in experience

> all our Knowledge is founded; and from that it ultimately derives it self. Our Observation employ'd either *about external, sensible Objects; or about the internal Operations of our Minds, perceived and reflected on by our selves, is that, which supplies our Understandings with all the materials of thinking.* (*Essay* 37 [bk. 2, ch. 1])

Therefore, Locke says, the proper business of the mind is to "think of every thing just as it is in it self" ("Of the Conduct" 50). Reasoning upon evidence provided by the senses is the goal of the new Natural Philosophers. Abraham Cowley put the turn from metaphor to mimesis especially well in his prefatory poem to Sprat's *History of the Royal Society*. He praises Francis Bacon as the great precursor of the Natural Philosophers: "*From Words, which are but Pictures of the Thought, / (Though we our Thoughts from them perversely drew) / To Things, the Minds right Object, he it brought*" (B2r). One might almost say that Behn's descent from high heroic to low realistic discourse follows the same trajectory.

As students can quickly see, the novel begins in the style of a familiar essay wherein Behn establishes the truth to experience her tale: "it shall come simply into the World, recommended by its own proper Merits, and natural Intrigues; there being enough Reality to support it, and to render it diverting, without the Addition of Invention" (8). The detailed descriptions of Surinam, the setting for most of the tale, are rendered in the analytico-referential mimetic, discourse that I have called "low realistic." This style first establishes an easy connection between narrator and reader that will enable the reader to see into characters and judge events through the narrator's eyes—to "experience" an encounter with the characters and to participate in the events that befall them. In addition, because rendered in strictly mimetic discourse, Behn's detailed descriptions of "Marmosets," "*Cousheries*," "*Parakeetoes*," and "a thousand other Birds and Beasts of wonderful and surprizing Forms, Shapes and Colours" (8) draw the reader into the landscape. That is to say, this mode of discourse causes the reader to imagine the physical landscape into being. In using it, Behn follows the recommendation of the Natural Philosophers that the language used to describe scenes should abjure "*Hieroglyphics, Emblems, Morals, Fables*" and reproduce only "what properly relates to their Natural History" (Ray A4r).

However, and most important, the new novelistic, mimetic mode admits the reader directly into the consciousness of the characters. With it, Behn can gradually disclose the evolution of subtle, sometimes conflicting, emotions within Oroonoko and Imoinda that build slowly but inevitably to Oroonoko's march to the sea, so that when the slave revolt occurs we see it as not just probable, but predictable. We experience the changes of feeling that take place in Oroonoko as he moves from heroic warrior prince who admires Europeans to slave robbed even of his name by his natural inferiors, the colonists, who repeatedly betray his trust and dehumanize him. Having shared the interwoven emotions and the evolution of sentiment that lead to the event, the reader enters the slave revolt when it happens in support of Oroonoko. We have shared Imoinda's despair as she "began to shew she was with Child, and did nothing but Sigh and Weep for the Captivity of her Lord, her Self, and the Infant yet Unborn; and believ'd, if it were so hard to gain the Liberty of Two, 'twou'd be more difficult to get that for Three" (51). We share Oroonoko's anxiety, the pressure on him to do something in response to Imoinda's despair and his own dishonor. What is more, we have seen for ourselves the degenerate viciousness of the colonists and have accepted the narrator's judgment of them as cowardly villains, the transported scum of England. Oroonoko's rousing speech to his fellow slaves, then, expresses our sentiments. With the help of the naturalized style in which it is spoken and the affiliation with the narrator that we have established—for the speech is embedded within the simple, low narrative style—we, the readers, become participants in the action.

Oroonoko, to my mind the first novel in English, stands at the cusp of the most profound change in language and epistemology in English history. It is an invaluable instrument for teaching students to recognize that change.

The Language of *Oroonoko*

Bill Overton

Surprising as it may seem, a lot remains to be discovered about the language of *Oroonoko*. Because most critical discussion focuses on thematic and historical questions, the linguistic complexity of the text is often overlooked, and thus detailed study of its language is useful as a teaching strategy. One of the best ways of motivating students is to give them the means to find things out for themselves. In the case of *Oroonoko*, detailed study of the language may even enable more advanced students to make their own discoveries.

By early modern standards, the language of *Oroonoko* is not especially difficult. The text has little recondite vocabulary, and its syntax is not unusually dense. Instead, its linguistic complexity consists in switches between different modes of discourse, and in the connotations of words and syntactic structures that are not in themselves striking, but that in context can reveal much. If such details are overlooked, it is easy to misread or read in blinders. In order to show how students may, with some help, inform themselves about the language of *Oroonoko*, this essay considers three types of narrative and linguistic choice: the way speech is represented; the implications of particular kinds of vocabulary; and the use of differing forms of reference for several of the characters.

Analyzing how speech is represented in the text requires basic knowledge of syntax and narrative theory. It is best approached by answering the first of two basic questions that Gérard Genette suggests should be asked of any narrative: who speaks (186)?[1] In any narrative, the primary speaker is, by definition, the narrator, since it is this figure who delivers the story to the reader or audience. The first word of *Oroonoko* refers to this figure with the personal pronoun *I*; and, repeating the word at the start of the next paragraph, the narrator claims authority to tell the story on the basis of having witnessed part of it and having heard the remainder from the hero. Because the narrator has the role of relaying the story, her status is different from that of the characters represented. A clear example of this is that the narrator is also represented as a character, interacting with the other characters of the story and as unaware as they of what twists and turns it will take.

The radical difference between the role of narrator and characters is also apparent in the form in which speech is represented. In the strict sense of the word, a narrator of a printed text, rather than of a story delivered orally, does not speak at all. The word *tell* is therefore more appropriate. But such a narrator may represent the speech of characters in three main ways. The most direct form of speech representation is verbatim quotation, or what is offered as such. In this form, the actual words that the character is supposed to have uttered are given by the narrator without modification, except in accidentals. As early modern printed texts normally use italics to indicate direct speech, nearly all the examples of this form of speech-representation in *Oroonoko* are easy to identify. At the other end of the spectrum is the narrative voice on its own, as when reporting, commenting, or describing. Between the two are forms that filter a character's voice through the narrator's. In passages of this type, the character's actual words are used, but are transposed into the narrative voice by a change of person from first to third and of tense from present to past. The stock term for this blend of voices is "*free indirect speech*," but I prefer to use different phrases to distinguish between the narrator's representation of words that are spoken, thought, or written: *narrated speech*, *narrated thought*, and *narrated writing*.[2] It is important to add that distinctions such as these are based on narrative conventions that are, broadly defined, mimetic. The narrator invokes such conventions at the start when she claims she is telling the story as it was told to her and as, in part, she witnessed it (8).

These distinctions prompt important questions. For example, the narrator's claim that she is to tell the story truthfully glosses over various choices that she has the power to make, including how she represents speech. The first, to repeat Genette's question, is, "Who speaks?" Whether or not a character's words are represented in a narrative is likely to indicate the importance of that character not only in the action but also in whatever value systems to which the narrative subscribes, explicitly or otherwise. By the same token, the extent to which the speech of a particular character is represented is also likely to be significant. The second choice is in what form to represent a character's speech: directly, indirectly, or in the mixed mode that I am calling narrated speech because it is transposed into the person and tense of the narrative voice. Again, such a choice may connote value, because representation of speech in direct form conveys greater impact. As a successful dramatist, Behn is likely to have been well aware of its implications.

The first task in analyzing with a group of students how speech is represented in a story is to ensure that these basic principles of narrative theory are understood. A good passage to use for this purpose is one near the beginning of the text that provides an early example of European social and linguistic practices in contrast with those of the Caribs:

> They once made Mourning and Fasting for the Death of the *English* Governor, who had given his Hand to come on such a Day to 'em, and neither came, nor sent; believing, when once a Man's Word was past, nothing but Death cou'd or shou'd prevent his keeping it: And when they saw he was not dead, they ask'd him, what Name they had for a Man who promis'd a thing he did not do? The Governor told them, Such a man was a *Lyar*, which was a Word of Infamy to a Gentleman. Then one of 'em reply'd, *Governor, you are a Lyar, and guilty of that Infamy*. They have a Native Justice, which knows no Fraud; and they understand no Vice, or Cunning, but when they are taught by the *White Men*. (10)

Students will easily see that this passage begins in the narrative voice, but that it includes other voices and perspectives. For example, the clause that starts with the word "believing" marks a shift toward the viewpoint of the Caribs, whose convictions about the binding nature of a promise the narrator goes on to state. The next shift is into indirect speech, introduced by the words "they ask'd him." However, this could also be interpreted as narrated speech, because it fulfills the condition of free indirect discourse in that it can be transposed back into the words that are supposed to have been spoken by converting the person from third to first and the tense from past to present. Transposed in this manner, the words uttered by the Caribs would be: "What name do you have for a man who promised a thing he did not do?" Such a way of interpreting the text at this point is reinforced by the simplicity of the vocabulary. The Governor's reply may also be read either as indirect or as narrated speech, and for similar reasons. Although it too is introduced by a phrase suggesting that it is indirect speech, it is equally open to transposition back into the tense and person of dialogue; and again the register, which is educated and genteel, is appropriate to the speaker. The third and most significant shift is to direct speech for the riposte by one of the Caribs to what he rightly understands as the Governor's hypocrisy. Aptly, the italics used for direct speech give this special emphasis.

Once these shifts in narrative voice and linguistic register are recognized, students may consider their implications. Following the lead given by the narrator in the last sentence of the extract, they might connect it with the episode of Oroonoko's capture, as this also highlights the "Vice and Cunning" of "*White Men*" in opposition to the honor and truthfulness of the African prince. Another possible response is that the Governor uses social and linguistic conventions according to which an acceptance of an invitation is not necessarily binding. This would enable discussion of the ethical and cultural values at issue, and of where the text might stand on these.

The short passage just considered not only allows some basic principles about narrative voice and perspective to be demonstrated, but also indicates their importance to interpretation. Analyzing it enables another kind of question. Once students are able to recognize shifts in narrative discourse, they can identify the characters whose voices are represented in the text, and then the modes in which their speech is rendered—direct, indirect, or narrated. This is likely to lead to interesting findings. One is the sheer number of voices—I count fourteen in all—represented in a text that seems dominated by the narrator's. The other is the fact that some of the voices are collective. This kind of finding creates opportunities for students to develop various arguments and interpretations. For example, the fact that Behn distinguishes between three different indigenous groups within Surinam supports her claim to have visited the colony while the fact that she represents their speech, even if only in the margins of the main story, suggests an interest in each group and its particular form of humanity.

Rich though the results of this kind of investigation may prove, analyzing the representation of speech is only part of the challenge. Equally important is attention to vocabulary, as the shifts in register between Governor and Caribs indicate in the passage just discussed. For example, early in her account of Oroonoko and Imoinda's relationship, the narrator draws attention to the kind of language the hero uses. She remarks:

> I have often heard him say, that he admir'd by what strange Inspiration he came to talk things so soft, and so passionate, who never knew Love, nor was us'd to the Conversation of Women; but (to use his own Words) he said, Most happily, some new, and till then unknown Power instructed his Heart and Tongue in the Language of Love, and at the same time, in favour of him, inspir'd *Imoinda* with a Sense of his Passion. (15)

The parenthetical "to use his own Words" indicates that the rest of the sentence is in narrated speech, but the vocabulary is equally significant. While the parenthesis re-emphasizes what the narrator claims is the authenticity of the story, the vocabulary ("soft," "passionate," "Heart," "Passion") establishes the characteristic register of heroic romance. Oroonoko has already been introduced as a hero through the narrator's praise of his "Greatness of Soul," "Notions of true Honour," and "absolute Generosity" (12), but this is the first occasion on which he is shown drawing on the discursive field of romance. In the Coramantien sequences that follow, he has several major speeches that display that discourse in action. Analysis of these should help define what is at stake in them: the principles of heroic love, honor, and integrity that the story is to show being betrayed.

Extracts for class discussion include the one in which Oroonoko denounces the Captain for not accepting his word of honor (32–33), and that in which Byam, using the language of courtesy, persuades Oroonoko to surrender following the rebellion (55–56). Interestingly, in the latter episode, even Oroonoko's stipulation that Byam put his promises in writing fails to hold him to them. However, as both passages are too long to analyze here, the example I will discuss is one that involves the narrator's speech while she is entertaining Oroonoko and Imoinda pending the much-promised but always deferred arrival of the Governor—a lapse that invites Oroonoko's suspicion. It begins with the narrator reporting her own speech indirectly: "For these Reasons, I had Opportunity to take notice to him, that he was not well pleas'd of late, as he us'd to be; was more retir'd and thoughtful" (41). However, the words that follow "and told him," imply a shift into narrated speech for the rest of the sentence, when the narrator says: "I took it Ill he shou'd Suspect we wou'd break our Words with him." Following Oroonoko's answer, which merely summarizes Oroonoko's doubt, the words "which made me ask him" suggest a further shift into narrated speech for the narrator's rejoinder to the end of the sentence: "what advantage it wou'd be to doubt? it would but give us a Fear of him, and possibly compel us to treat him so as I shou'd be very loath to behold: that is, it might occasion his Confinement" (41). Finally, after a retrospective comment from herself, "Perhaps this was not so Luckily spoke of me" (41), the narrator uses narrated speech once more, this time to represent Oroonoko's response: "he assur'd me, that whatsoever Resolutions he shou'd take, he wou'd Act nothing upon the White-People; and as for my self, and those upon that *Plantation* where he was, he wou'd sooner forfeit his eternal Liberty, and Life it self, than lift his Hand against his greatest Enemy on that Place" (41–42). Here, as in other examples, the words that may be read as narrated speech can be converted plausibly into direct speech by altering third person to first and past tense to present. Especially interesting is the final shift into narrated speech that features Oroonoko's characteristic heroic language in his undertaking to "forfeit his eternal Liberty, and Life it self" rather than rebel. By quoting herself, the narrator in effect highlights her divided loyalties. It therefore raises further questions about her role not only as the teller of the tale but as a character within it.

These questions may be explored further by considering other aspects of the vocabulary, which is surprisingly mixed. The diction is sometimes plain or, as in the closing pages, brutally direct, but elsewhere, though the language of commerce sometimes makes its appearance, as when the narrator gives an outline of the slave trade (11), the dominant linguistic code is that of heroic romance. Students can be invited to classify the different types of language within sections of the text, or even, using an electronic edition, to carry out word-searches and word-counts.[3] Such inquiry may draw attention to a subordinate code of heroic romance related to the language of courtesy. Words in this category and their cognates that appear in the text (as distinct from the Dedication) include "honour," thirty-one times; "grace," eleven times; "civil," seven times; "conversation," seven times; and "condescend," four times. An especially interesting example is "oblige" because of the range of meanings it encompasses. During the sequence in which the narrator tells how she tried to entertain Oroonoko and distract him from his grievances, she uses the verb five times out of a total of eighteen occurrences in the entire narrative. In two of these instances, "oblige" has its courtly sense of gratifying someone, as when the narrator declares "I oblig'd 'em in all things I was capable of" and "obliging him to love us very well" (41). However, even these suggest the ulterior motive made explicit by the *OED* definition of this sense, the first part of which reads: "To bind or make indebted by conferring a favour" (def. 9a). The other three examples are in the stronger sense of "constrain" (defs. 12–14). The first is applied to the narrator early in the passage when she states: "I was oblig'd, by some Persons, who fear'd a Mutiny (which is very Fatal sometimes in those Colonies, that abound so with Slaves, that they exceed the Whites in vast Numbers) to discourse with *Caesar*, and to give him all the Satisfaction I possibly cou'd" (41). While this suggests that she had no choice but to act as she did, the next occurrence indicates the kind of complicity on her part already revealed by her divided loyalty: "After this, I neither thought it convenient to trust him much out of our View, nor did the Country who fear'd him; but with one accord it was advis'd to treat him Fairly, and oblige him to remain within such a compass" (42). "Convenient" is the kind of euphemism used earlier in saying she did not want him treated in a way that she would be very loath to behold, but on this occasion she does not put it in plain words. Evidence such as this may lead students to explore the relation between the language of politeness and the exercise of power. In the same episode, Oroonoko applies *oblige* to his own influence over the colonists: "*Caesar* look'd upon it as a Mark of extraordinary Respect, and was glad his discontent had oblig'd 'em to be more observant to him" (42).

In referring to the hero as "*Caesar*," the remark just quoted points to a further approach to the language of *Oroonoko*. Jacqueline Pearson has shown how significant the pronoun can be in Behn's narrative (185, 187–88), and the same principle applies to proper names too. Examples are the shifts between African and slave names for the two central figures, especially Imoinda, whose slave name is dropped completely only a few pages after it has been introduced, and is used only ten times out of the thirty occasions when she is named. Students might be asked to consider whether this suggests that she is less assimilated than Oroonoko to European codes of value, even heroic ones, just as her more extensive body-markings seem to make her appear more "other."

Another significant example of naming concerns the figure whom the text most often designates "the Governor." In most instances the term almost certainly refers to William Byam (54), though he was deputy to the actual Governor, who was Francis, Lord Willoughby of Parham (Gallagher, "Colonial Life" 337). Students might be asked to consider why the text refers to Byam in various ways: twelve times as "Governor," eleven times by his surname, and once as "Deputy Governor"; while she never refers to Willoughby by name, but five times as "Lord Governor" (a term unlikely to be applied to Byam), and five times as "Lord." There are also three occasions when the word *Governor* could refer either to Byam or Willoughby, who is known to have been in Surinam in 1651 and 1665 (LaCombe, "Willoughby"). These all occur in the episode when the Governor fails to honor his promise to visit the local people. While such variations might be explained by carelessness on Behn's part, it is possible that they follow contemporary usage in Surinam, so offering further potential evidence that Behn spent time there. More interestingly, they also furnish data for analysis of different kinds of reference to those holding executive power, especially when the distinction between governor and deputy is blurred. In particular, the narrative casts unmistakable doubt on Byam's ability to govern.

Encouraging students to analyze forms of reference is, then, not only a productive exercise in itself. Like analysis of vocabulary, narrative voice, and perspective, it also opens up a whole range of critical and thematic questions. Some of these involve Behn's representation of gender and ethnicity, while others bring into focus the systems of value that the text endorses, and others still highlight matters of power and agency. Because these questions are often interrelated, detailed study of the linguistic texture enables closer and more accurate judgments, and also furnishes textual evidence that students can deploy on their own.

NOTES

[1] Genette's second question concerns narrative perspective and is "Who sees?" Although answering this question is for the most part beyond the scope of this chapter, it is also an invaluable analytical as well as teaching techñique.

[2] For a properly theorized account, see McHale or Rimmon-Kenan for a more accessible source.

[3] The edition used for this purpose in this essay was downloaded from *Early English Books Online*. Other electronic editions may produce slightly different results.

Oroonoko and the Heroics of Virtue

Shawn Lisa Maurer

Much of the way we read, understand, and teach *Oroonoko* depends on our acceptance of the text's delineation of the eponymous protagonist as a hero—not only in the sense of his centrality in this purportedly "true Story" but also in his possession of qualities defined by literary convention as heroic. Handsome, noble, and honorable, Behn's African prince epitomizes the victorious warrior as well as the devoted lover. Indeed Behn's narrator presents her "Royal Slave" (7)—the oxymoronic phrase that will itself bear importantly on Oroonoko's heroic status—as superhuman: this "young *Mars*" (14) is "belov'd like a Deity" (30) in his native Coramantien; he is treated with similar awe and reverence on the slave ship to Surinam and in the English colony there. At the same time, the narrator's reiterated claim of being "an Eye-Witness" to most of the history and her direct connection to Oroonoko as both confidante and narrator—"what I cou'd not be Witness of, I receiv'd from the Mouth of the chief Actor in this History, the *Hero* himself" (8)—combine to establish Oroonoko as necessarily mortal, endowed with temporal as well as spatial specificity. Although a biographical precedent for Oroonoko has yet to be discovered, his all-too-human nature in the text, culminating in his gruesome death, becomes essential to the narrative's elegiac celebration of a fallen hero and a lost world.

Larger than life and tragically human, the virtuous hero Behn hopes to immortalize remains a complex and contradictory figure. The heroic status of this "Great Man" (7) serves as the literary and moral foundation of the narrator's account, since Oroonoko's unsung greatness establishes the necessity for and the value of his ostensibly true story. Yet his ability to function as hero is severely challenged by his often bizarre responses to forces he cannot control or countermand: the absolutist demands of his grandfather, king of Coramantien; the deceptions of the ship captain; the empty promises of the Surinam leaders. In particular, Oroonoko displays—on many occasions—a self-destructive passivity that undermines his heroic identity.

How, then, are we to understand Oroonoko's problematic heroic status? What might attention to moments of textual contradiction reveal about the period's changing attitudes toward heroism, virtue, aristocratic honor, masculinity? For Mary Beth Rose, Oroonoko's behavior typifies an ideological shift from the late sixteenth to the late seventeenth century in which a "heroics of action," associated with an aristocratic male warrior class, is increasingly replaced by a "heroics of endurance" that "privileges not the active confrontation with danger but the capacity to endure it, to resist and suffer with patience and fortitude, rather than to confront and conquer with strength and wit" (xii). By the late seventeenth century, as the English Civil War and its aftermath had rendered traditional forms of heroism obsolete, this new form of passive valor, "gendered normatively as female," becomes "the primary model of literary heroism," in Behn's *Oroonoko* and other Restoration texts (85–86). While Rose's reading offers compelling insight into Oroonoko's stoicism during the novel's deeply troubling final scenes, her approach cannot account for his many suicidal impulses, nor does it address the patriarchal underpinnings of his actions—in particular the honorable killing of Imoinda that precipitates the self-mutilation and subsequent dismemberment that he withstands with such fortitude. Ultimately, Rose's feminization of passive heroism as "always a female position, the position of the woman" (111), part of her laudable desire to acknowledge the previously obscured cultural importance of the female in representations of the heroic (xxi), itself functions, ironically, to erase one of the text's most significant components: the emergence of a new form of virtuous masculinity in the noble yet ultimately defeated Oroonoko.

Oroonoko is an excellent text through which to teach students about the changing nature of heroic virtue as well as about the ways in which a masculine gendered identity was itself constructed in relation to heroic ideals. In his vexed and often contradictory manifestations of heroism, Oroonoko can be seen as representing a transitional figure, one who must negotiate between a notion of honor derived from the aristocratic ethos (privileging birth, aggressive courage, competition, reputation, and revenge) and, competing with that notion, a new, sentimental bourgeois ideal in which a man's ability to love and protect his family becomes the measure of his worth. Drawing students' attention to the changing and often fractured codes of heroic male virtue depicted throughout *Oroonoko* can help students focus on the prior, often eclipsed, sections of the novel and show connections between the work's seemingly disparate parts. Spanning both halves of the novel, Oroonoko's heroic virtue is shown most powerfully in three key areas: first, extraordinary physical courage; second, faithful love for Imoinda; and third, "true Honour" (12), a moral uprightness displayed most powerfully in the verbal integrity that makes Oroonoko incapable of deceit. Yet these heroic qualities ultimately subvert one another as Oroonoko must navigate the competing demands of love and war, as the text simultaneously reveals how each area is itself already compromised.

Thus physical bravery, a hallmark of the aristocratic male code of honor, must rest on a blatant disregard for one's own well-being: although "animated with Despair," thinking Imoinda dead, Oroonoko fights fearlessly, doing "such things as will not be believ'd that Humane Strength cou'd perform" (29). His love for Imoinda also suffers ideological contradiction. Demonstrating "right Notions of Honour," he pledges a monogamy that runs "contrary to the Custom" of his polygamous society (15). As students tend to forget, the Coramantien section of Behn's text centers on male rivalry—in particular Oroonoko's efforts to liberate Imoinda from his grandfather, the all-powerful king of Coramantien. While Oroonoko's love for Imoinda seems to epitomize the kind of mutual affection that would increasingly distinguish bourgeois marriage from arranged aristocratic unions, Oroonoko is no less the possessor of Imoinda than his patriarchal and polygamous grandfather. Indeed, the narrative acknowledges such absolute power near the end of the novel, as Imoinda embraces death at the hands of "him she so tenderly Lov'd, and so truly Ador'd . . . for Wives have a respect for their Husbands equal to what any other People pay a Deity" (60).

Equally problematic is that the idealized honor of Oroonoko simultaneously criticizes and upholds aristocratic codes. Initially, his honesty, his "honorable inability to lie and consequent inability to perceive lies" (Chibka, "Truth" 223), allies him with the Surinam natives, who believe that "when once a Man's Word was past, nothing but Death cou'd or shou'd prevent his keeping it" (10). Sharing their belief in the direct correlation between word and deed, Oroonoko partakes as well in their prelapsarian virtue, which represents to the narrator "an absolute *Idea* of the first State of Innocence, before Man knew how to sin" (10). Therefore Oroonoko frequently functions as a noble savage whose naïveté serves to expose the hypocrisy and corruption of the civilized European Christians. At the same time, his steadfast fidelity to honorable ideals necessitates that he take revenge on those who have wronged him. In this way, he is not the scourge but the defender of an aristocratic code of honor founded on the need to protect, at all costs, one's reputation. This defending is most explicit in his exchange with the ship captain, who refuses to trust the word of a "*Heathen*" unmotivated by fear of damnation in the afterlife. Reversing the usual hierarchy, Oroonoko contends that "eternal Torment in the World to come" necessarily pales before disgrace in this world: the "*Man of no Honour . . . dies every day ignominiously in his Fame, which is more valuable than Life*" (32–33). In elevating a man's "Fame" above all other concerns, he upholds an aristocratic ideology that, in its inexorable demand for revenge, stands notably at odds with Christian teaching.

The novel repeatedly shows how Oroonoko's particular combination of integrity and naïveté, though it distinguishes him from men "of no Honour," also makes him especially vulnerable to these same men. Such "open trustfulness," as Joanna Lipking notes, is curiously absent from seventeenth-century travelers' accounts of West Africans, who were known for being "only too shrewd" ("'Others'" 171). By contradicting historical representation and making naïveté an integral part of Oroonoko's heroic persona, Behn sets up his downfall. As an adherent of the code of honor, Oroonoko must revenge himself on those who have betrayed and humiliated him. Yet he also must kill the pregnant Imoinda, to protect her from those betrayers, an action that contradicts an emerging sentimental ethos in which the family is not a site of conflict but a place of refuge.

The novel depicts an irreconcilable clash between love and war. In Surinam, Oroonoko makes the painful discovery that the heroic ideal that had so successfully rallied his Coramantien warriors to a "Manly Defence" (28) on the battlefield does not produce a similar effect on the slaves he attempts to lead in escape from Parham.[1] Driven to desperation by Imoinda's pregnancy and his fear that their child will be born into captivity, he is twice betrayed by the words of others—first by the slaves who abandon him after having "Vow'd to follow him to Death" (54) and then by Byam, who promises to pardon him but instead subjects him to a brutal whipping. Oroonoko succumbs to the desire for revenge he overcame before, with his grandfather and with the slave ship captain. In this final section of the novel, revenge is Oroonoko's raison d'être.[2]

What thwarts the ability of Oroonoko to fulfill his heroic goal is not cowardice but intense feeling. After having killed Imoinda but before he can carry out his revenge on Byam, he is rendered powerless by "excess of Grief" (61), which also threatened to destroy him on two previous occasions—when he believed Imoinda dead and when he was imprisoned on the slave ship. At the end, he is undone by the same love and familial connection that made him powerless and self-destructive—indeed suicidal—in those earlier scenes, scenes that reveal not "passive Valour" (50), a term associated with the Surinam warrior captains and with his final stoicism in the face of dismemberment, but an active and unbearable anguish. In all these instances, his sorrow is manifested in an increasingly debilitating prostration, both physical and emotional.[3]

Examining the three scenes of prostration can help students understand how a heroic model based on relationships of dominance and submission increasingly gives way to sentimentality. Characters other than Oroonoko manifest the earlier, more traditional sense of prostration as marking "humility, adoration, or servility" ("Prostration," def. 1)—for example, when Imoinda, in entreating the king to withdraw the royal veil, "threw her self on the Marble, on the Brink of the Bath, and besought him to hear her" (17) or when the messenger bearing news of Imoinda's death throws "himself at the Prince's feet, . . . with all the Submission of a Man that had something to implore which he dreaded to utter" (27). Later, the plantation slaves display their reverence for Oroonoko as they "cast themselves at his Feet" (37). His prostrations, by contrast, display less a deferential physical posture than a distraught physical and emotional condition. In each of three scenes, he is "abject, defeated or powerless" ("Prostrate," def. 2a) and suffers "extreme physical weakness" or "mental depression" ("Prostration," def. 3). As the first of these scenes transpires in Africa, it is clear that his prostrations are not exclusively the result of his enslavement, although the lack of autonomy inherent in his oxymoronic situation as a "Royal Slave" powerfully exacerbates the torment and melancholy he earlier suffered.

The first suicidal impulse occurs after Oroonoko learns that Imoinda has been taken to his grandfather's palace, and "they had much ado to save him from laying violent Hands on himself" (17). However, his followers soon convince him of the king's sexual impotence and of the "solemn Contract" that sanctions his pursuit of Imoinda (18). Only later, once Oroonoko has learned of Imoinda's death, does his prostration occur: on the eve of battle, he "laid himself on a Carpet" for two days, refusing food and drink (27). Yet his grief cannot overpower the realization that his soldiers are ineffective without him: he rouses himself with the heroic idea of dying "*the noblest Way*"—actively in battle against his rival, Jamoan, rather than "*lazily, on a Couch*" in a "*Love-sick*" daze (29). In contrast to his previous depressed state, when he had believed himself *"the most wretched, and abandon'd by Fortune, of all the Creation of the Gods"* (28), he arms himself and turns "the Tide of the Victory" (29).

Despite his victory and subsequent friendship with Jamoan, Oroonoko continues to suffer the "Disease of Melancholy and Languishment" (29). While faithful to his lost Imoinda, he eventually revives, especially with the arrival of an English slave ship, whose cultivated captain quickly gains "upon the Heart of this gallant young Man" (31). But as Oroonoko was betrayed by the king, he is similarly taken advantage of by the captain, who uses the bonds of friendship and hospitality to capture the prince and "an hundred of the noblest of the Youths of the Court" (31). Oroonoko, responding to his confinement like a "Lion," attempts suicide but is prevented by the way his captors "had so wisely manag'd his Fetters, that he cou'd not use a Hand in his Defence, to quit himself of a Life that wou'd by no Means endure Slavery" (31). Instead, he "resolved to perish for want of Food: And pleased at last with that Thought, and toil'd and tired by Rage and Indignation, he laid himself down, and sullenly resolved upon dying, and refused all things that were brought him" (32). His second prostration lasts four days, at which point the captain, fearing the loss of both Oroonoko and his attendants, who similarly "refus'd all manner of Sustenance," agrees to release the prince from his chains while aboard ship and promises that Oroonoko and his warriors will be freed at "the first Opportunity" (33).

As in the battle scene before, Oroonoko inspires his men, who are "transported with Excess of Joy at the sight of their Darling Prince" as he assures them of their imminent release. While he directs his followers to "bear their Chains with that Bravery that became those whom he had seen act so nobly in Arms" (33), he suffers recurring melancholy, blaming himself for having abandoned Imoinda to her death. Yet his depression does not overwhelm him, as it did not when he thought he had lost Imoinda forever. Foolishly, he trusts in the captain's promise of freedom, and his "thousand Griefs" for Imoinda's "eternal Loss" are mitigated by his recollection of "a thousand Thoughts of past Joys" (34).

Such alleviation is not possible in the third, most devastating prostration scene. Once again Oroonoko has been deceived, this time by Byam, the "Fawning fair-tongu'd" deputy governor (54), who, like the captain before him, pretends a friendship that he will later betray. Having incited the colonists to pursue the fugitive slaves, the duplicitous Byam promises to pardon Oroonoko but instead has him whipped by "every one of those *Slaves*, who, but a few Days before, Ador'd him as something more than Mortal" (57). Oroonoko vows revenge, fully aware that it will mean his death—either at the hands of the English mob or by his own hand. But he recognizes that his death will leave Imoinda vulnerable. Although she is eager to die by her husband's hand, her death precipitates vastly different emotions in Oroonoko. Having responded like a noble lion to his earlier capture, Oroonoko here reacts with a frenzy that turns him into a raging beast who must again fight the impulse to destroy himself: "[H]e Tore, he Rav'd, he Roar'd, like some Monster of the Wood, . . . a thousand times he turn'd the Fatal Knife that did the Deed, toward his own Heart, with a Resolution to go immediately after her." He is roused only by the thought of "dire Revenge, which now was a thousand times more fierce in his Soul than before." Yet rage and revenge give way to paralyzing grief: lying by the side of the dead Imoinda, whose face he waters with unaccustomed "showers of Tears," he is prostrate for two days. Attempting to rise in order to complete the "great Work" of revenge, he finds "his Strength so decay'd" that he remains on the ground six days further. From two days of prostration on the African battlefield to four on the slave ship to eight in the Surinam woods: each incident doubles the one before, resulting in a situation in which not lack of nourishment but "excess of Grief" (61) brings about his final, and ultimately fatal, prostration, which also prevents his revenge.

When Oroonoko does finally arise from his stupor at the sight of his pursuers, he turns his rage not on them but on himself, first slashing his throat much the way he had killed Imoinda and then disemboweling himself. Although still capable of killing an "English" who attacks him in his weakened state, he is transformed from superhuman being to symbol of mortality, "a Death's Head black'd over; nothing but Teeth, and Eyeholes" (63). The dejection that plagues the dying Oroonoko is transferred to the narrator, who reports that "his Discourse was sad; and the earthly Smell about him so strong, that I was perswaded to leave the Place for some time (being my self but Sickly, and very apt to fall into Fits of dangerous Illness upon any extraordinary Melancholy)." Although the noble Trefry pledges to stay behind to protect Oroonoko, Trefry is himself deceived by Byam and lured away from Parham, so that Byam's agent, Banister, a "wild *Irish* Man" and "a Fellow of absolute Barbarity" (64), can execute Oroonoko.[4]

Byam, like the slave captain before him, betrays the honor code egregiously, but the narrator also is complicit in Oroonoko's betrayal, absenting herself during his torture and execution. Although she asserts her authority in Surinam, claiming in the novel's "Epistle Dedicatory" that she "had none above [her] in that Country" (7), as a woman she is necessarily excluded from masculine structures of power, in particular the code of honor dependent on personal reputation—reputation gained in part through aggression against other men, in part through protection of women. In Behn's world as in Oroonoko's, honor for women is situated in chastity, a quality associated not with the narrator but with "the Brave, the Beautiful, and the Constant *Imoinda*" (65). By contrast, the narrator's reputation is not personal but professional: she concludes by hoping that the "Reputation of [her] Pen is considerable enough" to preserve, for posterity, the "Glorious Name" of Oroonoko and his beloved Imoinda (65).

Published near the end of Behn's life, *Oroonoko* in fact promoted Behn's literary standing by depicting a hero whose reputation—for courage, glory, and love—also revealed the corrupt code of honor that marked the English ruling classes. Prevented by his position as slave from mastering other men and mastered, in turn, by his concerns for his family, Oroonoko falls fatally between the cracks of two overlapping and contradictory systems of heroic virtue.

NOTES

[1] Anita Pacheco notes that Oroonoko's speech is curious in that the ideals of honor he espouses do not actually apply to the slaves he is addressing, since those slaves have been captured in battle—many by Oroonoko himself (498).

[2] In this section, the word *revenge* appears eleven times in six pages (55–61), as opposed to eight times in the previous forty-six.

[3] Derek Hughes calls attention to "over twenty prostrations" in Behn's text ("Race" 9).

[4] This scene marks the second time that Trefry is deceived by Byam. During the attempted escape, Trefry, "believing the Governor to mean what he said," uses "Wit and Reasons" along with tears to convince Oroonoko to surrender (56). When instead Oroonoko is brutally beaten, he is able to forgive Trefry, acknowledging that Trefry was unable to intervene for fear of being himself attacked by the slaves (58).

CULTURAL CONTEXTS

Oroonoko and Blackness

Derek Hughes

I started thinking and writing about *Oroonoko* many years before I had an opportunity to teach it. The opportunity first came when, in 2004, I moved to the University of Aberdeen in Scotland, where my responsibilities included coordinating a large second-year core course on literature of the long eighteenth century as well as devising final, fourth-year options, each with a maximum enrollment of fifteen students.

When I arrived, the second-year course was a straightforward eighteenth-century great-books course, with hardly any acknowledgment of the topics that have produced so much innovative work over the last thirty years: for example, colonialism, slavery, the rise of the woman writer. *Oroonoko* had been included before I arrived but was dropped because of unpopularity with the students. I reintroduced it, to bring the course more into line with current scholarly preoccupations. *Oroonoko* is now studied in relation to a number of other narrative works, starting with *Paradise Lost* and ending with *Sense and Sensibility*. In this way students are shown—as they must always be—that content and point of view can be shaped by genre and tradition at least as powerfully as by racial politics—which is not to say that generic expectation may not be modified by particular context. Students are told, for example, that the description of Surinam's perpetual spring continues a tradition of portraying perfect places that goes back to the description of Alkinöos's gardens in Homer's *Odyssey* (bk. 7) and that it is not the first time that the convention has been used ironically.

Studying *Oroonoko* in a history of the development of narrative forms—surely no uncommon thing—invites stress on the artifice of convention. Like many scholars who think about the work, I draw attention to Behn's juxtaposition of romance convention with nonromance conduct and settings. Although Oroonoko's heroism against tigers recalls, for example, Lysimachus's bare-handed slaughtering of a lion in La Calprenède's *Cassandre* (2.2.126), the former's exploits in Surinam are not freely exercised heroism but a licensed diversion allowed him by his captors: an artificial oasis of romance in a world of brutal commercial realism.

Oroonoko has been enthusiastically received in both the second- and the fourth-year course, so much so that I find its earlier poor reception difficult to understand, especially as the text is not, for students in the United Kingdom, morally problematic. This is particularly so in Scotland, which has a very separate sense of national identity and where *Oroonoko* is not tainted by the sins of the past. Scottish universities naturally teach their country's role in the British Empire, acknowledging the empire's many iniquities but also seeing creditable motives and achievements. Awareness of Scotland's part in the slave trade is, moreover, offset by pride in the many Scots who worked for its abolition.

For most of my students, therefore, *Oroonoko* seems remote from any living heritage of hatred and injustice. It is a brilliant record of a distant period, and I have to inform them about the passionate and nonliterary debates that have surrounded its moral and ideological status for many years now. It is important for them to recover a past that is unfamiliar but equally important for them to choose the right past to recover: they should not assume that the racial injustices of the seventeenth century were driven by the prejudices and theories of the nineteenth.

For the senior option, I devised a course on the representation of racial difference in seventeenth-century literature, based on my anthology *Versions of Blackness*. *Oroonoko* naturally occupies a central position in this course. It is preceded by *Othello*, by *The Tempest* and its Restoration revision by John Dryden and William Davenant, and by Dryden's *The Indian Emperour* and Behn's *Abdelazer*, and it is followed by Behn's *The Widdow Ranter* and by the dramatic versions of *Oroonoko* by Thomas Southerne and 'Biyi Bandele. As background for each class, the students also read contextualizing extracts from *Versions of Blackness*: discussions of colonialism, slavery, and racial difference by writers ranging from Bartolomé de Las Casas and Juan Ginés de Sepúlveda to John Locke and the authors of the Germantown Protest. In this final-year course, the only text that has met with any reservations as to its quality is Southerne's. Bandele's version is well liked, but the chief surprise has been the popularity of the Dryden-Davenant *Tempest* (read in conjunction with Henry Neville's *The Isle of Pines*). *The Indian Emperour* is also enjoyed, though more as an intellectual document than as a theatrical masterpiece.

Each week, the principal text is read along with several extracts from *Versions of Blackness*. Along with *Othello*, in the first week, students read passages from José de Acosta's *On Spreading the Gospel among the Savages* (D. Hughes, *Versions* 293–94) and from Richard Ligon's *True and Exact History of the Island of Barbados* (300–06). Acosta argues that the apparent differences of nature between Europeans and black Africans are purely products of education; Ligon gives a simple and stark story of African jealousy and superstition, which illuminates by contrast the immense complexity of *Othello*. In the second week, *The Tempest* is paired with extracts from Michel de Montaigne's idealistic discussions of Native American culture in "Of Cannibals" and "Of Coaches" (287–92), which are recalled in the play, and Sepúlveda's earlier and contrastingly brutal dismissal of the indigenous peoples as "homunculi"—less than men (285–86). The Montaigne passages provide the source of the imaginary ideal community about which Shakespeare's Gonzalo fantasizes. In addition, the contrasting extreme images of the primitive in Sepúlveda and Montaigne provide a context in which to see Shakespeare's anagramming of the cannibal in the figure of Caliban. I also show students Aristotle's discussion of those who are slaves by nature (*Politics*, bk. 1), on which Sepúlveda draws.

Montaigne's influence extends far beyond Shakespeare. His description of the infant continent "naked in the Mothers lap" (D. Hughes, *Versions* 292) is versified by Dryden in the opening scene of *The Indian Emperour*, and he compactly brings together many distinctive and recurrent aspects of early modern representations of the primitive: aspects (such as the recurrent contention that Europeans are more barbarous than the peoples they conquer) that students often find surprising. There is, for example, an exemplary brief exposition of cultural relativism: "[E]very one gives the Title of Barbarity to every thing that is not in use in his own Country: As indeed we have no other level of Truth and Reason, than the Example and Idea of the Opinions and Customs of the place wherein we Live" (288). Montaigne also sees the New World as both realizing and exceeding the perfection of the classical golden age, a view that was to be powerfully but also skeptically echoed by Behn.

The passage from Montaigne that may have the most complex influence is the characterization of New World cultures as lacking the sign systems that sustain European civilization: there is no writing, number, or money and no conception of verbal falsehood. Behn used the idea of a culture without lies in portraying the Native Americans in *Oroonoko* (it was to recur in book 4 of *Gulliver's Travels*). This detail is part of something larger, a tendency to conceive of alien cultures in terms less of alien bodies than of alien sign systems. In "Of Cannibals," Montaigne's evocation of a utopian anarchy with "no [knowledge] of Letters, no Science of Numbers" (D. Hughes, *Versions* 290) gives no hint of the presence of great civilizations in the newly discovered continent. In "Of Coaches," Montaigne does provide a respectful account of Aztec artistry and morality, but this account is initiated by another description of a world without its full quota of sign systems: "[I]t knew neither *Letters, Weights,* [nor] *Measures*" (292). Partly because of Montaigne, the strangely organized symbolic system fascinated Behn far more than the strangely colored body.

Not that there was any desire to convey the actual systems of the newly discovered peoples—to use, for example, Roger Williams's *A Key into the Language of America* (1643). The alien peoples are imagined as semiotic mirror images of Europeans, reversing familiar systems rather than inhabiting ones that are completely unrelated to ours. In *Oroonoko* Behn describes how Native American competitors for high military office compete by lopping off parts of their faces: the one who inflicts the most damage on himself wins. This description is probably a fiction. Accounts of the New World describe painful rites of initiation for chieftains, involving scarification or flogging but not self-amputation, though Behn may have read about a ritual of sacrificial self-amputation in the Indian province of Quilacare (Ramusio 2: 667–78; Purchas 421). She appears to have invented the chieftains' use of this practice, both to show its being exceeded in the barbarity by the European treatment of Oroonoko's body and to exemplify the idea of a culture with no forms of symbolism beyond the body, a culture in which the only imaginable currency is body parts. Carib society is imagined through a reversal of European forms rather than through the direct appropriation of travelers' narratives. Nevertheless, sign systems are the primary points of differentiation. The three peoples in *Oroonoko*—Europeans, black Africans, and South Americans—are distinguished at least as much by artificial body modification and artificial dress as by innate physical appearance. That is, they are presented as the recipients of signs. The bodies of the Europeans are not described at all; the one exception, the fisherman who has "become a perfect *Indian* in Colour" (48), proves the rule.

Oroonoko is read alongside four passages in *Versions*: Antoine Biet (313–14) and Jean-Baptiste du Tertre (327–30) both document the brutality and dishonesty of the slave trade, George Warren describes the fauna and ethnography of Surinam (331–38), and *Great Newes from the Barbadoes* narrates the brutal suppression of a slave rebellion and rather incongruously concludes with a description of the rich and unspoiled natural resources of the island (339–43). This description, however, is not of a Montaignesque golden age but of an economic paradise ripe for exploitation. After the enthusiastic cataloguing of "Wood Pidgeons, Turtle-Doves of several kinds, [and] wild Fowls" comes the curt and sober reassurance that the forts are "well mounted with store of great Guns" (343).

By the end of the course, students have read ten major texts and encountered the diversity of seventeenth-century opinion on questions such as the morality of colonialism and the human status and rights of indigenous peoples and black Africans. Their knowledge is still sketchy, but they have enough to avoid rash simplification or generalization.

I feed into class discussion the results of my own study of later theorists of race, notably the Comte de Gobineau (1816–82) and Houston Stewart Chamberlain (1855–1927), and of early European responses to Aztec culture. I quote, for example, Bernal Díaz del Castillo's moving and wondering account of the Spaniards' first glimpse of the beauty and refinement of Tenochtitlán (2: 37). I ask students to think about the relative importance of race and culture in *Oroonoko*. For Gobineau in the mid–nineteenth century, culture was completely determined by race and degrees of racial intermixture. What was the situation in the seventeenth century?

I take as a starting point Oroonoko's explicitly European nose (13), which has aroused strong and strikingly opposed reactions. For Margo Hendricks, Oroonoko's partly European appearance "schematizes an optic dichotomy," hinting—she improbably suggests—in a kind of reverse code at Behn's own fearfully preserved secret: that she was partly black ("Alliance" 269). For other critics, the nose reveals not Behn's blackness but her whiteness: it is a "deprecation of the African phenotype" (Reinhardt 28), betraying her lack of sympathy "with Oroonoko as a black character" (Twagilimana 15). It reveals "the failure of Behn's novella to see beyond the mirror of its own culture" (Brown, *Ends* 37). Oroonoko's executioners cut off this troublesome facial feature. What should we do with it?

Certainly, the nose appears with remarkable frequency in seventeenth-century writing as a distinguishing feature of European beauty. Du Tertre mentions "Indian" Warner's aquiline nose (3: 82) and William Penn describes the "Roman" noses of the Pennsylvanian Indians (5) in passages not dissimilar to Behn's description of Oroonoko. Despite the importance of the nose in the aesthetics of racial appearance, many writers believed that the flat African nose was artificially induced in early childhood, that it was another cultural modification of the body. Du Tertre relates that a colleague dissuaded a black African woman from flattening the nose of her first child but that she was so horrified by the ugliness of the resulting European nose that she surreptitiously flattened the nose of her next child. He also asserts that the plump black African lips—another feature that Oroonoko lacks—are artificially induced (2: 508).

Some bodily differences that later ages attributed to race were in the seventeenth century considered the result of cultural management. It is unquestionably true that artificial body modification, by cutting or painting, is at least as important a factor as skin color in the differentiation of peoples, both in *Oroonoko* and in works of seventeenth-century ethnography. In this context, I show students some of the illustrations from the 1590 edition of Thomas Harriot's *Briefe and True Report of the New Found Land of Virginia*, in which representations of Native Americans are complemented by imaginary pictures of heavily tattooed Picts. The clear implication is that the body modifications of "primitive" tribes illustrate a cultural stage occupied by our own local ancestors in the relatively recent past, a point made explicitly by Morgan Godwyn (*Negro's and Indians Advocate* 34–35).

So is the African nose for Behn a racial phenotype (as it is for Reinhardt) or a cultural artifact? Probably the former, since Behn describes the flat nose and full lips as "natural" to black Africans (13). Yet students need to be reminded that the question is real and that the existence of divergent opinions itself may diminish the power of the nose as an absolute racial sign: the boundaries of culture and what later ages would call *race* were drawn differently. Nor is it only in the sphere of body modification that "primitive" cultures correspond to earlier stages in our own cultural history. In her plays, Behn traces a development from feudal and patriarchal militaristic societies (*The Forc'd*

Marriage [*Works* 5: 1–81]) to modern commercial societies (*Sir Patient Fancy* [6: 1–81]), showing that the redistribution of power among men makes no impact on the position of women. The two historically successive stages of European development are, in *Oroonoko*, set synchronically side by side: the militaristic patriarchy of Oroonoko's Coramantien and the commercial culture of Surinam. Yet European culture has been where Behn's Coramantien now is.

I ask students whether they can identify any essentialist criteria of racial difference in the text, and their answer is generally no. Are the non-Europeans, for example, more sexually voracious and menacing than their civilized counterparts?—an aspersion often cast on allegedly primitive peoples, then and later. Margaret Ferguson observes, to Behn's discredit, that the women flee in terror from the threat of rape during Oroonoko's rebellion ("Juggling" [Hendricks and Parker] 215–16). Her censure seems overdone, because these fears are reported in retrospect, after their baselessness has become clear, and the report states only that the women feared "he wou'd come down and Cut all [their] Throats" (57). Sexual violence is, in fact, remarkably absent from all three cultures portrayed in the novel. The only exception is the sexual tyranny of the centenarian king of Coramantien, and he is no threat, being impotent.

Although interracial liaisons are not at issue in *Oroonoko*, it needs to be stressed that they are a regular feature of romance and drama. The points of reference for a seventeenth-century London writer, even one describing slavery from firsthand observation, are not necessarily the plantation and its inevitable interracial tensions. Susan Andrade sees the novel as infused with fear of interracial coupling (201–06), yet not only does such coupling never take place, it is never explicitly in prospect. True, in the 1696 "Memoirs on the Life of Mrs. Behn," the author, "a Gentlewoman of her Acquaintance," feels obliged to deny that there was an "*Affair between that Prince and* Astrea" (Behn, *Histories* b1r). But this denial proves my point: the reason given is that there is absolutely no evidence of an affair in the text. In any case, the aim of the "Gentlewoman" is clearly to discourage romantic speculation about the pair, not to keep at bay the horrific specter of miscegenation.

Ferguson ("News" 170) and Hendricks ("Civility" 234–37) detect fear of miscegenation in another Behn work, *The Widdow Ranter*, which does feature an unfulfilled romance between an Englishman and a Native American, even though to the ordinary reader the romance might appear idealized—as the love of the Englishman Towerson and the East Indian Ysabinda, in Dryden's *Amboyna*, clearly is. Southerne has been blamed for his timidity in portraying a white Imoinda in his 1695 dramatization of Behn's novel, and it is certainly true that the Restoration stage never featured a black-skinned heroine, however ready dramatists were to portray the indigenous peoples of India, Africa, or America. Whatever his motives, the end result is that he provides an exemplary interracial marriage and reminds readers that, in the seventeenth century, enslavement was not uniquely practiced by white Europeans on black Africans.

To counter readings that impute fear of miscegenation to Behn, it is useful to review the history of legislation against interracial marriage (with reference, for example, to Hodes and to Rinaldo) and distinguish between the treatment of Africans and that of the indigenous peoples of the Americas. Particular historical instances I cite are the marriage of the French governor of Santa Lucia with a Native American woman, who was praised for her beauty by Charles de Rochefort (252), and the career of Thomas "Indian" Warner, son of an English father and Native American mother, who was made governor of Dominica in 1664 (LaCombe, "Warner"; Du Tertre 3: 82–86). I also stress the prevalence of interracial love in epic, romance, and heroic drama. The terms of reference of a London readership can be shaped at least as much by the utopian fantasies of nonrealistic literature at home as by anxieties that were taking shape over three thousand miles away.

What of religion, a key difference in a world where there was still widespread resistance to the baptism of black slaves? In *Oroonoko*, all three communities use religion deceitfully and self-servingly, and there is no sense that Christian Revelation is superior to pagan darkness. Oroonoko derides the doctrine of the Trinity, which for missionaries was an essential mystery of Christianity, difficult for simple savages to grasp but indispensable. If Oroonoko re-creates the stereotype of the savage bewildered by the elaborate theology of the Trinity, however, he does so for unexpected reasons: his mockery is not the incomprehension of an uninstructed savage but the sophisticated skepticism of a man of the early Enlightenment. The boundaries between African and European are again drawn in unexpected places.

The Trinity is a theological mystery and—for Oroonoko—a mathematical absurdity. His skepticism highlights something that is worth exploring: the extent to which mathematical systems can be markers of cultural differentiation. The seventeenth century was fascinated with mathematically primitive cultures. Writers about the New World comment less frequently on the substantial mathematical achievements of the Aztecs than on reports that certain Native American communities had no abstract numerical system and were incapable of comprehending numbers that exceeded—or even reached—the total of their digits. These reports are used by Behn in her portrayal of Native Americans who can record the passage of time only with knots on cords and who, when confronted with the inexplicable sight of clothed Europeans, spread out their hair and cry, "*Numberless Wonders*, or not to be recounted, no more than to number the Hair of their Heads" (48). In her constant play on counting, accounting, and recounting, she elaborates systems of difference that are based not on color of skin, penetration of intellect, or ratio of lust to reason but on the development of symbolic systems. Oroonoko is led onto the slaving ship by his interest in the captain's mathematical instruments. Yet the greater mathematical sophistication of the Europeans leads simply to the quartering of Oroonoko's body. So *Oroonoko* can be studied in relation to the seventeenth-century revolution in science and chronometry, a revolution that shaped criteria for defining the alien but also led to a selective understanding of advanced non-European cultures. I have found this approach successful in engaging student interest.

My teaching thus emphasizes relativism and the different cultural forms that can be assumed by the same human material—differences of symbolic systems and of generic expectation. I move forward from the seventeenth century to suggest that our systems of interpretation are not Behn's and that we stand on the other side of systems of interpretation that are not Behn's either. My purpose is to suggest not that the lot of the black American was better in 1688 than in 1930 but that the oppressions of the seventeenth century were driven by different imperatives and anxieties and that it is a mistake to read the earlier period entirely in the light of a later one. At the same time, the evil of slavery is an unchangeable absolute, however mutable its justification, and we see the foreshadowing of later prejudices. In attacking the idea, common among Barbados planters, that black Africans were not descended from Adam, Godwyn shows that polygenism was already rearing its head (14–19). He also shows that, from the standpoint of a London readership, it was a quaint belief whose existence they would not readily have suspected.

Students respond to *Oroonoko* as a great, complex, and profoundly experimental landmark in the development of prose fiction. They also learn that the past operates according to rules and assumptions that are different not only from those of the present but also from those of the intervening and more recent past.

Economic *Oroonoko*

Karen Gevirtz

The undergraduates I teach are remarkably diverse—ethnically, socioeconomically, geographically, even religiously—but most share a concern about money: having it now for things like tuition, having it in the future for themselves and their families. This preoccupation is understandable, given the sacrifices they and their families are making for their college education, but it also can be a formidable hurdle in getting students to encounter, understand, and relate to eighteenth-century texts. If a text does not look immediately relevant and useful, they do not think they can afford (pun intended) to give it attention. I turn this mind-set to advantage by "following the money"—that is, taking the development of capitalism as the theme for readings in the long eighteenth century. This approach allows me to focus discussion of *Oroonoko* on its exploration of the effect of colonialist capitalism on morality. I use a combination of primary source readings, research projects, and clips from the PBS historical reenactment-reality series *Colonial House*.

Taking the fight to the students, so to speak, is a well-established classroom tactic, and drawing on the economic concerns of the British eighteenth century to reach students has succeeded with other texts. Although I developed this approach for my undergraduates, I have since found that others have applied similar principles and techniques. Cheryl L. Nixon, for example, describes using *Robinson Crusoe* for nearly the same effect in a freshman writing class at a business school. As if describing my students, Nixon writes that her undergraduates "often see little connection between their business aspirations and their required liberal arts courses." However, facing "this supposed schism" allowed her "to recognize that their business interests can provide a foundation for . . . a complex appreciation of literature's role in the construction of the idea of the self" (207).

Although, as Gillian Skinner points out, the word *economics* did not take on its current meanings until at least the middle of the eighteenth century (4–5), the novel picked up on the connection between social values and the circulation of wealth early on. Without an established vocabulary or genre for considering the changes wrought by the rise of mercantile capitalism, writers created or adapted texts for that task, among them the fictional prose narratives that eventually became the novel. My study of social values, emerging capitalism, and the novel, *Life after Death*, tracks the effect of the changing economic system on morality in such early works. I argue that novelists used the figure of the widow, the only woman with autonomous economic power in the late seventeenth and eighteenth centuries, to establish proper behavior for women when morality and money intersected. Increasingly over the century between Daniel Defoe's *Robinson Crusoe* (1719) and Jane Austen's *Persuasion* (1817), different classes of widows appear in novels to demonstrate that domestic, limited economic activity was the only morally acceptable option for women, even those endowed by their society with the ability to inherit a business or start one and to sign contracts for themselves. Representations of the widow—her relationships, her use of money, the kinds of work she does, even what she looks like and to whom she is attracted—show how eighteenth-century novelists responded to the crisis of economic change and morality by using widows to argue that unregulated, self-interested commercial behavior was unnatural for women and immoral for all.

Moira Ferguson and Gary Gautier both undertake a similar project with *Oroonoko*, linking Behn's economic times to her ambivalent and nuanced exploration of slavery. While primarily concerned with issues of class, Ferguson's and Gautier's investigations of slavery in *Oroonoko* reveal that for Behn, the economic motives behind slavery had significant consequences for value systems. In Ferguson's analysis ("*Oroonoko*"), Behn shows that a society that simultaneously bases its morality in a hierarchical social structure and supports slavery ultimately undermines its moral foundation, since class cannot protect people from being treated as a commodity. Gautier writes that in *Oroonoko* "slavery is naturalized by its universality. It becomes corrupted, however, by the all-corrupting commercial order" (163). Ferguson and Gautier thus expose how sensitivity to class, which is writ large in the text, reveals anxieties about how economic changes were disrupting previously stable systems for classifying and interacting with others.

Approaching *Oroonoko* through an economic perspective challenges several factors that limit students' ability to engage with the text. One is the difficulty in recognizing the shared humanity of people who lived in the past. Another is the cherished myth about the colonization of the Americas: that it was done by people seeking freedom, especially freedom of religion and of conscience. I oppose this difficulty and this myth with reality television: PBS's *Colonial House*, a series that follows two dozen volunteers in a replica of a Maine colony over four months as the "colonists" grapple with the challenges of not only subsisting but also turning a profit for their corporate sponsors in England. Using *Colonial House* exploits students' familiarity with visual media and attraction to reality television to make the life of the seventeenth century real to twenty-first-century undergraduates. The opening scenes of *Colonial House* show the colonists traveling by sea to their new colony and allow the students to encounter real people, in period dress, expressing the same anxieties that seventeenth-century colonists felt about going with a group of strangers to a new, strange place. Students are shocked by the small size of the ship and by the fact that the colonists must sleep under blankets on deck during their journey, and students recognize the human dimension of colonization when they see the wife of one of the colonists weep as her husband rows to shore to scout the new colony. This recognition is readily applied to Behn's text.

Colonial House also overtly explores the financial aspects of a corporate-sponsored colony. The colonists confront economic life on a daily basis—for example, how they allocate time and labor both to earn a profit for their corporate sponsors and to ensure survival for themselves—and in their moral lives. Students are stunned when a representative of the corporation shows up in episode 5, part 1 ("The Shake-Up"), and makes the colonists gather goods for the corporation to sell in Europe; they are outraged that his authority trumps the governor's and the lay preacher's; and they are shocked to discover that regardless of the colonists' motives for joining the colony, the corporation is using them as tools to make money. In episode 8, part 2 ("Measuring Up"), assessors from the twenty-first century evaluate the viability of the colony to determine if it can survive the winter and if it can be profitable to corporate underwriters.

Even more powerful for my students is the departure of the one African American man among the colonists. As the narrator reports in episode 5, part 2 ("An Easy Slide"), for Danny Tisdale, "the direct descendant of African slaves, 1628 is becoming an uncomfortable place to be." Tisdale, reflecting on slavery that a few decades later was to arise from conditions in some of the colonies, explains, "I'm sure [slavery] evolved from the same kind of complaining that we have today about work, about economic ventures, about somebody else doing the work. Cheap labor. And here in a very strange way, I'm part of it." Tisdale is a central figure in the community; his departure not only stuns the colony but also reinforces how *Oroonoko* personalizes the economic pressures to commodify people. After viewing this episode and other clips, students confront the historical and economic conditions and the individual decisions that led to slavery. As an African American, Tisdale is more alert to the "easy slide," as Governor Jeff Wyers puts it, from grumbling about labor and financial obligation to solutions that minimize hardship and maximize economic output. Every complaint of the twenty-first-century colonists with whom he works and lives is the same as that of the seventeenth-century colonists. Tisdale's point is that people chose to enslave others because they lived under certain conditions, not because they lived hundreds of years ago. The choice arose from a human nature shared by the original colonists with *Colonial House*'s colonists, with Danny Tisdale, and as we discuss, with the students in my classroom. Many students now see how their own choices and values in their historical and economic situation—including their dismissal of voices such as Behn's—have a moral dimension.

The clips punctuate our discussion to introduce issues, deepen our insights, and transition to other questions. In the class before the one devoted to *Oroonoko*, I show the opening scenes of the colonists aboard their tiny ship, to help prepare students for the reading. With the humanity of seventeenth-century people before them, we can discuss the ethics of the story less clinically. I ask students the night before to write an answer to the question, "Is Oroonoko a hero?" It gives them an easy way into the text but also immediately reveals the clash between economic and moral systems in the narrative. Students proceed to Oroonoko's slave trading and to his killing of Imoinda. "Can you be a hero and also sell human beings?" they demand of one another. We debate whether Oroonoko's speech to the slaves inciting the rebellion is heroic or self-serving, because he sold slaves, and we interrogate the distinction between people enslaved through military defeat and people enslaved through kidnapping and deception. That interrogation raises the issue of complicity with an economic system. Does it matter, someone inevitably asks (not always I), if the people sold as slaves accept the system? Carried by the momentum of their animated answers, students move through the connection between integrity and slavery, a connection made explicit when the English captain kidnaps Oroonoko, to the deeper question of the connection between integrity and a commodifying economic system. Does being a slave trader compromise the English captain's integrity? Behn suggests that it does. Does it compromise Oroonoko's? His speech to the slaves to incite them to revolt is less clear. Is he using them for his own purposes, or is he trying to liberate them from an unjust situation? The debate over this question reveals how the students' ideas about the value of individuals differ greatly from Oroonoko's, the narrator's, and Behn's. Students also see how, in the behavior of the English captain and in Oroonoko's speech to the slaves, self-interest can be justified by any number of cultural discourses, including religion, romance, and heroism. As they debate whether the captain and Oroonoko are all that different in their comfort with other peoples' enslavement, students consider how economic concerns shape values and the language used to express them and consequently consider what the role of literature, including texts such as *Oroonoko*, might be in codifying behavior in an economic system.

Evaluating the behavior of Behn's characters shows how Behn explores what a commodity-driven world is like to live in. In response to the question of Oroonoko's heroism, many students also point to his killing of Imoinda. They wonder which characters, if any, respect her as a person, and they question the treatment of women in the narrative. Behn's description of the otan, for example, uses suggestive language, placing the "Cast-Mistresses of the old King" in charge of the "young Ones" while the older mistresses take care of the "Business" of teaching the younger ones the "Arts of Love." Repeating the word "pay'd" emphasizes both the immaterial acquisitions of beauty ("Caresses" and "Gallantries") as well as the material ones ("Honours" and "Presents") of which the younger women "rob" the older (21). Here emotional and material vocabularies combine to describe the commodification of beauty not just of Imoinda (her abduction into the otan, her treatment by the king) but of women in general.

The treatment of people in Coramantien leads to Surinam and the precarious balance that Behn's narrative shows between colonizer and colonized. Students tend to ignore the Caribs as players in the narrative, but highlighting the economic purpose for the British presence in Surinam brings these indigenous people into better focus. As we discuss the shape of slavery in Surinam and address the question of whether Oroonoko is really a slave, students remember that Africans, like the British, are imports, and that the Africans are there because the Caribs cannot be exploited unconditionally. Summarizing the British relationship with the indigenous people, the narrator reports, "So that they being, on all Occasions, very useful to us, we find it absolutely necessary to caress 'em as Friends, and not to treat 'em as Slaves; nor dare we do other, their Numbers so far surpassing ours on that *Continent*" (11). Here the language of dependence and fear (the Caribs are "absolutely necessary" to British survival because of their generosity and their forbearance) undercuts the language of exploitation (the Caribs are "useful"). Scenes of equal exchange balance reminders of exploitation and rebellion. As the narrator explains in introducing the Caribs, "those we live with in perfect Amity, without daring to command 'em; but on the contrary, caress 'em with all the brotherly and friendly Affection in the World" (8). Behn emphasizes this economic interdependence by repeating "trade," "trader," and "trading" almost exclusively in episodes where the British have direct dealings with the Caribs. Throughout the introduction of the Caribs, the narrator describes first what the British gain—necessities such as "Fish, Venison, Buffilo's" as well as "Rarities," including "Marmosets . . . and *Cousheries*" and the famous "Feathers" that became "the Dress of the *Indian Queen*, infinitely admir'd by Persons of Quality" (8–9)—and then, in a passage as detailed and nearly as extensive, what the Caribs gain (9). This emphasis on "trade," balanced exchange, occurs again in the narrator's journey with Oroonoko to a distant Carib village. The "Fisherman" who guides them is known to the villagers "as trading among 'em," and the trader is the intermediary between the villagers and the narrator's party, "for they love not to go far from home, and we never go to them" (48–49). The conclusion of the encounter is that Oroonoko "begot so good an understanding between the *Indians* and the *English*, that there were no more Fears, or Heart-burnings during our stay; but we had perfect, open, and free Trade with 'em" (50). Elements such as the contrast between the slavery posited in *Oroonoko*'s opening paragraph and the trading described immediately after or the recurring use of "trade" and its implications in English dealings with the Caribs encourage students to confront the commodification of people for different reasons and by different standards and, like Behn's narrator, to consider their role in such a system, especially if they benefit.

The economic perspective raises a number of questions. How is the text an example of an emerging rather than emerged genre? Is it a novel? An autobiography? Why is the narrator ambivalent about England, Oroonoko, and Imoinda and even about her own actions? The text's positions on slavery, race, gender, and class can be hard to pin down. An economic approach to teaching *Oroonoko* reveals a tension between economic and moral goals but also offers useful ways to discuss the formal elements, especially when they can be understood as innovations or ambiguities. When students start to praise the narrator, we break into groups to analyze the main characters: Oroonoko, Imoinda, and the narrator. The narrator is ambiguous, ambivalent, and surprisingly unreliable. We look at how she is not congruent with Behn, then discuss Behn's appropriation of other genres—the pastoral, the epic, the romance—that students encountered in the earlier sections of the course.

The theme of the relation between economics and culture is applied to further readings of eighteenth-century British texts. Issues of the *Spectator* (Addison and Steele), such as 69 (about the Royal Exchange) and 11 (about Inkle and Yarico); John Gay's *The Beggar's Opera*; Jonathan Swift's "A Modest Proposal"; images from William Hogarth's *A Rake's Progress*; and poems by Behn, Alexander Pope, and Lady Mary Wortley Montagu permit the repeated investigation of ideas involved in emerging capitalism. Hogarth's and Gay's blunt concerns with money and morality compare with Swift's outrage over the subjugation of the Irish in "A Modest Proposal." Swift's satire also forces students to articulate how the commodification of Irish babies in terms of price (How much for a fat toddler?) and productivity (How many people can one feed?) can also serve as an analysis of colonialism's submerging the moral in the economic: people stop being considered people as they are redefined as sources of income. Similarly, poems like Pope's "The Rape of the Lock" associate the female body and the mercantile motive behind colonization, as Laura Brown has pointed out (*Ends* 103–34). It also, like Montagu's reply to Swift's "The Lady's Dressing Room," explores the different values of the physical body and the character within ("Reasons"). In this context, Behn's narrative seems both thematically and generically innovative.

Throughout the course, students give presentations on topics that deepen the class's understanding of this period. Students each choose one topic assigned to a class meeting. Many of the topics for the unit on the long eighteenth century involve economic developments: the day we read "Inkle and Yarico" in *The Spectator*, students research the Bank of England, the Royal Exchange, and paper money; for *Oroonoko*, they present on aspects of global expansion, including the triangular trade, the spice trade, and Captain Cook. This ongoing history lesson for students from their peers keeps texts comprehensible, compensates for a survey's lack of critical editions, and generates a cadre of students familiar with the issues I wish to emphasize in the period.

For twenty-first-century students, eighteenth-century British literature, to quote *Colonial House*, "is not a comfortable place to be" at first. When students see people of the period, like themselves, struggling to reconcile morality and economic values, it becomes much more familiar. Behn's *Oroonoko* asks—but does not always answer—serious questions about the relations between money and morality, yet Behn's struggle with these questions can be made to ring true to students born over three hundred years after her death. In answer to their implied question, "What has the long eighteenth century got?," this approach to *Oroonoko* answers, "You."

The Traffic of Women: *Oroonoko* in an Atlantic Framework

Laura M. Stevens

What does it mean to teach transatlantically? Such a term verges on the obvious when we consider *Oroonoko.* After all, how would one teach such a text without attending in some way to the transoceanic movement and interrelation of people, objects, and people as objects? The Atlantic itself is so inextricable from Behn's narrative that the text divides it almost evenly: to open the narrative at midpoint is to find Oroonoko concluding the Middle Passage, being sold off to Trefry—and embarking upriver in Surinam.

Genres and images identified with either side of the ocean mix with almost equal proportionality, so that the eyewitness testimony and bewilderment that fill European accounts of the Americas alternate with the heroic conventions of European romance. Objects and practices of Africa, Europe, the Americas, and Asia circulate throughout the narrative. The skin of the Coramantien Imoinda, now transported to Surinam, is described as "Japan'd" (40); the "Taffaty Cap" worn by the narrator and the "Stuff Sute" on her brother contribute to the "Amazement" with which the natives greet Oroonoko's embassy (48); and a pipe of tobacco serves as central prop to his gruesome execution (64).

Nor is this transoceanic movement in one direction. As with nonfictional travel narratives, the presence of the published text shows that one person has returned to tell the tale, and Behn's narrator emphasizes this return to Europe by referencing the dress of feathers she presented to the King's Theatre (9). A story of encounter, colonialism, and enslavement, *Oroonoko* also is a text of transatlantic, even global, traffic. It embodies, even as it describes, the transport of commodities—including people—that helped constitute the early modern Atlantic world as a cluster of diverse regions conjoined by the ocean as watery highway.

Recently I had the opportunity to teach undergraduate and graduate versions, separately but simultaneously, of a course I titled Women and Writing in the British Atlantic World. The classes were organized around the study of women as both objects and authors of writing in a world that dramatically expanded, for better and for worse, the experiences available to them. This movement beyond the boundaries of a course on women writers was important to me, for I worried that a class focused only on female authors in transatlantic context would convey an incomplete narrative of unfettered opportunity. I wanted my students to encounter not only the Aphra Behns and Judith Sargent Murrays of the Atlantic region, blazing paths both literally and literarily, but also the women not positioned to tell their stories. Alongside the work of Mary Rowlandson, Phillis Wheatley, and Mary Wollstonecraft we read texts by John Smith, Daniel Defoe, and Thomas Paine. With the exception of early exploration accounts and some manifestations of the Inkle and Yarico story collected in Frank Felsenstein's anthology, the course focused on anglophone writers and texts—a regrettable limitation but one that fit the purview of an English literature curriculum and imposed some limits on an already broadly defined course.

Texts varied between the two courses. The graduate seminar naturally tackled a more ambitious reading list, including Margaret Cavendish's *The Blazing World*, Susanna Rowson's *Charlotte Temple*, several captivity narratives, and many secondary readings. Both classes read *The Female American* (by the pseudonymous author Unca Eliza Winkfield) and Leonora Sansay's *Secret History*. For many texts, the undergraduates read excerpts and the graduate students read the document in its entirety, so there was significant continuity between the discussions.

With its female authorship and narration, its juxtaposition of white women and women of color, and its consideration of women travelers even while in forms of captivity, *Oroonoko* was a centerpiece for both courses. For the undergraduates, it was bracketed by two texts connected with New England: Rowlandson's captivity narrative and Sarah Kemble Knight's account of her journey from Boston to New York in 1711. My graduate students encountered Behn's texts just after studying a group of women's funeral sermons and right before reading *Moll Flanders*. These geographic and thematic leaps were sometimes abrupt, but they facilitated my efforts to keep the attention of the students moving vertically and horizontally from week to week as I prompted them to think about women in vast systems of traffic.

I asked the students to consider *traffic* in both the early modern and contemporary senses of the word, as commerce and as the movement of people. My goal was to have them think of women participating in circulation but with their ability to act as agents of their own fates augmented or hampered by the writings that proceeded from or about them. More broadly, I wanted to see what happened to women—as authors, objects, and metaphors—when considered in the context of this supranational region. Organizing questions included the following: How did the colonization of the Americas and the transportation of several million African slaves there affect the lives, imaginations, and writings of European, African, and Native American women? What influence did the cultural and commercial intertwining of four continents play in representations of women? How did gender inflect colonial encounter, and how, in turn, did images of women catalyze conversations about matters ranging from theology and landscape to politics and trade, extending what Louis Montrose has described as "the sexualizing of [the New World's] exploration, conquest, and settlement" (178)?

In designing this course, I had access to a growing body of scholarship but not to many model syllabi, anthologies, or documents designed for pedagogy. A comprehensive body of work on transatlantic literary teaching had yet to emerge at the time I taught this course, although some literature has appeared afterward. A notable example is *Teaching the Transatlantic Eighteenth Cen-*

tury, edited by Jennifer Frangos and Cristobal Silva. Myra Jehlen and Michael Warner's *English Literatures of America* was the closest I could find to a transatlantic anglophone anthology for my undergraduates, and they had to scramble for used copies when we learned it had just gone out of print.

Transatlantic teaching considers literature as interwoven with comparable or contiguous genres and texts in a wider arena. A benefit of such an approach is that historical narratives emerge to reflect more accurately the lines of influence that shaped literary production. We can more easily ascertain what the authors we are studying were reading, what was on their minds, and how their writings fit in the worlds that initially received them. For example, historical study that takes a fuller view of the Atlantic region recently repositioned the American Revolution in a cluster of struggles throughout the Americas between colonial societies and the European bureaucracies struggling to manage their sprawling empires (F. Anderson; Egerton et al.). Attendance to an Atlantic context in literary study makes visible the textual density of transatlantic correspondence, the vibrancy of colonial literary cultures, and the full impact of colonial settlement on the literary production of Europe (see, e.g., Bannet; Giles). An Atlantic framework, as well as some focus on the topics of intercontinental contact and movement, can make literary innovation more visible. Pamela J. Albert has noted that "as a consequence of global exploration, conquest and trade, the early modern era witnessed the emergence and transformation of many literary genres," the novel being foremost among these, and *Oroonoko* was a central document in that genesis (7). A national literary history thus emerges from the shadow of a nationalist one.

By the time they encountered *Oroonoko*, my students already had read early descriptions of the Americas and at least one captivity narrative. With this background, they were positioned to consider not only how Behn echoes the accounts of exploration and conquest but also how what William Spengemann calls the genre of the "Brief True Relation," with its emphasis on experience, created authorial space for a woman (390). Their grounding in these nonfictional narratives also prepared them to assess Behn's experiments with form. Whereas students in the many surveys of British literature in which I have taught *Oroonoko* had breezed through the opening description of Surinam, these students were eager to trace its revisions of purportedly nonfictional accounts of America, especially in relation to gender. They pored over Behn's description of Edenic native bodies, compared her account of native modesty with the sexual laxity at which Amerigo Vespucci marveled (50), and considered her description of Surinam's bounty in the context of Walter Raleigh's infamous promise to Elizabeth I, "*Guiana* is a Countrey that hath yet her Maidenhead" (96). They noted with some surprise that Behn did not share Vespucci's fascination with the athleticism of native women but rather stressed modest courtship practices. Here the Atlantic context yielded one pedagogical benefit I had not anticipated: I did not have to work as hard as I normally do to dissuade students from mapping Behn in simplistic ways onto a modern feminist sensibility.

The same applied to discussions of slavery. Over the preceding few years, I had developed some reluctance to teach *Oroonoko*, partly because of exhaustion with what Srinivas Aravamudan has termed "oroonokoism" and its variant, "imoindaism" (30, 31). As he writes, "*Oroonoko* responds to trends in new historicism, criticism of empire, and race and gender studies, and these approaches rely on it, in turn, to satisfy a checklist of political concerns" (32). Especially in a survey of British literature, where the impetus is to move quickly while charting paths of development through genre and era, I have found it a struggle to steer my students away from the sense that our attitudes toward slavery, gender, colonialism, and race are the fulfillment of Behn's anticipatory take on these issues. Key to this struggle is the critical bracketing of what Aravamudan describes as the "transferential relationship between the novella's female first-person narrator . . . and its black hero" (30). Historical detachment and context strike me as key to moving past enchantment with the liberal and counterimperial potential of Behn's text. Aravamudan's fascinating reading of *Oroonoko* in the context of the English aristocratic practice of keeping ornamental slaves as pets does much to undermine an uncritical appraisal of Behn's female narrator's sympathy for Oroonoko and Imoinda. The Atlantic framework also helps. Having witnessed the nonchalance with which the capture and transport of people takes place in the literature of exploration and captivity, the students were quick to consider the larger affective and economic frameworks that surround Behn's treatment of one couple's enslavement.

Better equipped to separate Behn's tonally flat description of the macroeconomic realities of the slave trade from the tragedy of Imoinda and Oroonoko, the students were primed to consider the story alongside parallel genres, such as captivity narratives. They wondered what made these two types of texts, relating circumstances that on a certain level were alike, so distinct in outcome and tone. Both Oroonoko and Rowlandson, for example, are captured by differently colored people and carried from their homes through a series of removes as they are bought and sold. Both swing between hope and despair in their quest for freedom, and both are granted occasional concessions by their captors. Both also experience the joyful rediscovery of loved ones in captivity and exile. Given these striking similarities, these two tales could hardly be more different in point of view, in hermeneutic framework, in moral overlay, in structure, and in style. Oroonoko's story is of a great man brought low by betrayal, of lovers who choose death rather than the torment of continued enslavement. Oroonoko's baseline response to his enslavement is rage, and the narrative tilts generically toward tragedy. In contrast, the core drama of Rowlandson's text is the testing of her soul, and all events serve that narrative of spiritual struggle. Her baseline response to her captivity is gratitude to God, and the text most closely resembles a sermon or a spiritual journal: "Oh, the number of Pagans (now merciless enemies) that there came about me, that I may say as *David*, Psal 27.13, *I had fainted, unless I had believed, &c*" (74).

To focus on these similarities is certainly to overlook the treatment of these two captives, whose fluid status in captivity could lead to assimilation, redemption, or death but who in the situation of chattel slavery were slotted into the increasingly race-bound category of the imprisoned and abject. Still, to read these texts alongside each other is to acknowledge the wide range of genres through which one can tell stories of human beings deprived of their autonomy and thus to call attention to Behn's decisions about genre and style. It is also to consider why and how stories of captivity and enslavement become vehicles for other sorts of stories and projects. Finally, it is to probe the significance of sexual practices and attitudes to the dynamics of chattel slavery versus Indian captivity.

A surprising point of correlation between the two texts is the turmoil of parental grief and fear. The emotions Rowlandson, Oroonoko, and Imoinda express at their captivity or enslavement are magnified beyond measure when they contemplate their offspring. Imoinda's pregnancy is part of what provokes Oroonoko's rebellion, while Rowlandson's narrative is steeped in the raw emotions of a mother torn from most of her children and forced to watch one slowly die: "I must sit all this cold winter night upon the cold snowy ground, with my sick Child in my armes, looking that every hour would be the last of its life" (73). To look at these texts together, then, is to consider how the possibility or the presence of offspring provokes an escalation of affect, and sometimes of resistance, for human beings deprived of freedom.

To this mix the graduate students added Cavendish's "Assaulted and Pursued Chastity" and *The Description of a New World, Called the Blazing World.* These two texts, respectively termed a "romance narrative" and a "utopian fantasy" by Cavendish's editor, Kate Lilley (xii), triangulated in fascinating ways with the other accounts of intercultural encounter, skin color, and race. Reading Behn after Cavendish made clearer how both writers map hyperchivalric codes onto stories of intercultural encounter, weaving a fantasy of a white woman's queenly status in foreign lands among differently colored and obsequious peoples. The pairing also showed how royalist nostalgia revives itself through colonial excursion. Finally, it helped students isolate the position of the white woman in the exotic wilderness as a heavily laden rhetorical construct performing varying forms of work for a colonizing people.

Just as the preceding texts were crucial to the discussion of *Oroonoko*, Behn's narrative did much to shape my students' examinations of later readings. *Moll Flanders* produced intriguing contrast with the narrator of *Oroonoko* as a white woman describing her colonial experiences. While for Moll the anonymity of the colonial world facilitates a self-fashioning that brings about moral downfall and then recuperation, Surinam presents a gilded cage to Behn's narrator, whose status as the daughter of the deceased lieutenant general elect brings entitlement but little true power. The most powerful linkages, however, were with other accounts of slavery. Foremost among these were Sansay's *Secret History*, a story of domestic abuse in a slave-owning household during the Haitian Revolution, and several retellings of the Inkle and Yarico story, which describe a Native American or African woman sold into slavery by the refugee she has saved and loved. These texts share with *Oroonoko* stories of courtship, marriage, and love that come into disastrous encounter with the economies of slavery. They all likewise intimate parallels between chattel slavery and the limitations imposed on white women by their societies.

One discussion of *Oroonoko* dealt with the energy circulating around Imoinda's body and the question of who will penetrate her body. The contest between a virile young prince and an impotent old tyrant to deflower Imoinda ultimately results in her enslavement. When Oroonoko discovers her in Surinam, she exists in a cloister-like cabin, architecturally echoing the Coramantien otan even as it amplifies the aura of modesty that has protected her from the advances of slave and slaveholder alike. Yet it is the fear of her rape, along with her unborn child's enslavement, that provokes Oroonoko's disastrous rebellion. Slavery thus enters the plot at the junction of sexual prowess and political power.

This triangulation of slavery, sex, and power became more visible to the students after they had read *Secret History*, with its intertwining of contests for sexual control, threats of rape, and competitions between white and mulatta women for the attentions of slave-owning males. In illustration of her assertion that before the revolution on Saint-Domingue, "[e]very inhabitant lived on his estate like a Sovereign ruling his slaves with despotic sway," Mary, author of most of the novel's letters, tells the story of a white woman who ordered that her female slave, Coomba, be beheaded, cooked, and served to her husband because she saw what she thought to be "symptoms of *tendresse* in [his] eyes" (70). This vignette of white-on-black atrocity, fueled by sexual jealousy, is more than matched by corpse-strewn narratives of "the horrible catastrophe which accompanied the first wild transports of freedom" (77), some of which feature sexually voracious black men preying on white women. In *Oroonoko*, Behn is always dangling before the reader the prospect of violence toward women, both black and white. Imoinda is perpetually in danger of rape, whether in Coramantien or Surinam, and the white women of Surinam swing between fascination with and terror of Oroonoko. *Secret History* realizes those awful possibilities. It forces us to contemplate the female bodies torn apart by a slave economy that brings out the otherwise suppressed tyranny and savagery of men.

One can productively read the women's deaths in *Secret History* alongside William Blake's famous engraving "A Negro Hung Alive by the Ribs to a Gallows," first published in John Gabriel Stedman's *Narrative of a Five Years' Expedition against the Revolted Negroes of Surinam* (1792 [*Internet Archive*]), or Shakespeare's *Titus Andronicus*, another text that links unwitting cannibalism to a woman's rape, although along a significantly different chain of causation. The pregnant Imoinda and the slaughtered Coomba stand in powerful counterpoint to Richard Steele's Yarico, whose pregnancy increases the profits of the cold-hearted Inkle (Felsenstein). Along with the mulattas, whose seductions drain the fortunes of Saint-Domingue's slave-owning families, these figures foreground the place of the reproductive body in the discourses of slavery.

Reading these texts together, students were struck that troubled stories of heterosexual love and betrayal often abut or catalyze those of slavery. One effect of this mingling was the triggering of elaborate emotions that sidestep the realities of the slave trade. Students were surprised to see Matthew James Chapman retell the Inkle and Yarico story in a defense of slavery in his poem "Barbados" (Felsenstein 269–76). Through such readings they contemplated not only how gender and race intertwine, slipping over each other as identity categories to redirect the viewer's sympathies, but also how gender amplifies the poignancy of slavery while deflecting emotion from its true object.

I like to think that my students took away from this class a more finely tuned sense of how intrinsic women were to the structuring of an Atlantic world. Just as women were crucial to the systems of trade that wove these continents together, supplying bodies for the gathering and consumption of new commodities, they also provided much of the vocabulary, imagery, and narrative to make this expanded world intelligible to those who sought to dominate it. *Oroonoko* did much to link the separate components of this vision for them. In turn, reading Behn's narrative in this Atlantic framework made visible certain aspects that tend to vanish in my other courses. Above all, the experience made clear that Behn's story develops through the placement of women at every stage of that transoceanic chain of commerce, including the creation and consumption of colonial fantasy. To read *Oroonoko* in this way is thus to contemplate the status of the reader as one entertained, however poignantly, by the miseries of faraway peoples crushed by the circumstances overtaking them. That alone seems a worthwhile pedagogical outcome.

Entering Atlantic History: *Oroonoko*, Revolution, and Race

Laura Doyle

In *Oroonoko*, Aphra Behn startlingly combines the high, tragic romance of kidnapped, noble lovers from Africa with exotic adventures in Surinam and a violent slave revolt, making for an odd yet strangely compelling text. I invite students to consider Behn's composition of these disparate materials as her grappling with historic transformations in the seventeenth-century Atlantic world. This approach heightens their sense of the novel's importance as a historical document and a literary text.

Teaching *Oroonoko* in the context of English and Atlantic history sheds fresh light on its contradictory representations of racial identity and the importance of its female narrator. It also links the novel to arenas with which students might be more familiar, such as the rhetoric of racial freedom or the ideologies of the American Revolution. In the classroom and in scholarship, when we understand *Oroonoko* as an Atlantic-world text, we do better justice to its pivotal place in the intertwined literary, racial, gender, and political histories of the anglophone world.

History writing in English blossomed in the late seventeenth century in part to make sense of a century of revolutionary upheavals. In 1603, the English people and Parliament welcomed the Stuart king James I, who united in his rule the kingdoms of Scotland and England. Soon, however, the English found themselves at odds with James I, then with Charles I, his son, who claimed a right to absolute rule without Parliamentary interference, a claim that was especially troubling for Parliament because of the kings' Catholic sympathies in this Protestant kingdom. By the 1620s and 1630s, the balance of political and financial power was shifting, as English merchants, who were aligned with the Protestant Parliament members, founded colonial settlements on the Atlantic seaboard and supported Puritan dissidents who also emigrated across the Atlantic. All these men interloped profitably in Spanish colonial trading, and reaped new wealth in American tobacco and other trades. After decades of political struggle, during which Parliamentary members vocally claimed their participatory rights and the Stuart kings in response imprisoned them and refused to call Parliament (at one point for eleven years), a civil war broke out. This war pitted loyal followers of the king against religious and political dissidents, both Parliamentary and more radical, with the Parliamentary side being significantly funded by the English Atlantic merchants (Brenner 114–20, 149–69, 500–07). Eventually Charles I was imprisoned, his army was defeated, and in January 1649 he was beheaded. The English Revolution had succeeded.

But in 1660, after roughly a decade of nonmonarchical but increasingly repressive Puritan rule, the English restored their monarchy, inviting Charles I's son, Charles II, to the throne. Behn was a Royalist—that is, an ally of this line of Stuart kings. By the late 1680s, as she was writing *Oroonoko*, Parliament was again at odds with the Catholic-leaning, debt-plagued James II, whose brother, Charles II, had fathered many children but left no legitimate heir. Parliament maneuvered to expel James II in favor of a more securely Protestant and Parliament-supporting king, finally accomplishing the Glorious Revolution, whereby the Dutch royal couple William (nephew of Charles II and James II) and Mary (the daughter of James II) ascended the English throne.

Over the course of the seventeenth century, these power reversals gave rise to two highly antagonistic political parties, the Tories (Stuart and king-aligned) and the Whigs (Parliament-aligned), and historians of each party began to write its version of England's history. Both sides championed freedom and considered the English Revolution of the 1640s pivotal. But while the Tories spoke of the king's freedoms, the Whigs spoke of the people's or Parliament's freedoms, and the Whig historians especially tapped into a discourse of "Anglo-Saxonism" that had come to the fore during the English Civil War (Doyle 27–73). According to this discourse, the English had descended from a race of Gothic peoples who migrated from Germany and brought with them a tradition of rights for freeborn men and of participatory government, after which Parliament was supposedly modeled.

Both the revolutionary-era pamphlets and the later Whig histories suggested that an Anglo-Saxon will to freedom was native to the English, and this freedom-loving nature compelled them to revolt against all political tyranny. The American revolutionaries would later tap this tradition, fashioning themselves as the true or radical Whigs (Horsman 1–186; Doyle 73–93). In championing the Anglo-Saxons as carriers of England's true inheritance (despite their being overrun in 1066 by invading Normans), this new racialist discourse began to displace an older ideology in which noble races rightly conquered and ruled over common peoples. Thus did a rhetoric of conquering Caesars, favored by Tories even as they also spoke of royal freedom, give way to a Whig rhetoric of righteous resistance.

Initially this Anglo-Saxonism had little to do with racist notions of whites as superior to people of color. Yet, as we glimpse in Behn's novel, by the seventeenth century's end and amid an expanded colonial economy increasingly made profitable by enslaved Africans, this early, nativist, Anglo-Saxon liberty discourse came to underwrite and intertwine with the white/black racism that is now so familiar. Together these forms of racial thinking fostered an ideology in which lower races or non-English peoples were considered incapable of desiring and managing political freedom.

When students encounter these intertwined discourses in *Oroonoko*, they are sometimes confused by the novel's apparently contradictory racialization of a royal slave. In class, I trace the ways that Behn labors to stabilize and compose these shifting discourses through emergent historical genres.

First of all she establishes her participation in contemporary Whig-Tory debates when she calls her text a history and then casts Oroonoko as a figure for both embattled Stuart kings. In framing this account as her personal recollection of historical events, Behn borrows from the seventeenth-century genre of an exile's memoir or secret history of the revolution, made popular by the Royalist earl of Clarendon's *History of the Rebellion* and expanded by such writers as Lucy Hutchinson. Furthermore (and signaling the unsettling reversals of nobleman and captive slave), she gives Oroonoko the slave name of "Caesar" (36), an honorific that Tories used to refer to Stuart kings and a tag carrying the older idea of noble races. Finally, as Laura Brown has argued, in the violent murder of Oroonoko Behn creates a "hidden figuration" of Charles I's beheading, which serves as a warning in the years of James II's succession crisis (*Ends* 58). George Guffey has highlighted the traces in Behn's text of James II's crisis (soon to culminate in the Glorious Revolution).

Most important, as we notice in class, in setting her tale of English history on the Atlantic, Behn also situates this national narrative of liberty, rights, and revolution in the colonial history of captivity and colonization. Her Anglo-Atlantic female narrator enters English history at the collision point of these stories in the colony of Surinam, in effect prefiguring the way that she herself, as a female writer, will enter the anglophone literary canon largely by way of this history and text of the Atlantic world. She also creates a prototype for later novels, in which plots of ruin leading to failed or successful liberation operate as microcosms for English history, although in later fiction the dimension of African-Atlantic revolt lurks more subtextually.[1]

Behn hints that a highly volatile Atlantic world of competition accompanies the Stuart experience of ruin. As Guffey shows, she alludes to the Dutch acquisition of Surinam and also to the threat in the late 1680s of usurpation of the Stuart throne by the Dutch-Protestant Pretender (as Tory Royalists liked to call William of Orange). Indeed, both Oroonoko's ordeal and the impending Dutch takeover in Surinam are prepared by a colonial succession crisis, as signaled in the absence of two key leaders: the narrator's father, designated Lieutenant-General, who has died at sea en route to Surinam (43), and the Lord Governor, presumably Lord Willoughby, who fails to arrive to undo the confusion of authority between the Royalist Deputy Governor Byam and benevolent, powerful, Whig-aligned plantation owners such as Trefry at Parham House. In effect, the story implies, the swallowing Atlantic and the violence of intra-European mercantile competition together undermine Stuart power. These conditions enable the wrongful kidnapping of princes, which in turn opens the gap in which a Royalist daughter steps into her role as white historian while shifting her allegiance toward slaveholding Whigs. In this Atlantic world, African noblemen become violent blacks while British women become ruling-class whites. These absences, schisms, and reversals signify the dispersion of inherited, royal power in a colonial, Atlantic context; and, as Behn's text hints, women writers and women characters step into the new breach.

Yet even before the climactic slave revolt, Behn sets up the parallel to English revolutionary crises in the Coramantien portion of the novel, with the unlawful romance of Imoinda and Oroonoko. In claiming the right to choose a lover over the king's right to decree and possess, Oroonoko and Imoinda set in motion a crisis of kingly authority, while also signaling the transatlantic source that both crises share. That is, the questions of obedience to a king and the rightfulness of dissent by subjects, catalyzed here by the couple's transgression of the king's prerogative, re-create the century-long, revolutionary Anglo-Atlantic question about proper authority and proper rebellion. This question was from the beginning linked to Atlantic colonization and wealth, as the couple's Atlantic deportation suggests. Thus although Oroonoko is aligned with the Stuart kings, he also emblematizes the transgressive activity that has brought down—and again verges on bringing down—those kings.

In effect, Oroonoko becomes a Leveler through his relationship with Imoinda.[2] Having married without the king's permission, they further transgress by keeping their marriage a secret and consummating it in the seraglio after Imoinda has been summoned as the newest royal concubine. When the king sells Imoinda into slavery as a punishment, Oroonoko, thinking the king has killed her, begins to question all monarchical, military forms of nobility and to adopt a dissenting or leveling Whiggish ideology in which aristocratic inheritance is eschewed. Called to a battle for the kingdom, at which he is urgently needed, he rejects the system of lineal nobility:

> He reply'd, He wou'd not give himself the Trouble [of choosing a new leader for the army]—; but wish'd 'em to chuse the bravest Man amongst 'em, let his Quality or Birth be what it wou'd. *For, O my Friends!* (said he) *it is not Titles make Men brave, or good; or Birth that bestows Courage and Generosity, or makes the Owner happy. Believe this, when you behold* Oroonoko, *the most wretched, and abandon'd by Fortune, of all the Creation of the Gods.* (28)

Here Oroonoko's illicit monogamous love has not only depleted his interest in the glories of war; it has also compelled him to question the validity of distinctions of birth and rank, all in the pursuit of happiness. This dissent from an aristocratic and Coramantien order of things is the first step toward his interpellation by an Atlantic-world, merchant-class order of things, and it will enable his kidnapping into the narrative of English history as it takes its Whiggish turn toward the ur-plot of liberty, disastrously in his case.

This new kind of leveling love eventually explains, as the narrator casts it, Oroonoko's and Imoinda's tolerance of slavery: even though Oroonoko "accus'd himself for having suffer'd Slavery for so long; yet he charg'd that weakness on Love alone, who was capable of making him neglect even Glory it self" (42). Likewise,

> *Caesar* swore he disdain'd the Empire of the World, while he could behold his *Imoinda*; and she despis'd Grandeur and Pomp, those Vanities of her Sex, when she cou'd gaze on *Oroonoko*. He ador'd the very Cottage where she resided, and said, That little Inch of the World wou'd give him more Happiness than all the Universe cou'd do; and she vow'd, It was a Pallace, while adorn'd with the Presence of *Oroonoko*. (39)

In effect, the slavery and political violence of Atlantic modernity are being recast here as the picaresque tribulations of sentimental lovers, whose nobility is now measured by their humbleness—thus establishing a prototype for future middle-class heroes and heroines in anglophone novels, from *Charlotte Temple* (Rowson) to *Uncle Tom's Cabin*. But if the novel cultivates a Whiggish sympathy for a nobly humble Oroonoko and Imoinda, it ultimately metes out a Tory punishment for their king-dissenting liberties. Behn shrewdly implies that the reorganization of culture around righteous liberty and leveling values leads to chaos, violence, and the end of properly noble races.

Underneath this dissenting drama lies a claim to Imoinda's body, which is central to the reproduction and succession of a particular race. Here too the novel gestures toward the contemporary succession crisis in England. Earlier in the story, when the king worries about having "disoblig'd" Oroonoko "by the Rape of his Mistress, or rather, Wife," he is concerned not only because he is no longer "able to defend himself in War" but also because he has "no Sons of all his Race remaining alive, but only this [Oroonoko], to maintain him on his Throne" (26). Oroonoko, for all his tender love, recognizes the same value in Imoinda, so that her pregnancy after their reunion in Surinam makes him "even adore her, knowing that he was the last of his Great Race" (40). Likewise, when Byam has Oroonoko whipped, he keeps Imoinda safely distant at Parham House, "not in kindness to her, but for fear she shou'd Dye with the Sight, or Miscarry; and then they shou'd lose a young *Slave*, and perhaps the Mother" (57).

Disobedience of kingly power and the accompanying Atlantic exile play out across Imoinda's sexual body, which is the linchpin for the transition from one racial order to another. It is not simply that Oroonoko and Imoinda's sexual transgression stands in for political transgression. Rather, Behn's novel indicates implicitly that a sexual plot is always political and racial, since it concerns the reproduction of proper social lineages, as Behn seems to have understood. Along with everything else that this perspicacious text ferrets out, it makes clear that the sexual liberties of Oroonoko and Imoinda thus trouble the whole political order. As a result of their implicit challenge to the aristocratic order, Oroonoko and Imoinda become, in effect, Atlantic subjects.

Behn makes a tableau of the moment when the lovers enter this new order: their mutual, dramatic swoon marks their interpellation into Atlantic modernity. At his first sight of Imoinda in Surinam, Oroonoko "stood without Motion, and, for a Minute, knew not that [his body] had a Being," while Imoinda "fall[s] dead in the Hands of *Trefry*" until he rushes to awaken her (39). Such swooning scenes, appearing in many novels to come, operate as condensed dramatizations of the racial remaking of Atlantic world subjects, as I argue in *Freedom's Empire* (6–9, 97–115). For Africans, as this scene suggests, the swoon sublimates and elides the near-death experience of an Atlantic crossing or Middle Passage.

This unmaking of Africans will be the making of whites, including white women. The female narrator's entry into history through African loss is signaled in the fact that she becomes a participant in the action just after Oroonoko and Imoinda's mutual swoon. That is, she enters the story as the vehicle that helps recast the couple as creatures of a timeless, place-transcending love in which they are simultaneously reborn as enslaved blacks.

We can see this process unfold in the narration. Early in the novel, Oroonoko's gallantry in love is a feature of his highborn soul—another sign of his racialized, noble position above the other Africans (13). But once he becomes a captive in Surinam, and especially as he begins to press for his liberty on the soil of an English colony, the narrator's racial terms shift. On the one hand, she keeps in play his noble attributes; on the other, she increasingly aligns him with the "Blacks" (11) as distinct from "the Whites" (51). She finds it no longer "convenient to trust him" and positions herself against him on the side of the white "Country who fear'd him" (42). She likewise exhibits contradictory alliances as a genteel female associated with an aristocratic Oroonoko, a friend who strives to "Soften" the language she uses in discussing his captivity (41), and a companion of Whiggish Englishmen (represented in Trefry).

Encoded here is the deep implication of Whigs, despite their rhetoric of freedom and rights, in the Atlantic colonial project, for that project is the source of their revolutionary power and wealth. As Behn seems to see, all kinds of English people are following suit—Tories, women, and middle class—because England's wealth as a nation increasingly depends on colonialism. Our white female narrator thus dramatizes the transformation by which genteel, ambiguously positioned English daughter becomes dominant white and by which a noble African becomes an enslaved black. The narrator draws readers into this new racial order, fostering their identification with a place far from England while also bringing them to a racialized sentimental vision of this violent, imperial English geography.

Although prefiguring white women's conflict-softening, class-straddling role in the colonial order, the narrator suffers from a sense of vulnerability: she feels that at any moment she could become prey to the violence catalyzed by this changing world. When Oroonoko leads the slave rebellion, she reports, "[W]e were possess'd with extream Fear . . . that he wou'd come down and Cut all our Throats. This apprehension made all the Females of us fly down the River, to be secur'd" (57). Later she reports that she is again "perswaded to leave the Place for some time (being my self but Sickly, and very apt to fall into Fits of dangerous Illness upon any extraordinary Melancholy)" (64). Oddly, in this parenthesis, Oroonoko's ordeal of fainting becomes hers. After her fit, she too reawakens, by way of Oroonoko's story, into the modern order of things—but as a writing subject rather than as a mangled slave-king. Again Behn's novel models a sleight of hand emulated by many later white novelists and called by Toni Morrison "American Africanism," wherein the presence and experience of African Atlantic persons are displaced by the historical experience and central literary presence of Anglo-Atlantic persons ("Black Matters" 6).

Like her narrator, Behn thus enters into canonical authorship on terms she does not wholly choose or endorse and with long-term implications she could not have anticipated. Given an opening through the Atlantic economy, a marginal yet pivotal place to stand, she rewrites Oroonoko and Imoinda's Atlantic story as a tale of Stuart England. Under the pressures of the expanding nation's reproductive, succession, and colonial crises, she labors to compose English history. In so doing, she begins the work of the anglophone Atlantic novel.

NOTES

[1] For elaboration of this point and of my full reading of Behn's novel, see my discussion in the introduction and first four chapters of *Freedom's Empire*. For important analyses of the emergence of anglophone novels in an Atlantic context, see White; Spengemann. Behn titled other texts as histories (e.g., *History of the Nun*), and after her, eighteenth-century novelists repeatedly titled their texts as histories, often secret histories—note Manley's *The Secret History of Queen Zarah and the Zarazians*, Richardson's *Clarissa; or, The History of a Young Lady*, and Defoe's *Roxana, the Fortunate Mistress; or, A History of the . . . Lady Roxana in the Time of Charles II*.

[2] The Levelers and, even more so, the Diggers were dissident groups of the 1640s that argued for equal or level distribution of rights, and thereafter anyone advocating such a challenge to inherited or propertied rights came to be known as a Leveler.

Writing War in *Oroonoko*

Sharon Alker and Holly Faith Nelson

War and its effects are repeatedly, almost obsessively, etched on nearly every page of *Oroonoko*. When the Royalist Aphra Behn composed the novel, England was still reeling from the violent civil wars of the 1640s, waged during Behn's formative years, and engaged in the Anglo-Dutch Wars, during which she served as a spy for Charles II. *Oroonoko* was also written against the backdrop of colonial warfare, as England's expansionist agenda demanded military action in colonial outposts. *Oroonoko* may therefore be read as a work that emerged from a culture of war and testifies to its consequences. Nigel Smith has argued that literature written during the English civil wars and their aftermath was "part of the crisis and the revolution, and was at its epicentre" (1). The civil wars, he notes, necessitated the invention of new literary genres that could accommodate "a massive destabilisation in the order of meaning" in the mid–seventeenth century (362). In the case of *Oroonoko*, written in the shadow of domestic and foreign wars, this emergent genre would be the novel, which was sufficiently heteroglossic, in the Bakhtinian sense, to record a range of competing voices on the nature and significance of war. Dissimilar perspectives of martial activity, and its unpredictable consequences, produce lacunae and tensions in the narrative, especially when epic visions and early modern realities of war come into contact. Moreover, by placing narratorial gender and the role of women in war in the foreground of *Oroonoko*, Behn adds a layer of complexity to the novel, reflecting the active part played by women in both fighting and memorializing the civil wars.

Since the nature of martial references varies widely in *Oroonoko*, it is useful to begin a class on *Oroonoko* as war narrative by having students list all the overt and covert references to war they can discover. For example, we read of war among the natives of Surinam, who are led not by a king but by a war captain (10). We are told of the past wars of Coramantien, concluded just before Oroonoko meets Imoinda, in which his grandfather lost thirteen sons (12). The deity of Coramantien is assigned a military title, "Captain of the Clouds" (26), Oroonoko is a general (12), and Imoinda is a general's daughter (14). New wars begin shortly before the sexual encounter between Oroonoko and Imoinda (22), and the hero temporarily withdraws from the fighting when he believes their affair has caused her death (28–29). There is the threat of civil war when Oroonoko's grandfather compels Imoinda to receive the royal veil (18, 26). Various forms of actual or potential violent conflict continue in the second half of the work, from the Captain's fears of rebellion on the ship (32) to the new name given to Oroonoko, Caesar, which calls to mind ancient Roman wars (36). The narrator herself is associated with war through the military title of her dead father, the designated "Lieutenant General" (43), and Surinam is a place of many colonial conflicts and an ongoing anxiety about rebellion (41). The English king's ultimate surrender of Surinam to the Dutch haunts the text (36, 43), hinting at an unheroic English failure to resist aggressive martial forces, which stands in contrast to Oroonoko's proactive incitement of his fellow slaves to rebellion. The relationship between the English community and the native community is unsettled by an emphasis on shockingly disfigured war captains (50) and an account of the monstrous deaths inflicted on the Dutch (47). On a more subtle level, the presence of Banister, the "wild *Irish* Man" (64), reminds us of battles in Ireland that occurred in the uncomfortably recent past and of associated English propaganda that presented the Irish as barbaric. The rebellion Oroonoko leads is inspired by references to the warrior Hannibal, the noted enemy of Rome, and the rebellion itself brings to mind, paradoxically, both Parliament's uprising against Charles I and the displaced king's military resistance to Parliamentary rule (53–56). The English civil wars are explicitly mentioned when we are told that Oroonoko has knowledge of them and sympathizes with the unhappy fate of Charles I (13), and the references to Oroonoko as a "mangl'd King" (65) at the end of the narrative could equally be applied to the executed Charles I, of whose "deplorable Death" Oroonoko speaks "with all the Sense, and Abhorrence of the Injustice imaginable" (13).

Once students have identified and cataloged references to war in the text, it is fruitful to step back and present the broader historical context. A brief lecture on the English civil wars is critical here. Emphasis should be placed on the disturbing nature of a domestic war that divided loyalties at every level of society; the horror of bearing witness to the evil within, as community members perpetrated acts of brutality on each other; the prevailing sense that the world had been turned upside down with the loss of the familiar and the known; the way conventional familial and gender roles had been destabilized and upended; the wave of communal guilt following the regicide (the killing of the father-king); and the failure of military might to effect the restoration of the monarchy. This lecture should convey the cruelty, terror, and mayhem of war that threatened to unravel the fabric of law and order in society and appreciably eroded the epic or heroic view of war. It should bring to the fore the horror of "Man's inhumanity to Man" (Burns 55 [line 55]), causing the class to question the essential decency or morality of human beings, because that questioning is fundamental to the representation of martial action in *Oroonoko.* An overview of the Anglo-Dutch Wars, which took place largely at sea, is also essential here, as Behn addresses in *Oroonoko* the struggle between the English and the Dutch to lay claim to the colony of Surinam. It should be made clear that this struggle was motivated chiefly by commercial interests and colonial ambitions, these two European powers vying for dominance in trade and empire building. The dehumanizing economics of war are thereby played out in a colonial context in *Oroonoko*, especially in terms of the objectification and commodification of prisoners of war.[1]

After this historical review, students should be given time to connect the information it provides with some of the significant moments they have uncovered in the novel. The ensuing discussion should demonstrate that literary texts respond to war in unexpected, complex ways and reveal that *Oroonoko* assumes neither a pro- nor antiwar position but rather examines and mediates among various positions on warfare, colonial or otherwise. For example, students might consider Behn's reaction to the Anglo-Dutch Wars, which is illuminated in five brief passages on the Dutch. They might relate the majority of these passages to the anxieties of colonial war, as the passages recount the horror of combat, with the Dutch imprisoning or hanging some of the English (59) and with the Indians hanging Dutch women and children and mutilating a footman left by the narrator in the colony (47). The threat of such violence under English rule is addressed when the narrator informs us, on the one hand, that the English live peaceably with the natives and, on the other, that it is "absolutely necessary to caress 'em [the natives] as Friends, and not to treat 'em as Slaves; nor dare we do other, their Numbers so far surpassing ours in that *Continent*" (11). Students might contrast this colonial apprehension with the narrator's lament at the peaceful resolution of war where it requires the surrender of land with great "Beauty and Use" (43). In response to the stipulations in the Treaty of Breda of 1667, which marked the end of the Second Anglo-Dutch War, when the English handed over Surinam to the Dutch in exchange for New Amsterdam (New York), the narrator declares, "[H]ad his late Majesty, of sacred Memory, but seen and known what a vast and charming World he had been Master of in that Continent, he would never have parted so Easily with it to the *Dutch*" (43). Anxiety about the consequences of colonial war and the desire to possess and defend colonies uneasily coexist in *Oroonoko*.

The novel also foregrounds what may seem an obvious point: that war narratives are contingent, dependent on the origins and survival of the narrator. In *Oroonoko*, the diplomatic resolution of the war with the Dutch and the subsequent colonial violence is associated with narrative failure—the disfigurement of story—because after the surrender of Surinam, the Dutch "kill'd, banish'd and dispers'd" those who could provide a full account of Oroonoko's life and violent death (36). A number of textual moments can be linked to the complicated relationship between narrative and war and the inability of language to capture the intricacies of a conflict, leading to another way of organizing the war-related material in *Oroonoko*. The war in Coramantien, for example, is apparently recounted to the narrator only by Oroonoko (8), who assumes the position of epic hero; thus we hear little about the brutality of the experience on soldiers and civilians, and more about the psychological suffering of a heroic member of the nobility. Many of the details of combat are elided. When Oroonoko refuses to fight during his depression over Imoinda's terrible fate, the narrator tells us only that the soldiers "flee before the Enemy, and scatter themselves all over the Plain, in great Disorder," making great "Out-cries" (29). She relates far more about Oroonoko's personal despair. Her account of events in Surinam, on the other hand, has multiple, sometimes competing, sources. While Oroonoko tries to position his uprising in heroic terms, alluding to the fearless Hannibal (53), she recalls hearing varied versions of this martial event, the first of which makes her so apprehensive that she flees with others for fear the rebels will "Cut all our Throats" (57). The story of the uprising is filtered through the perception of a princely leader and also through the consciousness of ordinary people. As with most who endure a siege or an attack during war, the slave women in the midst of Oroonoko's revolt feel dread and suffer, though the narrator portrays them as cowardly: "[T]he Women and Children, seeing their Husbands so treated, being of fearful Cowardly Disposition . . . they all run in amongst their Husbands and Fathers, and hung about 'em, crying out, *Yield, yield*" (55). That accounts vary according to their sources teaches readers to recognize biases and elisions in the numerous and partisan war narratives of the period.

In revealing bias in narratives of war, Behn troubles the border between noble military action and debased slaughter. In *Oroonoko*, this is intensified when the narrator draws on classical epic notions of heroism only to hint at their limited relevance to the actuality of war and its aftereffects. This pattern will become evident when students read passages from *Oroonoko* alongside excerpts from classical epics, the epics providing a context for the rules and customs of combat depicted in and interrogated by *Oroonoko*. For example, students are often disturbed by the accepted practice in Oroonoko's Coramantien of selling the unransomed enemies captured in battle as slaves (11, 30), but relevant sections of the *Iliad* show them that the enslaving of men and women as spoils of war was an accepted practice of the Ancient Greeks. At the beginning of *Oroonoko*, students observe that warriors in Coramantien gladly sell as slaves "a great many Captives" taken "in Battel" (11) for profit, but toward the end they come across a speech by Oroonoko in which the taking of prisoners of war, the selling of these prisoners as slaves, and the harsh reality of enslavement are uneasily juxtaposed. Although Oroonoko attempts to differentiate honorable enslavement following battle from the selling of slaves to "Rogues" and "Runagades" who administer the colony, his speech elides the fact that most of the slaves he addresses were presumably won in battle and sold to the highest bidder (52). Students are also confronted with the ghastly consequences of enslavement (regardless of its cause): the defacement and murder of Imoinda and the torture and dismemberment of Oroonoko.

Students who have not read the *Iliad* may also have difficulty seeing Oroonoko as a military hero when he insists, on hearing of Imoinda's death, that "henceforth he wou'd never lift a Weapon, or draw a Bow; but abandon the small Remains of his Life to Sighs and Tears" (28). However, Achilles's refusal to fight in book 1 of the *Iliad* reveals that Oroonoko is actually conforming to a classical representation of epic heroism. Nonetheless, the heroic ideal is scrutinized shortly after Oroonoko is described in epic terms as "one of the most expert Captains, and bravest Soldiers, that ever saw the Field of *Mars*."

The narrator expresses surprise that, surrounded by "fighting Men, or those mangl'd, or dead" in his youth, such a warrior could exhibit "Greatness of Soul," humanity, honor, and generosity (12). She goes on to attribute his civilized nature partly to the "Care of a *French*-Man of Wit and Learning" and partly to his postwar contact with English and Spanish gentlemen traders, whose language he has learned (12–13). Behn seems to share the concern raised by Niccolò Machiavelli in *The Art of War* that soldiers trained solely in warfare who cannot acquire new social roles when war is over pose a significant threat to a nation at peace (16).

The ambiguous, sometimes enigmatic, response to war and the principles that inform it in *Oroonoko* occurs in other early modern literary works. Students should read *Oroonoko* in conjunction with mid- to late-seventeenth-century works of poetry, drama, and fictional and nonfictional prose that recount experiences of war. The unique nature of war fiction will be underscored by contrasting it with other literary genres, as the novel was hardly the only genre to emerge from and be shaped by the civil wars and Anglo-Dutch Wars. Abraham Cowley's *Civil War*; Lucy Hutchinson's *Memoirs of the Life of Colonel Hutchinson*; John Milton's *Paradise Lost*, *Samson Agonistes*, and sonnets on military figures; John Bunyan's *Holy War*; and any of the many heroic dramas dedicated to war offer rich, multifaceted portraits of war. Like *Oroonoko*, these works record the experience of war and its aftermath. They address the joys of victory and the depth of mourning; they expose, even when using war in allegorical ways, the brutality of combat and commemorate acts of heroism; and they bear in mind the ethical or moral dimension of the battlefield.

If a comparative approach is taken, the works of Margaret Cavendish will prove particularly fertile in an undergraduate setting. Cavendish, like Behn, is a Royalist woman who produced a considerable amount of material on war in nearly every genre. Her military drama *Bell in Campo* has two overlapping plots, both of which bring into focus the relation of women and war. In the first, a female band of warriors led by Lady Victoria follow their husbands to war. After the defeat of the male army, they overpower the enemy, save their husbands, and return home to adulation. Epic heroism is regendered in the main plot by this all-female militia. The military actions of Lady Victoria and her army might make an interesting point of comparison with the Amazonian tendencies of Behn's "*Heroick Imoinda*," who during the rebellion "did nevertheless press near her Lord" in battle, "having a Bow, and a Quiver full of poyson'd Arrows, which she manag'd with such dexterity, that she wounded several, and shot the *Governor* into the Shoulder" (55).

The second plot in *Bell in Campo* contrasts passive and active female mourning in response to war, privileging the female mourner who deploys her grief as a cultural weapon. Madam Passionate's attempt to prevent her husband from fighting is presented as emasculating, and her excessive grief after hearing of his death is proved superficial. She may appear analogous to the cowardly slave women in *Oroonoko* who cause their fathers and husbands to abandon

Oroonoko during the rebellion. In contrast, *Bell in Campo*'s Madam Jantil, faced with the loss of her husband in battle, engages in "remarkably innovative and transformative cultural work" by producing "a living monument, a textual performance engendered by suffering . . . in order to give meaning to the private and public loss" caused by war (Nelson and Alker 15). Her ultimate death after completing this work might fruitfully be compared with Imoinda's pleas for death at Oroonoko's hands to save her virtue and prevent reenslavement (60).

Bell in Campo is itself a "work of mourning" produced by a woman intent on responding productively to "royalist military losses during the civil war" (Nelson and Alker 15). Likewise *Oroonoko*, narrated by a grieving woman, could be read as an assertion of the importance of an active, and specifically female, Royalist grief not only for Charles I but also for the suffering of the British nation during and after the civil wars. In the very moment that the narrator insists on the limited "Reputation of [her] Pen" (65) to do justice to her grief, Behn also makes clear that following wars in which renowned women such as Henrietta Maria and Brilliana Harley vigorously participated, the field of letters had also become more flexible with regard to the female sex.

Cavendish's poetry offers an even more intensely mournful awareness of the destructive force of war. "An Elegy on My Brother, Kill'd in These Unhappy Warres" engages directly with war-related grief, and "A Description of the Battle in Fight" is deeply concerned with the grotesque nature of violent conflict. The second poem could be profitably connected to Oroonoko's fate or to the customs of the native war captains. Its opening lines elucidate aspects of martial violence in *Oroonoko*:

> *Some* with *sharp Swords*, to tell, O most accurst,
> Were above halfe into the bodies thrust:
> From whence fresh streams of *bloud* run all along
> Unto the *Hilts*, and there lay clodded on.
> Some, their *Leggs* hang dangling by the *Nervouse* strings,
> And *shoulders* cut, hung loose, like flying wings.
> Here heads are cleft in two parts, *braines* lye masht,
> And all their *faces* into slices hasht. (lines 1–8)

Perhaps the mutilated bodies that Cavendish lingers over on the battlefield foreshadow Behn's maimed hero. Regardless, this comparison of works by Behn and Cavendish will encourage students to think about the role gender plays in the representation of war in literature.

Once *Oroonoko* has been mined for references to war, contextualized by a review of pertinent historical material and apposite excerpts from classical epics, and compared with contemporary works on combat, students will be better prepared to formulate a governing theory on the representation of military action in the novel and to trace the role of gender on its treatment of war. This is not to say, however, that they will discover a unified perspective on warfare in

Oroonoko, because Behn is inconsistent in her imaginative rendering of colonial conflict, armed rebellion, the enslavement of prisoners of war, the ethics of the battle, and the decency of combatants. She reflects the ambivalence toward war in many early modern treatises in which theorists struggled to envisage a righteous war, in which no "*Injustice* with Regard to an *Enemy*" would be committed (Grotius 136). *Oroonoko* suggests that a righteous war is nothing more than wishful thinking.

NOTES

Thanks are due to our research assistant Nanda Maw Lin (Whitman College), for his invaluable assistance in gathering and assessing primary materials for this project.

[1] The instructor who prepares a background lecture on the historical and literary significance of the English civil wars and the Anglo-Dutch Wars might consult Charles Carlton's *Going to the Wars: The Experience of the British Civil Wars, 1638–1651*, Diane Purkiss's *Literature, Gender and Politics during the English Civil War*, Nigel Smith's *Literature and Revolution in England, 1640–1660*, Roger Hainsworth and Christine Churches's *The Anglo-Dutch Naval Wars, 1652–1674*, and J. R. Jones's *The Anglo-Dutch Wars of the Seventeenth Century*.

Oroonoko as a Caribbean Text

Thomas W. Krise

Oroonoko is not often thought of as a Caribbean text. It is associated more commonly with Restoration literature or the literature of imperialism or the rise of the novel. When viewed from the imperial center, the novel's African and Caribbean characters seem to be merely exotic props in a drama about issues of concern to the audience at home in England, not representatives of traditions that created the Caribbean culture of today and have spread their influence throughout the world.

Caribbean literature as a category is usually thought of as originating in the early twentieth century, with the works of writers such as C. L. R. James, Claude McKay, and George Lamming. Caribbean writers and critics today tend to establish exclusive criteria for what constitutes a legitimate Caribbean text, limiting the label narrowly. Kenneth Ramchand suggests these limits:

> What makes a novel a West Indian novel? and what do we mean when we say that a writer is a West Indian writer? A safe enough generalisation to begin with is that those literary works are West Indian which describe a social world that is recognizably West Indian, in a West Indian landscape; and which are written by people who were born or who grew up in the West Indies. (93)

This definition admits some writers, like Jean Rhys of Dominica or V. S. Naipaul of Trinidad, both of whom left the Caribbean at an early age and rarely returned, but excludes much writing from the first several centuries of settlement, when most people who wrote about the Caribbean were not born and raised there. By contrast, the category of American literature has admitted many writers who were born elsewhere but who lived or spent time in the United States or in the colonies that later formed it. Captain John Smith, Anne Bradstreet, J. Hector St. John de Crèvecœur, Thomas Paine, and Saul Bellow all come to mind. English speakers in the Caribbean also have a claim to the English literature that precedes the colonization of the Americas. Derek Walcott points to this view from England when he writes:

> The colonial claim to English recedes as far back as Anglo-Saxon; part of its inheritance lies in deciphering the surviving fragments of its literature, and the claim revolves on whether a West Indian should write "their" or "our" when he is writing about English fiction or poetry. (61)

Oroonoko is a Caribbean text in that it describes "a social world that is recognizably West Indian, in a West Indian landscape." It was written by a person who was not born or raised in the Caribbean but very likely spent time in the West Indies. Furthermore, it presents us with one of the earliest literary representations of the people, cultures, and issues that would join to make the Caribbean the unique place it has become, and it touches on issues that were central to the experience of the Caribbean for centuries.

What makes the Caribbean unique? To begin with, no other place on earth has suffered the effects of colonialism as much as the territories of the Caribbean Sea. The near eradication of the native Caribbean peoples was one of the most complete exterminations in history. Today the only surviving communities of Caribs are in Dominica, Saint Vincent, and on the South American mainland; the populations of native peoples in the rest of the eastern Caribbean and most of the Greater Antilles were either eliminated or assimilated into the dominant European colonial cultures (Cunningham). Those populations were replaced by the largest forced migration in history, as between twelve and fifteen million people were taken from Africa to the Americas to work and live as slaves (Segal 4; Rediker 347; Davis and Mintz 32). The form that slavery took in the Americas—and most prominently in the Caribbean—was radically different from the forms of slavery that existed in the rest of the world for thousands of years: it was large-scale and commercial and involved colonies in which the enslaved vastly outnumbered the free population. This slavery was more brutal and deadly than any that had gone before. The territories of the Caribbean also changed hands between different empires more often than any other place on earth. Tobago changed hands at least twenty-two times between 1654 and 1815 (Rahim). A further distinction about the Caribbean in the time of *Oroonoko* is that the sugar-and-slave system was the world's first example of a society dependent on the world trading system for survival. In the eastern Caribbean especially, the desire to raise as much sugar as possible led planters to cover their islands with sugar cane with no provision for food crops, instead relying on imports of grain and salted fish and meats to feed the enslaved population.

The Caribbean has been a place represented by outsiders more than anywhere else—and the representations in fiction often take the form of imaginary islands. Daniel Defoe had thousands of real islands to choose from but decided to put his Robinson Crusoe on an imaginary island near Tobago. From Thomas More's *Utopia* and William Shakespeare's island of *The Tempest* to Robert Louis Stevenson's *Treasure Island*, Toni Morrison's Isle des Chevaliers in *Tar Baby*, Rhys's unnamed Windward Island in *Wide Sargasso Sea*, Lamming's unnamed native island in *The Castle of My Skin*, or Naipaul's unnamed native island in *The Mimic Men*, the Caribbean stands as an imagined, imaginary, and imaginatively colonized place.

Another thing to keep in mind when considering the Caribbean and its culture is the central role it has played in the making of the modern world. The Caribbean in the seventeenth and eighteenth centuries contained the most valuable agricultural property in the world, thanks to the immense value of sugar, molasses, and rum. In the decade preceding the American Revolution, the West Indies were worth more to the British imperial economy than all thirteen North American colonies combined (Price 103). On the eve of the Haitian Revolution in the early 1790s, Saint-Domingue (the French name for Haiti) was the most valuable colony on earth (Sheridan 407; Craton 45). The Dutch traded New Netherland (renamed New York) for English Surinam after the Second Anglo-Dutch War in 1667. In 1763, the French chose to keep Martinique and Guadeloupe instead of all of Canada after the Seven Years' War. In his *Capitalism and Slavery*, the founding prime minister of Trinidad and Tobago, Eric Williams, argued that the sugar plantations of the West Indies were the first examples of large factories, supplying not only a model for the industrial factory system that developed in the nineteenth century but also the great wealth that fueled Europe's rise to world domination in both commerce and military power.

One challenge for students is the tendency to assume that slaves were all alike—and unlike ourselves; that they would do as they were told without murmur or complaint; that they, by and large, accepted their enslavement as the way of the world. In fact, we find that enslaved people resisted continuously and creatively—just as we would if we were in their situation—from their first capture, through the Middle Passage, and throughout their lives in the New World. Another thing we tend to overlook is that enslaved people made full lives for themselves. They had families and relationships, hierarchies, traditions, customs, stories, music, moral codes, and habits—both those they brought with them from Africa, as Oroonoko and his companions did, and those they developed in the new cultures they created in the New World. Not only did slaves hold positions of skill and authority in their societies, but they also participated and contributed to the building of their societies, even when that work actually helped keep their fellow slaves enslaved.

Another challenge for students is the idea that, until about the middle of the eighteenth century, few considered slavery immoral. The first condemnation of slavery in the English language came in a sermon by an Anglican bishop, Robert Sanderson, in 1638. Sanderson was actually condemning the Spaniards for their harsh colonization of the Americas and condemning Spanish slavery as just one instance of the black legend of Spanish cruelty that the English used against their imperial enemies. One does not find much objection to slavery again until George Fox established the Religious Society of Friends, known as Quakers, and began to question the morality of slavery later in the seventeenth century. Antislavery sentiment remained on the fringe of religious extremism until the early eighteenth century. The first attack on slavery that did not emanate from a strongly religious point of view was "A Speech Made by a Black of Guardeloupe" in 1709. The first attack on slavery from a secular, natural rights point of view came in the "Speech of Moses Bon Sàam" in 1735. The Quakers issued a ban on the practice of slavery by their members in 1761 (H. Thomas 460), but it was not until the 1780s that antislavery was a widespread sentiment in the English-speaking world. The high point of its rhetoric came in the five years between 1787 and 1792. It subsided in the wake of the Reign of Terror in France and the Haitian Revolution but rose again in the period 1805–07, when the slave trade was abolished in the British Empire, and in 1808, when it was abolished in the United States.

So Behn's *Oroonoko* entered the scene a full century before antislavery feeling became widespread. Readers in the twenty-first century are quick to note that Behn's text laments not slavery itself but the idea of the unjust enslavement of a highborn prince. Despite the fact that Prince Oroonoko endorses and facilitates slavery and thus would seem an unlikely hero of antislavery, his character—in Behn's novel as well as in Thomas Southerne's dramatized version—presents the English-speaking public with an enslaved character with whom they can sympathize.

In some ways, *Oroonoko* is a representative Caribbean text and Oroonoko a representative Caribbean character: he is brought to the region against his will, as were approximately ninety percent of those who went there in the first two centuries of settlement. He both resists slavery and participates in it, as did so many enslaved people in all slave societies in all eras—for slavery of a majority of a population is impossible without the acquiescence and collaboration of at least some of the enslaved. The text is written by someone from Europe who visited the region rather than by someone born and raised there. The text links Europe, Africa, and America in a way suggestive of the mixture of cultures that characterizes the Caribbean both in the early period and in the present. And the text provides interesting grounds for the discussion of race, gender, and class that is characteristic of Caribbean literature throughout its half millennium of literate culture.

Behn foreshadows the important role of women in the abolitionist movement by being one of the first writers to present a sympathetic enslaved character to the English-speaking world (Moira Ferguson, *Subject* 27–49). Her representation of the culture of the native inhabitants of Surinam, moreover, is typical of those given by other European travelers to the region. When Behn describes the inhabitants as being "extream modest and bashful" (9), she echoes early reports, such as Thomas Harriot's account of the first English attempt at colonization in Roanoke, in which Harriot suggests to readers in England that the native inhabitants were childlike and not to be feared. Behn also presents the Caribs as remote and primitive, not sharing the time frame of Europeans. If such people are relegated to a distant, even pre-Edenic, past, then the colonizers feel justified in their encroachment and domination. Note the idyllic tone when Behn says that the Caribs "have a Native Justice, which knows no Fraud; and they understand no Vice, or Cunning, but when they are taught by the *White Men*" (10). While the reader might think that Behn is here suggesting that white men could learn something noble and valuable from these native people—and this sentiment can be heard from Edmund Hickeringill's *Jamaica Viewed* (1661) to Thomas Jefferson's *Notes on the State of Virginia* (1785)—the conviction that the natives are so primitive implies that they are doomed to extinction in a real, modern world where imperialism, commercial exploitation, and the attendant culture of deception are inevitable.

Behn further complicates the idea that modern European imperial culture is inevitably dishonest when she describes Oroonoko's African culture as more honest and honorable than that of the Europeans:

> [Oroonoko] was very sorry to hear that the *Captain* pretended to the Knowledge and Worship of any *Gods*, who had taught him no better Principles, than not to Credit as he would be Credited: but they told him the Difference of their Faith occasion'd that Distrust: For the *Captain* had protested to him upon the Word of a *Christian*, and sworn in the Name of a Great G O D; which if he shou'd violate, he would expect eternal Torment in the World to come. *Is that all the Obligation he has to be Just to his Oath?* replied *Oroonoko. Let him know I Swear by my Honour, which to violate, wou'd not only render me contemptible and despised by all brave and honest Men, and so give my self perpetual pain, but it wou'd be eternally offending and diseasing all Mankind, harming, betraying, circumventing and outraging all Men. . . .* (32–33)

Oroonoko's Coramantien culture is presented as more primitive than contemporary European culture, but it is also less remote and primitive than the Carib culture. Thus two of the components of Caribbean culture, the Carib and the African, are portrayed as more noble than the dominating European culture. The criticism of European imperialism and its attendant slavery and exploitation inherent in Behn's descriptions of both Carib and African cultures is a common feature of texts from the early Caribbean. Echoes can be heard in the many variations on the story of Inkle and Yarico (Seymour; Felsenstein) and in Thomas Tryon's *Friendly Advice*.

The representation of the superior nobility of the subaltern culture extends to the conclusion of *Oroonoko* when the enslaved prince endures his gruesome execution with nearly superhuman calm (64). Stories of such stoicism among Africans persist throughout the period of slavery, culminating in the remarkably similar description of the execution of the freedman Neptune, also in Surinam, in the 1770s (Stedman [*Internet Archive*] 2: 306–07). These accounts remind us that people were criticizing the imperial enterprise from the beginning and that the Africans who were forced to settle in the New World and the indigenous peoples who were assimilated, displaced, or wiped out all had vibrant and ancient cultures that both resisted the spread of imperialism and contributed to the richly mixed culture that developed in the Caribbean over the centuries since the first contact between the Old and New Worlds in 1492.

A challenge presented by Behn's *Oroonoko* and much Caribbean literature that follows it is our modern desire to read these texts from a postcolonial perspective—that is, to see empire and colonization as entirely negative forces in which European power is projected onto subordinate others who must struggle to reclaim or re-create their ancient cultures and agency. Such a perspective assumes that the twenty-first century is a postcolonial period and that people in earlier times were firmly rooted in a colonial mind-set, when in fact much of the Caribbean region today continues under either formal or informal colonialism and when the seeds of postcolonialism were planted at the very beginning of the colonial enterprise. One way to avoid the binary colonial-postcolonial prism is to look at both early and modern Caribbean literature from a point of view dubbed "paracolonial" (Newell). In its simplest definition, *paracolonial* means "arising alongside or accompanying colonialism." So, for example, European racism targeted toward dark-skinned Africans was not so much a deliberate policy developed to advance and promote the European exploitation of Africa and of African descendants in the Americas as something that developed alongside the colonization and exploitation of those regions. For another example, the development of distinctive cultural forms such as reggae, calypso, and the West Indian dialect of English happened as a result of the mixing of people and cultures in the colonized Caribbean, not as a deliberate policy. The music, language, and art of the Caribbean cannot be described as precolonial, postcolonial, or even simply colonial, because they have both roots and present existence in each of those periods of time and ways of thinking. Thus the term *paracolonial* offers us the opportunity to see cultural forms, including texts, as products of a complex network of relations in which apparent hierarchies are turned on their head or elements of later culture are forged not by the deliberate agency of the colonizer alone but as a dialectical product of power, resistance, preservation, creolization, cultural identity formation, and so forth (Newell; Archer).

Because *Oroonoko* takes place early in the period of English colonization of the Caribbean, we are shown a social situation in which the various racial groups—Europeans, Africans, and Native Americans—are distinct. It is a time before social intermingling would result in mixed-race people and the dynamic and distinctively mixed culture that becomes the Caribbean. Behn offers us vivid descriptions of Coramantiens and Caribs in what might be called their autonomous, premixed state, followed by descriptions of all three groups brought together by the forces of European colonization. So it presents the major constituents of the Caribbean culture that evolved over the centuries. Her portrait of English colonization in Surinam highlights the new, crass, commercial version of slavery and contrasts it with the slavery that Oroonoko's home culture practiced in Africa. Before the advent of Europeans into the slave market, enslavement was understood to be the result of defeat in a just war and was seen as a humane alternative to death. Oroonoko's own story demonstrates that the new transatlantic, commercial form of slavery led to abuses of the old martial form of slavery and resulted in kidnapping, betrayal, and profiteering. Oroonoko highlights this fact when he cries out to his fellow slaves, "*Have they Vanquish'd us Nobly in Fight? Have they Won us in Honourable Battel? And are we, by the chance of War, become their Slaves?*" (52).

Advocates of antislavery in the eighteenth century took care to emphasize that the African slave trade was rooted in kidnapping and chicanery. Part of what makes the plight of Oroonoko worthy of Behn's readers' sympathy is that he is a prince wrongfully sold into slavery and that this form of slavery is encouraged by England's management of its colonial empire in the Americas. Besides presenting English-speaking readers with a sympathetic character who would be an emblem of the wrongs of slavery for more than a hundred years, *Oroonoko* raised questions about the form and nature of the new commercial and territorial empire that England was building. Reading Behn's text through the lens of paracolonialism can help us appreciate the agency that previously overlooked groups of people brought to the development of culture in the Caribbean and elsewhere. It can also remind us of the complex social forces at work in the period of European expansion.

PEDAGOGICAL CONTEXTS

How Big Did She Say That Snake Was? Teaching the Contradiction in *Oroonoko*

James Grantham Turner

Oroonoko is not only a locus classicus of feminist and postcolonial reading but also an ideal training text for readers at all levels. Before anything else, I want to foster a close reading of those passages where contradiction is most revealing and authorship most active. Since hunting and fact-finding expeditions play a crucial role in the narrative—as diversions from but also reflections of the tragedy—I want the readers to hunt for themselves, to share the excitement of discovering the slippages and mutations of meaning, oscillating between contrary subject positions, that perceptive critics find in the details of the narrator's language, down to the very pronouns. My method could be called materialist poetics or poetic materialism, making the smallest details speak, letting the larger ideological tensions and imaginative contradictions echo from their fissures. So I use a sustained, unfolding reading of *Oroonoko* in a section of our introductory course English 200, which deals with "approaches to literary study, including textual analysis, scholarly methodology and bibliography, critical theory and practice" (https://schedulebuilder.berkeley.edu/explore/courses/FL/2012/1568). While designed for entering doctoral students, this reading serves equally well for honors or other advanced English or comparative literature majors.

For me the most important features of *Oroonoko* are the truth claims and the stretching of realism through marvelous details, the assertion of Behn's authorship and voice, the vivid manifestation of divided consciousness, and the critique of European values and religion. In this short essay, I can illustrate only how the first of these features might be brought out in class, but I point to the others.

Any class must confront the notorious European elements in Oroonoko's person and what could seem a racist concession that Oroonoko, like the Caribs, was beautiful "bating his Colour" (13). Such effects are provisional, reader-responsive, and subject to alteration in retrospect. I induce this awareness, however, not by lecturing but rather by reciting counterexamples and prompting questions of the form "Yes, but what happens next? What about . . . ?" The point is not to vindicate colonialism or exonerate Behn—as if literary historians were judges or thought police and imaginative writers could be held accountable—but to gain a sense of how imaginative writing reveals double consciousness or perhaps triple in Behn's case. Students should grasp that we have here two personae, not one: the young Behn present at the events narrated (or, if not present, ready to explain how she came to know them and why she did not prevent them) and the mature novelist putting into print a tale told over many years, while advertising her own career as an author. The narrator appears impossibly divided between the "we" of the callous and fearful slave owners and the "we" of the slaves: so terrified that Oroonoko will "Cut all our Throats" that she flees the scene with all the other white women (57) but horrified at what "they" do to maintain their rule over the slaves. What matters is the utterly conflicted relation between the narrator and the colonial world, embodied in its chief prize and victim, the "Royal Slave"—a contradictory mix of passion and exploitation, of terror, indifference, and adoration. I aim to set off in the student the same oscillation between credulity and suspicion, wonderment and calculation, that features so largely in the main characters.

Untrained readers tend to skip descriptions in prose fiction, but in *Oroonoko* the meaning lies more in the descriptions than in the story itself, which can be starkly summarized.

I ask students to visualize the New World "Rarities" (8) that Behn purports to have brought home, some literally, some by re-creating them in the mind's eye and relating them to the familiar: friendly, innocent Indians living in paradise! a grove of citrus trees as beautiful as the Mall in Westminster! feather costumes that the reader has actually seen on stage in another drama about noble natives tortured to death by cruel Christians! Students should think about what she could have seen, since these *National Geographic*–style objects serve as guarantees of all the other truths she tells. To help the witnessing process, I evoke (with reference to local museums) actual examples of feather artifacts and what Behn calls "[butter]flies . . . as big as my Fist," specimens of which could apparently be seen on the London stage and in the museum of "His Majesty's *Antiquaries*"—her donations (8–9). We move on to the skins of snakes, allegedly seen by Behn in Surinam and on view in the same Royal Society collection, palpable and permanent evidence of her truthfulness. I ask students to translate her measurement—"threescore Yards in length" (8)—into feet and pace it out along the classroom walls. Can we imagine the world's largest snakes, the boas and anacondas that really do live in that region, but almost twice as long as a blue whale? What is going on here? Either those cunning Caribs have sewn a lot of snakes together to impress gullible English anthropologists or Behn has invented a magic realism where details seem intensely factual but measure is unmoored from measurement. To stretch our capacity for belief to the scale required for *Oroonoko*, she gives us lions ten times smaller than natural yet somehow without loss of identity ("it is it in *Miniature*" [8]), snakes ten times larger than any known to science, and a river called Amazon almost as wide as the Thames (51).

Before any secondary research is done, it is essential to involve the class by vivid out-loud readings of important passages, unpacking the most loaded images and phrases. Leading questions prompt comparison with other episodes, juxtaposing contradictory evidence ("we" dare not treat Indians as slaves [11], but "our *Indian Slaves*" row the party upriver [51]). This comparison is greatly helped by tracking key images and even key words through the novel, using a computer-legible text. Each hit can be copied with its immediate context, giving access to the aura of significance around each usage; taken together, this database can show the shifts in the meaning of images and words as the narrative accelerates. These searches can be done online by students in a rapid-fire chase or in class on a projected computer screen (with some rehearsal).

A few examples show how such a search can work. Though Behn is fascinated by the texture of the Indians' bare skin, they object to "being touch'd" (9), presumably by her, yet this relation is reversed during the anthropological trip, when the "whites" are on display, and "[the Indians] touch'd [them]" (48). *Melancholy* (29) recurs as the explanatory term for Oroonoko's strange fits of excessive grief, when he becomes so paralyzed that he fails in his martial quest for victory (in Africa) or for revenge (in Surinam); the same word diagnoses Behn's even stranger moments of panic, when she flees the scene just as some terrible punishment happens to Oroonoko, which in retrospect she claims she could have prevented ("being my self but Sickly, and very apt to fall into Fits of dangerous Illness upon any extraordinary Melancholy" [64]). This affinity between the hero and the narrator hints at associations of melancholy with both creativity and blackness.

I assign a paper that explores the production and self-presentation of the text, especially how it manifests authorship. First, I highlight passages where Behn draws attention to her identity, claiming both social and literary status. The older Behn posts her name proudly on the title page, establishes her links to the Catholic aristocracy in her dedication, and then from the first page of the narrative engages us with her speaking voice. In the main text, she cites her younger self as eyewitness to what she insists is not fiction but fact, as occupant of the "best House" (44) and as daughter of the designated "Lieutenant-General" (43), whose death at sea, combined with the continued absence of the Governor, leaves the colony in the hands of unspeakable degenerates. Research has uncovered no evidence for this relation, but other allusions, biographical and autobiographical, are entirely plausible: William Byam (Behn's villain) and George Marten (brother of the revolutionary Henry Marten) really did live in

Surinam, and, as she says, Marten did feature in her next play (57–58). Behn frequently refers to her authorship—gendered as her "Female Pen" (36) and therefore having a special authority to evoke the passions—as well as to her intense emotions at each stage of the story, from her first meeting with the hero to his grisly end.

The title page displays not only the author's name and the claim that the tale is "A True History" but also the exotic name Oroonoko and the subtitle *The Royal Slave*, the greatest of her hybrid rarities, the master oxymoron or conjunction of opposites that sets up all the others. That doubleness is confirmed by a key-word search of the hero's names. *Oroonoko*, sounding suspiciously like the South American river Orinoco, is unlike anything documented in West Africa, yet we are asked to believe that it is his authentic African name. Searches of *Oroonoko* in Behn's text show that it is overlaid by the slave name Caesar for many pages, during the idyllic "diversions" and the rebellion itself, but *Oroonoko* is then fiercely reasserted after the scene of betrayal and whipping: "*you shall see that* Oroonoko *scorns to live with the Indignity that was put on* Caesar" (58). So we find precise evidence, in the alternation of names, for the insight that slavery splits the character into two, each antagonistic to the other: as the imposed identity of Caesar changes the meaning of the name, from idealized nobility to the alienable flesh that can be tortured and humiliated, so "Oroonoko" must assert his original self even if it means rending and destroying that slave's body. Yet the authentic name seems to be already hybridized, a mysterious offspring of native elements from both Africa and Amazonia. How can the hero grow up in Africa but have a Carib name?

This puzzle leads us to consider the African love-triangle episode early in the novel, which likewise seems utterly hybridized—African princes with orientalist harems, orange groves, and marble bathhouses. Here the question can be raised for future research: How far is this Behn's fantasy, how far is it the product of cultural mingling in Africa established long before Behn's time? Contemporary documents, gathered in the Norton and more fully in Catherine Gallagher's indispensable Bedford Cultural Edition, record inland kings living in splendor with Turkish carpets and festive architecture, a corrective to falsely homogenized and simplified conceptions of what the "African" should be.

Hybridization and authorial self-consciousness can be shown working together in a fascinating passage about the body carving of Imoinda, which identifies her as a member of the elite and as fit company for the colonial ladies. Her standing is indicated by the remark that "we paid her a treble Respect; and though from her being carv'd in fine Flowers and Birds all over her Body, we took her to be of Quality before, yet, when we knew *Clemene* was *Imoinda*, we cou'd not enough admire her" (40). In the next paragraph, this description follows:

> I had forgot to tell you, that those who are Nobly born of that Country, are so delicately Cut and Rac'd all over the fore-part of the Trunk of their Bodies, that it looks as if it were Japan'd; the Works being raised like high

> Poynt round the Edges of the Flowers: Some are only Carv'd with a little Flower, or Bird, at the Sides of the Temples, as was *Caesar*; and those who are so Carv'd over the Body, resemble our Ancient *Picts*, that are figur'd in the Chronicles, but these Carvings are more delicate. (40)

That single word *raced* conveys both the cutting technique and the marking of a specific ethnic and caste identity; it gives us a fruitful opportunity to understand *race* as a verb or process, something made rather than genetically fixed.

Despite the mention of Picts, this body scarification is irreducibly other, non-Western, indeed specifically West African, since it involves not tattooing or henna but actual raising of patterned welts. A handout could bring in Olaudah Equiano's description of the cutting and scarring of the forehead that produced the mark of the prince in the kingdom where he grew up. Yet Behn assumes without the slightest hesitation that "we" recognize this as a sign of "quality." Though the white ladies' skins were neither raced nor embroidered like their dresses, Imoinda's voluntary scars are assimilated as perfectly and appropriately beautiful, with none of the apologetic or "bating his Colour" rhetoric that marks the earlier introductions of Carib and African beauty. They identify her—and identify with her—as a luxury artifact, partly something exotic and imported ("Japan'd") but more like the specifically gendered and classed "Works" of a lady's own hand, fine high-point embroidery. Such embroidery was relegated to the status of a minor female art in the patriarchal scale of values, but for Behn it became a vital analogue to her life work, her authorship. Word hunting reveals, just after this passage, how she induced the newly married couple into her female circle by sharing literature, history, and needlework: "I oblig'd 'em in all things I was capable of: I entertain'd him with the Lives of the Romans, and great Men, which charm'd him to my Company; and her, with teaching her all the pretty Works that I was Mistress of; and telling her Stories of Nuns" (41). Those "pretty Works" include her own compositions, since Behn would shortly publish *The History of the Nun*. This cultural capital makes her "*Mistress*," exercising power, in and through the work of words, over the hero as well as the heroine: "obliging him to love us very well, we had all the Liberty of Speech with him, especially my self, whom he call'd his *Great Mistress*; and indeed my Word wou'd go a great way with him" (41).

Many discussions can open up here—for example, this description can be set against those of the Caribs and of Oroonoko himself. Behn apparently excepted his "Colour" (and his facial marking) from her earlier canon of beauty. But attentive reading of tone and image suggests that the color ("new Brick" [9] or "perfect Ebony, or polish'd Jett" [13]) is not the least but the most attractive aspect of these beautiful others, making them more like precious artifacts or "pretty Works." Again I push the idea of an affinity between hero and narrator. Behn identifies artifactuality with the hard-won work of her authorship, which she proudly maintains at every turn against misogynist essentialism. Having crafted her life work as art, she is well placed to know that, in the marketplace of gender, becoming a highly wrought artifact is a promotion above the status of mere chattel, working body, or biological function. This promotion is particularly significant when art is applied directly to the body, hence her fascination with both Amerindian and African body-marking customs.

At this point students normally raise an important objection, and if they do not, I do: that Behn's positive evaluation of the person as artifact merely replicates the objectification of slavery at a more genteel level, trading in gorgeous noble savages as one might bring back to Europe dead butterflies or trade for feathers and marmosets. This powerful point is an essential strand in the text's drama, articulated quite consciously when Oroonoko exhorts the slaves to rebel: African slavery by being honorably captured in battle is presented as wholly acceptable, but "*we are Bought and Sold like Apes, or Monkeys, to be the Sport of Women, Fools and Cowards*" (52). The dramatic irony of this magnificent speech cuts both ways. It anticipates the outcome, when he denounces the cowardly Africans as genetically inferior, "by Nature *Slaves*" (56), but it also retrospectively defines the young Behn, with her pet marmosets, gushing idealism, and sudden fits of panic, as all three—woman, fool, and coward. Do the contradictions here disintegrate the text or deepen it, sweeping away its diverting premise and transforming it from romance to tragedy?

Oroonoko is violent, but that violence is always a version of body art, alternately fascinating and ghoulish but always meaningful. Recurrent scenes of mutilation are arranged across a spectrum according to different levels of honor and agency: the Indian war captains' self-mutilation as badge of courage; the punitive horror of Oroonoko's whipping, hated not for the pain so much as for the status-canceling humiliation, which forces Oroonoko to consider his body as "Caesar" rather than "Oroonoko"; his love sacrifice of Imoinda, which severs her face from her body, once again a delicate cut; his self-mutilation, clearly modeled on the war captains'; his self-disemboweling, a version of Antony's Roman suicide; his decomposition into "a Death's Head black'd over" (63); the final execution, which, as it corresponds to the official dismemberment of a traitor, gives him the status of a grand enemy of the state. At the head of these body interventions is the voluntary, aesthetic, and status-conferring scarification of the princely face and torso.

Behn's description of Imoinda's body carved and "Rac'd" with ornamental markings leads us to other scenes involving the heroine, first in Africa and then in Surinam. "Imoinda" is in fact the very last word of the novel, and though she is often condemned as a flat character or mere cipher, an object of African as well as colonial patriarchy, it is important to bring out the moments when Behn "works" her in high relief. Her assenting death, horrible as it seems at first to the naive whites who stumble upon it, embodies the dreadful wisdom that life under slavery is unbearable when a child is born into that status (shades of Toni Morrison's *Beloved*). The pregnant Imoinda takes the most active part when she wounds the villainous Deputy Governor Byam with a poisoned arrow (55); she has been learning from the war culture of the Indians, not only from the genteel embroidery and light fiction classes in Behn's salon. Imoinda may start as a boring "beautiful *Black Venus*, to our young *Mars*" (14), but in the battle she becomes something the classical world could hardly dream up: a black, pregnant Amazon adorned with Pictish symbols and armed with the deadly arrows of the other Amazon. At each of these dramatic moments, I encourage the class to test the work of earlier critics (usefully selected in Lipking's Norton edition)—for example, the assertion that Behn, following "the conventions of heroic romance, allow[s] Imoinda no feature that marks her as distinctly African" (Sussman 251).

Pondering this battle scene opens a further line of inquiry. Wounding the vile Byam—a vivid emblem of Behn's own venomous satire, since he is her main target—leads not to his death and the resurrection of her plan for the repatriation and Restoration of King Oroonoko but to Byam's recovery, thanks to his Indian mistress, who sucks out the poison (55). I ask the class if this episode rings a bell. Often Chicano students will be the first to respond, for it resembles the story of La Malinche, Cortés's Aztec translator and mistress, alternately reviled as a traitor and celebrated as the founder of a new mestizo culture. From there we can set up yet a third level of discussion: of these two figures of female agency—the fierce Amazon archer and the go-between who detoxifies the confrontation and allows British governance to survive—which of the two more resembles what Behn herself does in this narrative?

An additional paper assignment situates the text in relation to its reception in or influence on its time. I encourage the search for internal anticipations of the reader's response. In the opening pages, when everything is unfamiliar, the narrator conjures up a reader quite explicitly—a jaded London sophisticate presumed to be blasé about New World wonders, supercilious about the female pen, and dismissive of Africans. By satirizing this kind of response, Behn sets up by implication a true model of readership, opposed to the racist treatment of aristocrats and properly attuned to the passions of wonder, sympathy, desire, and grief—the exact opposite of those contemptible listeners who assume that black people cannot blush (19) or who think the Captain did the right thing to trick Oroonoko into captivity on board his ship (31). This interpellation and education of an audience assumed to be revolted by barbarism and prejudiced against the African must be managed tactfully, as we learn from another feature of the description of Imoinda's body carving: its timing. Behn does not mention it when she first introduces her characters but slips it in after the lovers have been reunited in Surinam, with a disingenuous "I had forgot to tell you. . . ." The narrator conveniently forgot because she needed to wait until the reader was sufficiently attuned to a new aesthetic of the body.

At this point, the offensive remarks about color and European civility can be interpreted as a sop to or bait for the imagined London reader. Key-word searches reveal that the *European* and *Christian* characters are uniformly treacherous and sadistic, continually undermining the superior values they pretend to uphold. Sympathetic but ineffectual characters, like Trefry, Marten, and the narrator, seem excepted from this criticism—one of them, the French tutor, is ironically banished from Europe because of his skepticism about Christianity (30), yet he cannot be enslaved because he is "a Christian" (40). I would emphasize that Behn's proto-Enlightenment assault on the lies and hypocrisies of Western culture is not an occasional dab of radical chic but a consistent and courageous motif from the first to the last page: the liar-governor (10), the vile treatment of cast-off mistresses in "*Christian*-Countries" (15), Oroonoko's sense of the absurdity of the Trinity (41), and the use of the afterlife to guarantee good behavior in this life (32–33). Every instance of betrayal is accompanied by devastatingly sardonic reminders of the "Christianity" of the perpetrators (and of course Oroonoko's recurrent trust in them, at least until his final speech). The very notion that Europe has the monopoly on honor and civilization becomes ridiculous, credible only to the most fatuous reader. Oroonoko's last remarks (64) prompt us to run a key-word search on *white*, which comes to mean "false to one's word."

So students master the "work" that Behn is mistress of. By reading for process and contradiction, they apprehend *Oroonoko* as a text embedded in the genres of romance, oriental tale, and colonial fantasy yet at the same time "inconceivable" and "unimitable" (9), stretching beyond those bounds, swallowing and breaking down those conventions—a real boa constrictor, three score yards long.

Teaching *Oroonoko* in a Literature Survey 1 Course

Ana de Freitas Boe

With the inclusion of *Oroonoko* in *The Norton Anthology of English Literature* (Greenblatt and Abrams), more and more professors are assigning Aphra Behn's novel in the first half of the year-long survey of British literature, where they may find themselves confronted by two obstacles. First, students often have difficulty making connections between texts from different genres. When they read sonnets one week and novels the next, their sense of literary history can be all too fragmented. Second, students often lack a nuanced understanding of the differences between historical periods. The phrase "since the beginning of time" is an all-too-common cliché of student writing—even in sophomore-level courses such as the survey. It testifies to the extent that students do not always recognize the alterity of the past, and even when they do, they often have trouble discerning that adjacent historical periods are different from each other. My students find it obvious that the 1960s and 1980s were different decades in American history; however, they find it less obvious that Renaissance, Restoration, and eighteenth-century works of literature record different conceptions of the world. By drawing their attention to Behn's depictions of beauty in *Oroonoko*, I help them understand that ideas can be historically specific. Indeed, Behn's novel underscores not just the historicity of conceptions of beauty but also how these ideas become inextricably bound up with changing theories of racial and cultural difference in the Restoration and the eighteenth century.

As readers of *Oroonoko* are sure to remember, Behn introduces her eponymous hero through an elaborate description of his beauty: "He was pretty tall, but of a Shape the most exact that can be fancy'd: The most famous Statuary cou'd not form the Figure of a Man more admirably turn'd from Head to Foot" (13). The narrator proceeds to praise Oroonoko's face, eyes, teeth, nose, mouth, lips, and hair before going on to commend his intelligence and political acumen (13–14). Roxann Wheeler has dubbed such conventionalized descriptions in eighteenth-century novels the character sketch. "Conventionally," she explains, "the character sketch interrupts the narrative for a more or less detailed physical description that makes a subtle transition into an interpretation of the character" ("Racial Legacies" 419). Behn's character sketch suspends the action of the plot to further establish Oroonoko's nobility through an extensive description of his beauty.

Behn's character sketch, my students point out, bears more than a passing resemblance to the descriptive logic of the Renaissance poetic topos of the blazon. "The blazon as a poetic form," Jonathan Sawday explains, "[is] usually understood as a richly ornate and mannered evocation of idealized female beauty rendered into its constituent parts" (191). The blazon narrates the loveliness of the beloved by reducing her to a list of beautiful attributes: face, hair, mouth, lips, teeth, skin, eyes, among others. In Philip Sidney's sonnet 9 from *Astrophil and Stella*, for instance, the blazon shares a descriptive logic with Behn's character sketch. Astrophil's description of Stella's beauty narrates a gaze that shifts from beautiful body part to beautiful body part before summing up her loveliness as a whole:

> Queen Virtue's court, which some call Stella's face
> Prepared by Nature's chiefest furniture,
> Hath his front built of alabaster pure;
> Gold is the covering of that stately place.
> The door, by which sometimes comes forth her Grace,
> Red porphir is, which lock of pearl makes sure;
> Whose porches rich (which name of cheeks endure),
> Marble mixed red and white do interlace.
> The windows now through which this heavenly guest
> Looks o'er the world, and can find nothing such,
> Which dare claim from those lights the name of best.
> (lines 1–11)

Sidney's blazon produces a verbal portrait of Stella as a classic fair-haired Petrarchan beauty with pale skin, red lips, white teeth, and blushing cheeks. Behn's character sketch reproduces the blazon's visual logic, narrating a gaze that begins with Oroonoko's face and shifts to his eyes, teeth, nose, mouth, lips, and hair. Both Behn's character sketch and the sonnet's blazon aestheticize the beloved, whose beauty is akin to the loveliness of great works of art (for Behn, a statue; for Sidney, a mansion). Some of Behn's similes even replicate the blazon's most conventional similes. Describing Oroonoko's eyes, she notes, "the White of 'em being like Snow" (13). To note that something about the beloved is as white as snow is so clichéd that Shakespeare lampoons this simile in his parody of the blazon in sonnet 130.

Of course, in the Renaissance sonnet, the characteristic that is usually as white as snow is the female beloved's white skin, not the whites of her eyes. While my students recognize how Behn's character sketch reproduces the descriptive logic of the blazon, they also point out how it departs from the blazon's conceptions of beauty. First, Behn deviates by describing a male beloved. The blazon almost exclusively trumpets female—not male—beauty. Like Sidney's sonnet, Edmund Spenser's sonnet 64 from the *Amoretti*, for instance, exemplifies the blazon's dedication to the depiction of the female body. Likening his beloved to a garden, Spenser commends "Her goodly bosome," "Her brest," and "Her nipples" along with the other parts of her body. Indeed, the *Norton Anthology* cites a passage from Spenser's *Epithalamion* as the epitome of the blazon (Greenblatt and Abrams B: A12). Like his sonnet, Spenser's poem celebrating his marriage reserves the blazon for his description of the bride—not the groom. However, as Sawday notes, Shakespeare's depiction of a beautiful young man presents a departure from the Renaissance conventions of the blazon (201). Thus, unlike almost all her Renaissance predecessors, Behn, like Shakespeare, embraces male beauty. Describing her eponymous hero, she notes, "There was no one Grace wanting, that bears the Standard of true Beauty" (13). Nor is Oroonoko the only man described as beautiful in Behn's novel. She portrays Aboan as "a Man extreamly well made, and beautiful" (21). If most of her Renaissance precursors treat beauty and the blazon as the province of women, Behn holds open the possibility that men can possess the one and have their loveliness immortalized through the other.

Second, Behn breaks with the conventions of the blazon by paying tribute to the beauty of the black body. The blazon reserves its praise for the white body—usually blondes and the occasional brunette. In the traditional blazon, the beloved's skin is likened to "alabaster" (Sidney, line 3), "lillyes" (Spenser, Sonnet 64, line 11), and "yvory" (*Epithalamion*, line 172). In sonnet 127, Shakespeare offers a defense of "black" as "beauty's successive heir," but what makes the Dark Lady dark is her "raven black" brow and eyes—not black skin (line 9). However, when he goes on to satirize the blazon's conventional comparison of white skin with snow in sonnet 130, he notes of the Dark Lady that "If snow be white, why then her breasts are dun" (line 3), questioning the blazon's impossible simile for white skin—not claiming that brown skin is beautiful. Kim Hall has located the origins of the equation of fairness with whiteness and ugliness with blackness around the 1550s (3). While Hall's insistence that beauty and ugliness are racialized in the last half of the sixteenth century may help illuminate Renaissance poetry well (2–4), it sheds less light on Behn's Restoration character sketches of Oroonoko and his beloved Imoinda. Behn never shies away from referring to Oroonoko's "native Beauty" (12) even as she draws attention to the exceptional blackness of his skin. Like Oroonoko, Imoinda's blackness never disqualifies her from being labeled "a Beauty" (14). To be sure, Behn's initial description of Imoinda plays with the irony of a "fair Queen of the Night" (14), yet this does not stop Behn from referring to Imoinda as "fair" nine times in the novel. By the second reference to the "fair Imoinda" (15), Behn has described the black heroine's beauty four times in less than half a page. Behn might replicate the blazon's descriptive logic, but her panegyrics to black beauty complicate its racial politics. Of course, some of my students express skepticism about whether Oroonoko is, in fact, black. Like Laura Brown (*Ends* 37) and Londa Schiebinger (127), they point out that Behn's praise of her eponymous hero seems premised on the Europeanness of his facial features and hair. Again and again, Behn's character sketch valorizes what distinguishes Oroonoko from his African compatriots. Describing the color of his skin, she notes, "His Face was not of that brown, rusty Black which most of that Nation are, but a perfect Ebony, or polish'd Jett" (13). Even as Behn extols the darkness of his skin, she uses it as a way to set him apart from other Africans. The same is true of her account of his facial features. "His Nose," she tells us, "was rising and *Roman*, instead of *African* and flat" (13). Behn even applauds his straightened hair: "His Hair came down to his Shoulders, by the Aids of Art; which was, by pulling it out with a Quill, and keeping it comb'd; of which he took particular Care" (13–14). From this vantage point, the racialized aesthetics of Behn's character sketch differs only slightly from those of her Renaissance predecessors. If Oroonoko is, as Brown aptly describes him, "a European aristocrat in blackface" (*Ends* 37), has Behn really distanced herself from the Renaissance blazon's privileging of white beauty?

Yet there is enough that is strange in Behn's description that defies our twenty-first-century assumptions about the meaning of Oroonoko's face. By having my students read Behn's novel alongside Nicholas Hudson's recent article on the changing conceptions of human difference from the Renaissance through the Enlightenment and John Ogilby's seventeenth-century natural history *Africa*, I highlight the ways in which Behn's assumptions about race are radically different from our own. When modern readers suggest that "Oroonoko's classical European beauty makes it possible to forget his race" (Brown, *Ends* 35), they are projecting what Hudson identifies as distinctly modern assumptions about race onto Behn's seventeenth-century text. They assume that Africans were considered part of a single race whose members are presumed to resemble each other. In "From 'Nation' to 'Race,'" Hudson explains that such conception of human difference did not emerge until the end of the eighteenth century, decades after Behn wrote her novel. In contrast to modern assumptions that human groups are divided into a few broad categories of "races," Renaissance thinkers saw the world (including the African continent) as divided into a boundless plurality of different "nations" (248). "Nation" is precisely the term that Behn uses to describe Oroonoko's people (13, 14) and is explicit in the use of the term when she explains specifically where he is from: "*Coramantien*, a Country of *Blacks* so called . . . that Nation is very war-like and brave" (11). Rather than lumping all Africans together into a single race, Behn's description displays a more nuanced understanding of the different peoples of Africa. I ask students to consider the possibility that Behn depicts Oroonoko as a Cormantine, not as Brown's "European aristocrat in blackface." Behn was not the only writer to think that Cormantines had facial features like Europeans. As the *Norton Anthology* points out, "Edward Long's 1774 *History of Jamaica* reports of the Cormantines that 'their features are very different from the rest of the African Negroes, being smaller, and more of the European turn'" (Greenblatt and Abrams B: 2187n4). Behn's praise of Oroonoko's beauty might be premised on the Europeanness of his facial features, but that does not mean that an African could not have looked like Oroonoko.

Reading Behn's novel alongside excerpts from Ogilby's natural history, my students get to experience how varied and diverse Behn's contemporaries found the multiplicity of "nations" of Africa. In one of his opening pages, Ogilby includes a diagram of the different parts of Africa. "*Africa* in general," the diagram explains, "stands divided into seven Regions, besides Islands" (between B1v and B2r). Ogilby finds the peoples in particular regions so heterogeneous that he further subdivides them into various kingdoms and realms. For instance, he describes "*Negro-Land*," the part of Africa that included Coramantien, as composed of "Nineteen Kingdoms" (9). Ogilby's natural history perfectly illustrates Hudson's argument that "Europeans were . . . keenly aware of the differences between African peoples or 'nations'" in the sixteenth and seventeenth centuries (249). Reading excerpts of Ogilby's natural history also disrupts my students' assumption that Europeans had only derogatory opinions of Africans. Describing some of the peoples of Negro-Land, Ogilby's account is reminiscent of Behn's description of Oroonoko: "The Natives are very black; but the Features of their Faces, and their excellent Teeth, being white as Ivory, make up together a handsom Ayre, and taking comeliness of a new Beauty: they are well limm'd" (318).While there is no way to know if Behn read Ogilby's *Africa*, both texts record conceptions of human difference that are different from our own. The lesson of both Behn's novel and Ogilby's natural history is that modern categories of race are not the only ways to see the world's peoples—or to read the beauty of Oroonoko's face.

As L. P. Hartley has noted, "The past is a foreign country: they do things differently there" (17). In this essay, I have argued that by teaching *Oroonoko* in the first half of the literature survey, professors can help students appreciate the differing degrees of foreignness of the literary works of the past. By having students consider the differing theories of beauty in the Renaissance sonnet and Behn's novel, students come to understand the historicity of ideas about beauty and cultural and racial difference in the Renaissance and Restoration and eighteenth century.

Teaching *Oroonoko* in a Literature Survey 2 Course

Ashley Cross

As someone who finds the survey mode useful for its map of literary history but also equally frustrating because of its fast pace, the effect of which can make students passive, I begin my survey by asking them to reflect on what we are doing and why, especially since this course is required for majors. Wanting them to be active surveyors, I emphasize the contradictory nature of the word *survey*: it means both getting the broad view and looking in detail, both mapping and exploring. According to the *OED* definition of the word as a noun (1a), a survey is an official view, the territory of those who study and have studied a subject. But the verb form also opens the door for students to be the examiners and mappers, even if it is territory that has been discovered before.

Students set forth on the journey of my second-semester survey by reading *Oroonoko*. The novel offers many novelties for British literary history: emergent genres, subjectivities, and subjects; new roles for women, for writers, and for women writers; new economic ventures and modes of authority; new worlds. Its obvious differences from what students have read in the first semester have a defamiliarizing role, and its liminal position makes it a productive portal to the second. As a travel narrative, Behn's novel also provides a rough metaphor for students' discovery of new literary, psychic, and geographic territory during the survey; it creates an understanding of a specific period, the Restoration; and it sets the agenda for what follows.

I approach Behn's novel through formal issues of genre and narrative structure to create a concrete framework that challenges students' commonplaces about women writers and that situates the work in its literary context, especially in relation to women's writing and the eighteenth- and nineteenth-century novel. This approach sets up comparisons with travel narratives like *Gulliver's Travels* and *Heart of Darkness* and with the slave narratives in the eighteenth century. It fosters a study of *Oroonoko* not only as a Restoration text but also as a text about the early stages of British empire building and bourgeois claims to power. It opens the door for many issues that can be returned to again and again throughout the survey. Though we spend only two and a half days on Behn's narrative, it serves as a model for the contextualized, close reading I expect of my students.

To alert students to the central importance of gender and foreground women writers as key players in dialogue with their male compatriots, I draw on Rachel Carnell's understanding of *Oroonoko*'s form. I divide our discussion into three sections: the first half of the text (to the point when Oroonoko is renamed Caesar), which critics discuss as primarily courtly romance (a genre pointing to earlier literature); the second half of the text, which we examine as a mix of heroic tragedy and realist novel, what William Spengemann calls a "[b]rief true relation" (390) (a genre pointing forward to the novels and slave narratives of the eighteenth and nineteenth centuries); and the role of the narrator, who prefigures fictional narrators like Gulliver, Jane Eyre, and Marlow. The section on the ship, a scene from the Middle Passage, provides a transition from one place and one genre to another, even though the romance is not resolved until Imoinda and Oroonoko reunite in the second half.

My main concern in presenting the first half of the text in terms of courtly romance is to have students think first about the portrayal of Oroonoko as a heroic figure and then about Coramantien as a culture. They should see the heroic and royal ideal that Oroonoko, an African prince, represents for the narrator but also understand that Coramantien is a complex, dynamic, courtly society that has its own conflicts, deceptions, and problems with authority. I ask students to reflect on why Behn explains Oroonoko's life in Africa before he is enslaved. In this discussion, orientalism and courtly romance become the key concepts for thinking about the action. But before we turn to Behn's retelling of Oroonoko's life, we examine closely the opening pages of the novel to see the tensions in it between romance and realism, invention-entertainment and history, lying and honesty. This helps students to see how the generic opposition of the two halves is at play thematically as well as structurally.

The betrayal by the slave ship captain and Oroonoko's response provide the turning point, generically and psychologically, as Oroonoko comes to understand white honor. Whereas Behn draws attention here to the hypocrisy of white ideals, Olaudah Equiano tells of his experience of the Middle Passage through the eyes of a child to invert the racial codes ("Interesting Narrative" [Damrosch et al.]). We turn to the brutal realism of the novel's second half but continually compare and contrast the second half with the first. As several critics have noted, the events of the second half mirror much of the first, yet the changes in locale, tone, and genre result in a different resonance. We chart the continuities and discontinuities on the board, then consider whether Oroonoko has changed and why the shifts are made. Although the narrative tries to carry the romance into the New World, romance is unsustainable in the reality of enslavement. The interpretive problem posed by Oroonoko's character in the light of the final, violent events produces interesting discussion about the beginnings of the British slave trade and requires students to think more closely about the issue of honor in the narrative.

Students may argue about whether Oroonoko's killing of Imoinda is an act of honor and whether it says more about his character or about the effects of slavery, but they have difficulty understanding why Behn makes these shifts in genre other than to show the evils of slavery or the tragic fall of aristocratic values. They do start to understand, though, the politics of genre. I ask them to think about what differences in genre and location might mean for a woman writer of the Restoration period—why a woman writer might write this particular story at this particular time in this way. On the last day of our discussion, we turn to the role of the narrator as the connecting link, the one constant (though not a very constant one!) through the narrative. We trace the moments where she comments on her relationship to Oroonoko, and students discover that she has, as Laura Brown claims, a "mediatory role, between heroic romance and mercantile imperialism," that can "generate and enable the mutual interaction of two otherwise incompatible discourses" (*Ends* 48). There is disagreement among students: some emphasize her powerlessness—she is trapped, like the enslaved African, in disabling patriarchal structures—and focus on her unkept promises, her affection for Oroonoko, her disappearance at crucial times at the end of the novel; others argue that the narrator lies to Oroonoko and is complicit with the oppressive social structures that result in his dismemberment. Gender functions as an "alibi," to use Jane Spencer's term (*Rise* 50), for not taking responsibility.

By now I hope they will see a third position and make a distinction between Behn and the narrator. I suggest that Behn, in the last line of the novel, is doing something subversive, seeing writing as a political act that counters the white woman's role as a helpless spectator. Behn's reclaiming and passing on Oroonoko's story re-members Oroonoko and the values he represents in a gesture that opposes the violence of slavery. But the conclusion of the novel also links "the Reputation of my Pen" to "his Glorious name" and that of "the Brave, the Beautiful, and the Constant *Imoinda*," whose name is the very last word. Therefore, in the colonial context, the white woman writer's voice and authority are constructed at the expense of the body of the African man and woman (Margaret Ferguson, "Juggling" [*Women's Studies*] 170–71; Athey and Alarcón 436–37).

As the semester continues, I return many times to these issues and images of genre, narration, gender, race, and class and hope that students will grasp their centrality, complexity, and changing value over the course of literary history between the Restoration and the modern period. One way to build on the issues of *Oroonoko* is to pair texts by male and female writers in each period. This pairing allows students to see both the possibility of a separate women's literary tradition extending from Behn to Virginia Woolf and the importance of reading women and men in dialogue. In the eighteenth century, book 4 of *Gulliver's Travels* and Lady Mary Wortley Montagu's *Turkish Embassy Letters* build well on Behn's novel: Jonathan Swift's satirical travel narrative, highlighting the political nature of literature, contrasts well with the more personal, descriptive letters of Montagu. Gulliver's interaction with the Houyhnhnms and Yahoos provides another colonial narrative that reveals the alienation of the Irish colonial subject, whereas Montagu's letters try to bridge cultural difference through their interest in women's behaviors and rights. Moreover, Montagu's ethnological approach extends Behn's portrayal of Coramantien, offering another British attempt to represent otherness. I ask students to think about how these narrative differences are shaped by gender, genre, and the writer's attitudes toward cultural difference. Montagu's exchange with Swift on "The Lady's Dressing Room," combined with Behn's "The Disappointment" and Rochester's "The Imperfect Enjoyment," forms another set of texts that develop the connections between gender and genre more explicitly, as women writers address male sexual attitudes. They also create a useful context for the mock epic battle of the sexes in Alexander Pope's *The Rape of the Lock*.

In the Romantic period, we build further on the connection between a woman writer's authority and racial politics by showing how the discourse of abolition parallels and enables the struggle for the rights of woman and how concerns about voice and politics lead to new genres and new voices. I pair Equiano's narrative with selections from Mary Wollstonecraft's *Vindication of the Rights of Woman*, William Blake's "Little Black Boy" with Mary Robinson's "The Negro Girl," Samuel Coleridge's "Kubla Khan" with Robinson's "To the Poet Coleridge." While Behn's narrative intertwines racial and gender concerns, Equiano's narrative and Wollstonecraft's *Vindication* show a splitting of the African other's and white woman's claims to authority, even as each text expresses similar concerns about representing the experience of the oppressed. Wollstonecraft uses the discourse of slavery and rights to make claims for the masculine woman. But her model of womanhood, with its emphasis on reason and domesticity, is very different from the Restoration model embodied by Behn. Robinson's "Negro Girl" conveys the tragic impact of slavery from a female slave's perspective, giving voice to the suffering of a marginalized character like Imoinda but without the mediating narrator. This ballad-like poem instead conflates romance and tragedy, effacing the female writer's role. The sympathy between Behn's narrator and Oroonoko is writ large in this and other Romantic lyrics that center on an identification with the other. The ambivalence of Behn's narrator toward her characters and the generic shifts in her narrative, however, are not found in the Romantic lyric's emphasis on the speaker's emotional responses or its developing conflict over abolition and rights. This contrast helps students see how Romanticism differs from the Restoration in its attitudes about gender and race as well as in the movement toward a more democratic politics. Like Behn, both Wollstonecraft and Robinson led public lives of some notoriety and used their writing to challenge masculine literary conventions. Wollstonecraft's criticism of conduct books and male-authored literature (chs. 2 and 3 of *Vindication*) and Robinson's representation of herself as hearing the voice of Coleridge's Abyssinian maid in "Kubla Khan" ("To the Poet") provide further examples of how women writers rewrite literary conventions to forge their own space of authority.

I continue these questions of gender and genre in pairings of John Keats's "La belle dame sans merci" with Felicia Hemans's "The Wife of Asdrubal" and of William Wordsworth's "Tintern Abbey" ("Lines") with Dorothy Wordsworth's journals and poems. Charlotte Smith's sonnets may also be paired with William Wordsworth's. Like Behn, Smith created a hybrid form, the elegiac sonnet, in which she conveyed social critique through her personal experience and a melancholic subjectivity, thereby transforming the sonnet genre into the Romantic form later refined by Wordsworth. Her "Written in the Church-Yard at Middleton in Sussex" may be read with Thomas Gray's "Elegy Written in a Churchyard"; her "The Sea-View" may be read with Wordsworth's "Composed upon Westminster's Bridge." With *Oroonoko* as a starting point for their journey, students attend to the relation between form and content and thus can map the complex dynamic of genre, gender, and race as it shifts with the growth of British imperialism.

The innovations we saw in *Oroonoko* come to fruition in the Victorian period, when the middle class was in power, the British Empire was at its peak, and the novel was the dominant genre. *Jane Eyre* in particular builds on *Oroonoko*, because Charlotte Brontë gives us a developed female narrator empowered solely by her voice, a voice that depends on the erasure of a West Indian other, Bertha Mason. Jane employs the discourse of abolition and rebellion to articulate her own development, but she marginalizes the imperialism that gives her claim authority. The division of public and private into gendered spheres is complete in Brontë's work. Behn's narrator seeks to bridge that division, but the narrators in Victorian novels isolate women from the larger political realm, constructing the white woman's identity in opposition to the black body and limiting female power to the domestic realm. Jane wants conversation but not with Bertha, whose animal madness places her far from the heroic ideal of Imoinda and Oroonoko. While Behn's narrator writes her story to remember Oroonoko and Imoinda, Jane tells her story to empower herself; while Behn's text reveals the failures of romance in the face of economic realities and the destruction of spirit through the brutal treatment of the body, Jane seeks to make romance more important than economics, the spirit more valuable than the body.

Rudyard Kipling's "White Man's Burden" and "Gunga Din" and Joseph Conrad's *Heart of Darkness* use narrative voice to articulate the contradictions of empire and British anxieties about racial otherness. Like *Oroonoko*, *Heart of Darkness* reveals the ambivalence of the storyteller, Marlow, and his final lie implicates women in imperialist discourse to show the horror of separate spheres. Examining, in the light of Behn's novel, the difference of Marlow's narration, his tortuous journey into unfamiliar territory, and his portrayal of Africans demonstrates how imperialism has become a fully corrupt cultural system. Elizabeth Barrett Browning's *Aurora Leigh* and Christina Rossetti's "Goblin Market" show women writers' ability to use genre to challenge the dominant narratives—for Browning the epic, for Rossetti children's literature. Finally, in the modern period, as the empire comes apart, the violence of poems like William Butler Yeats's "Leda and the Swan" and "Easter 1916," the luxury of Mrs. Dalloway's interiority and upper-class life in Woolf's *Mrs. Dalloway*, and the alienness of Buenos Aires to Eveline in James Joyce's "Eveline" have a more profound significance in the context of a literary response to imperial brutality that stretches back to 1688.

Oroonoko works well as the beginning of the second part of a British literature survey because it raises questions that are central to the study of literature: What is literature, and what role does it play in culture? What relation does literary form have to literary content? How does one create an inclusive literary tradition that is historically specific and yet gives voice to all subjects? How does one explore a subject or map a territory without colonizing? I hope that my students will continue to ask these questions when they leave the safe territory of the survey and travel to other classes where they will surely find other novelties and have to make their own maps.

NOTE

Most of the literary works referred to in this essay are from *The Longman Anthology of British Literature* (Damrosch et al.), in excerpted form.

Teaching *Oroonoko* in the Travel Narrative Course

Margarete Rubik

Oroonoko passes itself off as an eyewitness report from the New World and has been called an "ethnographic," anthropological, or protoanthropological text (Campbell 221, 264), fusing romance with scientific travel writing and the sensational. As such, the novel invites comparison not only with various accounts of slavery (an issue frequently addressed by scholars) but also with reports of exotic travel and cross-cultural encounters from the early modern period to the nineteenth century. Reading *Oroonoko* in the context of travel and exploration literature gives interesting insights into Behn's discursive strategies and colonial attitudes, showing that Behn anticipates stylistic features characteristic of imperial travelogues, especially those of the nineteenth century, but also introduces surprising and unusual elements. For such a comparative reading, it is irrelevant whether her account of her journey to Surinam is imaginary or authentic. In fact, the texts I select for comparison include genuine travel reports of Captain James Cook and Christopher Columbus along with fictional or semifictional narratives, such as Daniel Defoe's *Robinson Crusoe* and Herman Melville's *Typee*. What is at stake is not the truth-value of these tales but the details selected for description and the cognitive frames enlisted to make sense of an alien world. What typical rhetorical features are employed? What popular tropes are disseminated? How do writers position themselves vis-à-vis the exotic other?

Travelogues typically merge a number of different literary genres. Like Stedman's 1796 *Narrative of a Five Years' Expedition against the Revolted Negroes of Surinam* and nineteenth-century travel reports, *Oroonoko* is a mélange of "ethnography, natural history, hunting stories, social description, survival tales, [and] anti-slavery critique" (Pratt 91). Behn styles herself as an adventurer who rubs shoulders with princes (Oroonoko) and savages (the Caribs), goes on tiger hunts, and is the only survivor of the colony's turbulent history left to tell the hero's story. What travel reports can never do, however, is convey to us the authentic feelings of the non-European counterpart in the cross-cultural contact. They tell us only about "the European practice of representation" (Greenblatt 7).

A course reading *Oroonoko* as a travel narrative will focus on the depiction of Surinam, which in its wealth of ethnographic, zoological, and botanical detail is quite different from the heroic romance of the Coramantien section. I start by asking students what details about the South American fauna and flora they find particularly impressive and memorable. The narrator obviously employs the popular trope of excess and abundance, painting the colony as a storehouse of spices, perfumes, fruits, exotic animals, and valuable timbers, "a vast and charming World" affording "all things both for Beauty and Use" (43), which the king had thoughtlessly bartered away to the Dutch. Characteristically, motives of strategic and economic profit and aesthetic appreciation are combined, and the favorable trading terms allowing British merchants to pay the natives for valuable overseas goods with a few beads and nails are seen as anything but reprehensible. There is even a hint in the text that treasures like cedarwood would otherwise go to waste (43) and are eagerly awaiting exploitation at the hands of European colonists—a trope in nineteenth-century exploration reports (Spurr 28).

Above all, as in so many travel reports, the New World is a place of wonders, of things defying description, so "unconceivable" are the tinctures, so "amazing" the forms, so wonderful the sights and smells (9)—although, by the end of the tale, we will also be treated to inconceivably cruel sights and horrible body smells. The narrator tries to bring this radical otherness of the colony under discursive control by composing lists of exotic animals, plants, or artifacts. She describes the animals in terms of species already known in Europe, such as the lion and the rhinoceros (8, 43). Like the famous eighteenth-century explorers Cook or Sir Joseph Banks—Benjamin West painted Banks surrounded by curios Banks brought back from his voyage—she collects artifacts such as the Indian feather headdress and natural curiosities such as the exotic flies (9) to serve back in London as "trophies" (N. Thomas 143), evidence of her visit and hence of the factuality of her tale. For eighteenth-century travelers, as Nicholas Thomas observes, "collected material attested to the fact of having visited remote places and observed novel phenomena" (141).

Among the exotic wonders, the "Eternal Spring" (43) in the tropics—the fact that trees bear blossoms and fruit simultaneously—was particularly impressive to European travelers and celebrated, for instance, in George Warren's *An Impartial Description of Surinam* (5) and Andrew Marvell's poem "Bermudas" (line 13). Yet a country in which time stands still, in which it is perpetually "*April*, *May* and *June*" (43), also seems to exist outside history—and this timelessness of background contrasts sharply with the history of the noble slave that unfolds.

In the course, special attention is paid to the description of the indigenous population of Surinam. At the beginning of the story, some information is given about the culture of the Caribs and about their relationship to the colonizers. These passages merge two different styles, which Mary Louise Pratt has identified as characteristic of "European narrative[s] of the contact zone" (75): some paragraphs are written in what is called the anthropological present tense, an impersonal style that signals scientific commentary and effaces the narrator as origin of the information; other sentences are written in the past tense, are predicated on personal experience, and foreground the narrating "I" (75–78). Students are invited to identify these two styles in the early parts of *Oroonoko* (9–11) and to consider how the scientific voice of the ethnographer and the traveler's eyewitness report tend to authenticate each other, establishing the female narrator as an authority on the subject.

I also ask students to analyze what images and cognitive schemas Behn employs to describe the Caribs and their relationship with the colonizers. Like Columbus (12, 225), she uses kinship metaphors, which became prominent in nineteenth-century imperialist propaganda, in which the colonized were often equated with children (e.g., Kipling's "The White Man's Burden"). The British colonists in *Oroonoko* are said to "caress [the Caribs] with all the brotherly and friendly Affection in the World" and to live with them in "perfect Amity" (8). But it is rare that the strategic nature of such a policy is made so clear: economic expediency and the force of sheer numbers make it necessary for the colonists to appease the natives, rendering suspicious even Trefry's appellation of Oroonoko as "his dearest Brother" (35). The power of language in the colony "resides in its capacity to misrepresent," as Derek Hughes has aptly said ("Race" 16).

Behn also uses biblical imagery: the Caribs are like Adam and Eve before the Fall, giving the narrator "an absolute *Idea* of the first State of Innocence, before Man knew how to sin," since "it is evident and plain, that simple Nature is the most harmless, inoffensive and vertuous Mistress," better than all the precepts of religion or the law (10). Nostalgic for prelapsarian innocence as these schemas may seem, both the image of Paradise and the trope of a golden age unspoiled by the corrupting influence of civilization place the indigenous population at a temporal remove from the speaker, so that travel to primitive societies is conceived as a journey back into the white man's or white woman's prehistoric past.

But it should be stressed that Behn never actually uses terms like *savage* or *primitive* for the Caribs—key markers of the past in anthropological discourse (Fabian 75). Her narrator feels no urge to civilize the Caribs, although she tries to introduce Oroonoko to the concept of the Trinity (41). The Restoration period did not as yet classify races on a hierarchical scale; "previously unknown societies merely further illustrated the diversity of the species" (N. Thomas 129). Columbus and most early travelers did speak about savages and frequently (Berkhofer 14), but Cook hardly ever used the term; neither, surprisingly, did Warren, although he described the indigenous peoples as "Cowardly and Treacherous" (23). To be sure, in Behn's Surinam paradisiacal innocence turns into barbarity when the Caribs massacre the Dutch colonists; the phrase "*below the wildest Salvages*" (53), however, is reserved for the whites and their shocking cruelty and treachery.

I then suggest to my students that the image of Paradise, with the natives as Adam and Eve, leaves two subject positions of the myth vacant: God and the devil. To whom are these roles allotted in the text? In travel reports, the position of devil is usually relegated to the savages, who in colonial discourse fulfill the double roles of innocents (if they are compliant) and demons (if they are hostile)—as illustrated in Columbus's writings but also in *Robinson Crusoe*, Victorian exploration narratives, and imperial romances like *King Solomon's*

Mines. In *Oroonoko*, however, it is the whites who teach vice to both the Caribs and the Africans, thereby playing the snake in the garden of the New World.

The Europeans were of course eager to assume the role of God in the discourse about the new Eden. Columbus famously reports how the Caribs were convinced that he, with his "vessels and crews, came from heaven" (8). Walter Raleigh tells of a similar superstition—namely, that the old Peruvian emperors ("Ingas") would one day be restored from "Inglatierra" (*Discovery of . . . Guiana*). The natives' belief that guns kill by magic is reported by Cook and exploited as a plot device in *Robinson Crusoe*, when Crusoe refers to Friday's terror at the "fire and noise" of a shot (ch. 14). During her visit to a Carib village inland supposedly never before visited by white people, the narrator remarks, somewhat condescendingly, that it would not be difficult to impose extravagant religious beliefs on these people, but she herself refrains from employing such tricks and prefers to gratify the Caribs with a flute concert, as she might do with European social equals (47–50). Her kinsman, however, gains a reputation as a magician by making fire with the help of a magnifying glass (49). All in all, the Europeans are anything but divine. As Oddvar Holmesland has pointed out, it is Oroonoko who is linked with images of Christ (71–72).

What usually and immediately catches the eye of travelers to primitive societies is the nakedness, which suggests the image of Eden in the first place. Warren takes a prurient interest in female bodies "too nakedly expos'd to every wanton Eye" (23). Yet few Europeans think and talk about their own clothing, which they naturalize as standard. Crusoe assumes that Friday, ashamed of his lack of covering, is glad to receive some old clothes (ch. 14). Behn's narrator, in contrast, acutely realizes that her glittering dress must look as strange to the inland villagers as their scanty coverings do to the English (48).

The expedition to the inland village is remarkable for a number of other reasons. Although vision is the means of perception generally adopted by explorers, anthropologists, and travelers to foreign countries, it has come to denote unequal power relations: the gazing-appraising subject is superior to the passive object of scientific or aesthetic contemplation. Crusoe observes the cannibals through his binoculars. Yet the explicit intention of Behn's traveling party is to surprise the inland villagers with "something they never had seen, (that is, White People)" (48), which allows for a reciprocal perspective: the whites come for "Diversion"—that is, touristic curiosity—but they are, in turn, willing to be stared at as "*Numberless Wonders*" (48). It is noteworthy that as late as 1846 the narrator of *Typee* quails at the reversal of power implied by the scrutinizing glance of a Polynesian chief: "[He was] looking at me with a rigidity of aspect under which I absolutely quailed. . . . Never before had I been subjected to so strange and steady a glance; it revealed nothing of the mind of the savage, but it appeared to be reading my own" (Melville, ch. 10). In an act of self-parody that inverts the Eurocentric perspective, Behn presents the spectacle of the jungle excursion from the viewpoint of the inland villagers, who now assume the objectifying gaze, wondering whether "*those things* [the Europeans] *can speak*," have "Sense, and Wit," and can "talk of affairs of Life" (49).

Vision is equated with comprehension in our culture, but it can apprehend only surfaces, not speaking subjects. It is therefore significant that the narrator of *Oroonoko*, inviting a dialogic cultural exchange, asks an interpreter to accompany her to the remote inland village, "imagining we shou'd have a half Diversion in Gazing only; and not knowing what they said" (48). What is most remarkable in this visit is the close bodily contact with the remote villagers the female narrator enters into (such physical contact never occurs in her relation to Oroonoko). She willingly offers the tribesmen her hands; she allows them to touch her face, breasts, and arms and to kiss her, after her kinsman has initiated this new fashion of saluting (48, 50). She even suffers them to lift her several petticoats and to look at her shoes, stockings, and even garters, "which we gave 'em, and they ty'd about their Legs, being Lac'd with Silver Lace at the ends, for they much Esteem any shining things" (48). Such a procedure would have involved a daring exposure of leg, with decidedly sexualized connotations. But it would be quite unjustified to infer from Behn's description the feelings of the Caribs—such as lust for the Englishwoman (Rivero 455–56). The scene does not suggest lechery, and the female narrator is not a passive erotic object but an agent who openly expresses admiration for the tribal *Peeie*, "as handsome as Nature cou'd make a Man." (49). Later, most women travelers were hesitant to comment on the attractiveness of men from other races (Foster 19), whereas for men like Raleigh ("I have seldom seen a better favoured woman" [55]), Warren ("so truly handsom" [23]), or Melville ("my Island beauty" [ch. 18]), acknowledging the beauty of a native female was acceptable. Descriptions of haptic contact are nonetheless rare. Many conquistadors and plantation owners, like Byam in *Oroonoko*, had African or indigenous mistresses, but sentimental tales of interracial love did not appear before the end of the eighteenth century. It is also interesting to compare *Oroonoko* with *Robinson Crusoe*, where the first contact consists in Friday's putting his head beneath his master's foot (ch. 14), or with *Typee*, where the narrator tolerates touch only out of physical necessity ("They felt our skin, much in the same way that a silk mercer would handle a remarkably fine piece of satin . . ." [ch. 10]).

While all these details make it clear that Behn "is not observing through the eyes of Todorov's Columbus or Cortés" (D. Hughes, "Race" 18), there is one scene of striking and revealing similarity: when the British party meet men from another tribe, she says that "[the men] cou'd not understand us"—that is, her Carib rowers could not communicate with the other tribesmen. Yet she claims that "as well as [the tribesmen] cou'd give us to understand," they told the whites where to find gold and invited them to come with them so that they could show them (51). Columbus too understood nothing yet confidently reproduced what the Caribs supposedly said—a case of what Stephen Greenblatt calls "authoritative certainty in the face of spectacular ignorance" (90). Sign language, as used by Columbus and in the scene from *Oroonoko* mentioned, is fraught with misunderstandings, since it wrongly presupposes "a shared gestural language" (89). The wish to be invited to the fabulous riches of the mythical El Dorado must have blinded Behn's narrator, as it blinded Columbus, to the absurdity of her claim.

Teaching *Oroonoko* in the context of other colonial travelogues sensitizes students to Behn's indebtedness to some of the generic features of travel literature but also to her originality. Her attitude toward cross-cultural encounters seems more open-minded than that of many contemporary and later writers on the subject.

Teaching *Oroonoko* at a Historically Black University

Leslie Richardson

Few of us find eighteenth-century English literature an easy sell in the twenty-first-century classroom. I have reeled through the usual gamut of cheerleading techniques, but before I started teaching at a historically black college-university (HBCU), I had never felt I needed to justify my field's validity. Of course, I had encountered students who rolled their eyes at *The Rape of the Lock*, but I never stopped to ask myself *why* my students should want to learn what I was offering.

At an HBCU, however, reflexive anglophilia is in shorter supply than at a majority institution, and I began to interrogate my own reverence for all things British. My home institution is a STEM-oriented school (STEM standing for "science, technology, engineering, and mathematics"), and students aspiring to medical school, for example, are not typically excited about spending their rare free time grappling with long and puzzling texts produced three centuries ago and a continent away. The greater challenge at my HBCU is that my students generally feel no claim to the British tradition and feel, reciprocally, that it has no claim on them. The colonial project and its ideological work are objects of skepticism to students whose core curriculum focuses on the legacy of the transatlantic slave trade. The period that espoused contract theory and liberal ideology also saw the rise of plantation slavery, the racialization of slavery, and ongoing attempts to wrest territory and resources from "savages" around the world. Students enter my classroom—and every classroom—well aware that certain self-evident truths about equality have been applied very selectively. How best, then, can I make this material meaningful to them?

I teach at a school where the student body is (as at many HBCUs) predominantly female, so it seems natural that gender informs my teaching. My students are particularly moved by the analogy between race and gender as categories of stratification, so my teaching addresses the conflicts between the Enlightenment rhetoric of "possessive individualism" (Macpherson) and the reality that women, slaves, and non-Europeans were all radically dispossessed from property and political freedom.

Courses on the eighteenth-century novel traditionally open with Daniel Defoe, spotlighting the genre's preoccupation with issues of identity and property. *Oroonoko* serves this purpose even better than *Robinson Crusoe* or *Moll Flanders*, by foregrounding identity and ownership, especially self-ownership, and exposing the fragility of these constructs even as Behn makes them central to humanity. Slavery robs Oroonoko of both his autonomy and his name, demonstrating how tenuous is possession of rights and self and leading to questions of whether humanity or identity can survive loss. Some would argue that degradation and symbolic feminization at the hands of European captors gradually transform Oroonoko from a noble warrior to a murderous madman. How has self been shaped by self-proprietorship—or by its loss?

Oroonoko explicitly interrogates what John Locke would call "property in his own person" (*Second Treatise* 19), demonstrating how property is complicated by race, whereas many other eighteenth-century texts examined instead dichotomies of gender. When I provide some information about seventeenth- and eighteenth-century concepts of marriage, often using *The Lawes Resolutions of Womens Rights* (facsim.), my students are quick to see how Behn's depiction of slavery draws disturbing parallels between the two institutions. They discern how rights, equality, and freedom have been distributed selectively and accept my argument that inequality between the sexes may offer a model for understanding inequality between races. Marriage, under early modern law, merely formalized a woman's alienation from property in her own person. Locke located freedom in self-ownership: the crux of what C. B. Macpherson labeled possessive individualism is found in Locke's declaration that "every man has a *property* in his own person: this no body has any right to but himself. The *labour* of his body, and the *work* of his hands, we may say, are properly his" (19). According to Macpherson, by Locke's model one can be truly an individual only through possession. Self is thus defined, and even produced, by self-ownership. A great many human beings, notably women and slaves (or peasants, or minors) lacked such rights over their own bodies. Locke sees the right to "dispose" of one's self, one's labor, and one's property (acquired, in the state of nature, by mixing one's labor with the matter of nature) as "freedom," which for him is both the reward and the prerequisite of human identity (32). When I offer my students this language, in a thumbnail lecture with a handout of salient passages from the *Second Treatise*, they have no difficulty identifying those passages where Behn's narrator demonstrates a painful awareness of this fundamental definition of humanity; they recognize what the denial of Oroonoko's freedom means: "[T]hough he suffer'd only the Name of a Slave, and had nothing of the Toil and Labour of one, yet that was sufficient to render him Uneasy" (42). Not only does Oroonoko understand that his supposedly benevolent owners view him like a captive tiger cub, to be admired and displayed, he also loses conviction in his own identity as a result of this enforced dehumanization. He tells his fellow slaves that "[t]hey suffer'd not like Men who might find a Glory, and Fortitude in Oppression; but like Dogs that lov'd the Whip and Bell, and fawn'd the more they were beaten: That they had lost the Divine Quality of Men, and were become insensible Asses, fit only to bear" (52).

Locke described the theoretical state of nature as a

> state also of equality, wherein all the power and jurisdiction [are] reciprocal, no one having more than another; there being nothing more evident, than that all creatures of the same species and rank, promiscuously born to all the same advantages of nature, and the use of the same faculties,

> should also be equal one amongst another without subordination or subjection. (8)

In the state of nature, he explained, man has "an uncontroulable liberty to dispose of his person or possessions" (9). At the same time, the legal status of women (particularly of wives) and the enslaved continued to deny them the rights that were coming to seem fundamental tohumanity. *The Lawes Resolutions of Womens Rights* explored woman's ambiguous status under law, explaining that "baron and feme [i.e., husband and wife] . . . are but one person, and by this a married Woman perhaps may either doubt whether shee bee either none or no more then halfe a person" (4). Under law, a wife's very identity was effaced by the marriage contract. Students see how Oroonoko is confronted with an analogous circumstance. When he formally enters a state of enslavement on his arrival in Surinam, he loses his name, much as a woman is renamed upon her marriage: "I ought to tell you," says the narrator, "that the *Christians* never buy any Slaves but they give 'em some Name of their own, their native ones being likely very barbarous, and hard to pronounce; so that Mr. *Trefry* gave *Oroonoko* that of *Caesar*" (36). Oroonoko is thus stripped of his identity and his history and christened as property. Here most students will notice that the ironic, grandiose title only underscores his subjection, like naming a dog Rex, and some may recall that Julius Caesar was betrayed by his friends and allies.

Further exploration leads to Mary Astell, whom my students invariably enjoy, and they are struck by her question: "If all Men are born free, how is it that all Women are born slaves? as they must be if the being subjected to the inconstant, uncertain, unknown, arbitrary Will of Men, be the perfect Condition of Slavery" (a1r). Reading Astell and Behn together, students begin to suspect that, conversely, slaves were both born and reborn as women. A woman under couverture could not enter a contract or earn her own wages. Unless carefully protected by marriage settlements that were generally negotiated by a father or other male guardian, all her property went automatically to her husband. Thus, by Locke's model, a married woman could assert no rights to herself. Again, Locke's concept of identity and his philosophical justification for private property are both founded on the assumption that an individual owned his experience and his exertion; hence he had a natural right to the fruits of his labor. That women did not stand in this possessive relation to their own persons was immediately apparent; more provocative is Astell's implication that perhaps they should. "Thus we are born free, as we are born rational," Locke asserts (34). And he adds, "The *freedom* then of man, and liberty of acting according to his own will, is *grounded on* his having *reason*, which is able to instruct him in that law he is to govern himself by, and make him know how far he is left to the freedom of his own will" (35). Following Locke's arguments to their logical conclusion, Astell asserts the rational power she undoubtedly possessed to argue that tyranny is "an Improper Method of Governing Rational and Free Agents" (a4v). Though in his *Second Treatise* he speaks of "men," Locke in his *Essay concerning Human Understanding* takes pains to define a person as "a thinking intelligent being, that has reason and reflection, and can consider itself as itself, the same thinking thing, in different times and places; which it does only by that consciousness which is inseparable from thinking" ([*EEBO*] bk. 2, ch. 27, sec. 9). Astell's arguments provoke this question: If a woman is clearly a person, why could she not be an individual in the political sense?

Behn presents us with the same contradiction: If a slave can dispute philosophy in English; if he can write a book, as Olaudah Equiano did a century after *Oroonoko*; if he is clearly a rational human being, why does he, or she, not possess the natural right to liberty? The cognitive dissonance produced by this paradox ripples through *Oroonoko*, as it does many works from the same period.

The tension between the ideals of equality made available by Locke's theory and the continuing subordination of women has been worked out in a variety of arenas. Thomas Laqueur argues that the discovery in the late seventeenth century of two separate, incommensurable sexes, displacing the ancient one-sex model of a continuum of sexual development, was a response to political theory's destruction of divinely ordained social hierarchy. Laqueur explains the newfound insistence on biological difference between the sexes as necessary to justify men's continuing dominance: "[T]he tendency of early contract theory is to make the subordination of women to men a result of the operation of the *facts* of sexual difference, of their utilitarian implications" (157). Gender differences were used to explain sexual differences, and vice versa.

Racial ideologies of slavery worked in much the same tautological fashion. In *Oroonoko*, that some Africans can be enslaved is obliquely used as a justification for their subjection. Behn gives this language to Oroonoko himself when he sneers at his former allies, calling them "by Nature *Slaves*, poor wretched Rogues, fit to be us'd as *Christians* Tools; Dogs, treacherous and cowardly, fit for such Masters" (56). My students invariably notice that while Behn condemns her hero's enslavement, calling our attention to some powerful contradictions, she avoids taking a position on the morality of slavery in principle. Her hero is idealized in terms of classical masculinity, described as Roman in appearance and nobility. Oroonoko, it often seems, deserves freedom because he is exceptional, whereas many of his fellow slaves are portrayed as deserving their fate. The slavers who take Oroonoko are deceitful, dishonorable rogues, but the novel reprehends their trickery and emphasizes Oroonoko's princely essence instead of grappling with slavery as an institution.

Regal Oroonoko disdains cowardice more than brutishness and equates loss of masculinity with loss of full humanity. "*Have they Won us in Honourable Battel?*" he asks. "*This would not anger a Noble Heart, . . . but we are Bought and Sold like Apes, or Monkeys, to be the Sport of Women, Fools and Cowards*" (52). Enslavement, Oroonoko suggests, is a form of feminization. In order to deny humanity, freedom, and self-ownership to enslaved men, the enslavers must recast them in the position of women. As Gerda Lerner points out, othering on the basis of gender may have been the first stratification, on which categorizations like race and class were modeled (86–88). Ownership of a slave was often far more brutal than marriage—so much so that the comparison may seem insulting to the descendants of slaves—but the relationship between slave and owner may be seen to take its cue, and its cultural justification, from an already accepted form of dominance. In both slavery and marriage, the body may be controlled, but the mind or spirit proves more difficult to command. Through rebellion, Oroonoko reclaims his identity before he meets his death—he refuses to accept the final dishonor of whipping, and vows revenge, insisting that "*you shall see that* Oroonoko *scorns to live with the Indignity that was put on* Caesar"(58).

Oroonoko's brutal mutilation offers the reader a titillating account of his loss of power at the hands of European men. Oroonoko disembowels himself to prevent his enemies from striking the first blow of his humiliation; he combines Roman suicidal honor with the stoicism of the war captains that Behn describes. But when he fails to die, his captors make "frightful Spectacles of a mangl'd King" (65). Tied to a whipping post, he is first castrated and then dismembered in stages, until "his Pipe drop'd; and he gave up the Ghost, without a Groan" (64). His superhuman courage upholds his noble masculinity, but the white men who lynch him to exorcize their own fears and to terrify the other slaves do their best to efface his manhood and his humanity. *Oroonoko* documents an early example of the ideological impulse to feminize nonwhite men in relation to European men. A provocative question for students of the text is how successful the endeavor proves. Behn paints no victors, but the men who degrade and destroy Oroonoko are left looking fearful, petty, and ignoble. Oroonoko remains the true prince.

If nonwhite men are so often emasculated in popular representations, it seems paradoxical, at first, that women of color should be denied the trappings of femininity. Although Imoinda is described as the embodiment of feminine perfection, ironically this perfection only serves to silence her. Her sentiments are assumed, reported by others, or paraphrased: she gets no direct voice in the text, and she cheerfully submits to her death at the hands of her husband to save her from the possibility of rape. My students are often frustrated by her passivity and regard her with a puzzled mixture of pity and disdain. But at least she exists—in Thomas Southerne's later dramatic adaptation, Imoinda is conflated with the white female narrator, and the black woman disappears entirely.

When I taught introductory women's studies courses at my degree-granting institution, I made use of the first class to ask students to list qualities they considered typically feminine and masculine. The listing generated the predictable binaries: weak-strong, emotional-rational, dependent-independent. I was able to point out stereotypes and explain that the culturally constructed roles we were registering were both dyadic and hierarchical, because the masculine qualities represented universally admirable traits. When I tried this simplistic trick at my

HBCU, however, the results were surprising, although they should not have been. My surprise simply reflected how oblivious I was to cultural and racial nuances. My classrooms of African American women typically identify femininity with strength, assertiveness, and stubbornness, not with delicacy. When pressed to consult Hollywood movies for their examples that first semester, my students eventually came up with "fragile" and "dainty," but they did not automatically associate femininity with any of the various euphemisms for weakness that my white students had so quickly generated. When I suggested these terms for weakness, they pointed out that I was thinking of *white* femininity. Black femininity, they explained, was identified with power and endurance. Semester after semester, such responses have remained consistent. This set of sweeping generalizations may be no more universally accurate than the stereotypes of feminine helplessness, but the white-black divergence raises intriguing questions. Being a woman does not necessarily involve submitting to early modern constructions of femininity, and the existence of enslaved and laboring women inconveniently deconstructs cherished binary oppositions between the genders.

I began to think about Sojourner Truth's question, "Ain't I a woman?" and the dearth of representations of nonwhite women in the eighteenth and nineteenth centuries.[1] British women were scribbling their stories everywhere, black men occasionally made their voices heard, but black women seemed almost entirely absent. Was their defeat so ensured that there was no need to vanquish them in print? They were subjected to dangers and degradations inconceivable to their propertied white sisters, so why were we never asked to feel *their* virtue in distress? There are entire conferences dedicated to excavating the connections among race, class, and gender, and many critics in English literature have pursued this question. Felicity Nussbaum has offered particularly useful insights into the effacement of nonwhite femininity, especially in her analysis of Southerne's adaptation of Behn's *Oroonoko*. I am not uncovering anything new, then, when I note that the femininity constructed in the eighteenth century, which cast women as delicate, domestic angels, was exclusively assigned to white, propertied women. We can take a closer look at a possible motive for this exclusiveness, however. With rare, sentimentalized, and usually short-lived exceptions, working-class women and women of color have never been characterized with the sort of femininity belonging to, say, Frances Burney's Evelina. Women whose productive labor was required in the fields or the scullery could not be too fragile to sweat and slave, leaving us to wonder how long Evelina would last in a cane field or even a milliner's shop. Nor could one reasonably expect working-class women and women of color to be dependent, passive, and naive. Their economic dependence on men was ensured by the shortage of well-paid work for women, and they posed no serious political threat. If the owner of a neighboring estate is a wealthy, educated heiress, she may present a conundrum, for she loses her right to vote or serve as magistrate only by virtue of her sex; but an enslaved woman, or a laboring-class woman, offers no problem, being doubly disenfranchised. There is hence no need to demonstrate to her her minority or debility, much less to make her embrace it. If femininity is a flattering construction of vulnerability, if women are "[f]ine by defect, and delicately weak," in Alexander Pope's construction of women's characters ("Epistle II," line 44), it is unnecessary to enforce that construction on women already dispossessed.

So why teach the British eighteenth century at an HBCU? Here is an answer that my students accept: The assumptions and ideals we take for granted were under construction during this time. The Enlightenment, however flawed, bequeathed us the language to appraise the world we live in today, and studying that language provides us a clearer mirror for examining ourselves. Humanity in the eighteenth century never lived up to the promise offered by its radical ideals: it granted liberty and equality only to a few. But its rhetoric makes available its own criticism. We can condemn its brutality because we embrace its virtues; we can assess its contradictions because we accept its principles. We better comprehend contemporary debates, conflicts, and injustices when we see their roots, and we can justly assess how much, or how little, has changed.

NOTE

[1] Sojourner Truth's short impromptu speech, delivered in 1851 at the Women's Rights Convention in Akron, Ohio, is usually given the title "Ain't I a Woman?" The account of it published in 1881 by Margaret Gage is probably distorted, but it is the most widely available version on the Internet and in countless anthologies. A different version, published first in the *Anti-slavery Bugle* in 1851, is less colloquial and likely to be closer to Sojourner Truth's words. For that version, see Stewart.

Teaching the Teachers: *Oroonoko* as a Lesson in Critical Self-Consciousness

Erik Bond

Oroonoko is a really messy book to teach. After teaching it at many different levels, I became aware of—and discomforted by—the content I was ignoring at the cost of presenting a single theory. For example, while helping students interpret Imoinda through a feminist lens, I found that we never had time to fully explore *Oroonoko*'s representation of race, even though race is essential to Imoinda's character. While discussing slavery through a postcolonial lens, we never had time to follow how Behn's transitional definitions of race point to changing conceptions of social class. It was clear that one, two, or even three lenses of literary theory did not generate satisfying interpretations, precisely because Behn's work denies that such an organically unified thesis exists. Although these different readings may productively coexist with, converse with, and even contradict one another, there frequently is not enough time in an introductory undergraduate survey course to model evidence for more than one approach, much less bring two fully introduced approaches into conversation. Repeatedly trying to sanitize *Oroonoko*'s messiness so that it would answer the questions theory asked of it, I left classrooms knowing something was wrong.

Laura Brown (*Ends* 61) and Margaret Ferguson ("Juggling" [*Women's Studies*]) would account for *Oroonoko*'s resisting a unified thesis since the boundaries of our oversimplified identity categories of gender, race, and class are, in Behn's seventeenth-century world, not clearly differentiated. Any attempt to interpret the novel using a single twenty-first-century lens (feminist, postcolonial, or Marxist) must therefore fail: we are asking questions it was never meant to answer. But how can we adequately teach *Oroonoko*—much less present a model to students for using closely read evidence to prove a thesis—if it points in so many directions simultaneously? How can we be responsible instructors if the interpretations we teach ignore complexity for the sake of proving a coherent interpretation in one class session?

I suggest two answers. First, *Oroonoko* can encourage students to reconceive and merge identity-based theories to discuss the otherness of the Restoration's social hierarchy. Because the story calls attention more to what falls outside those theories than to what is clarified by them, an unfortunate side-effect of this approach is that we are tempted to move *Oroonoko* to the syllabi of upper-level, specialist courses. But, second, if we consider the career goals of students taking their first or only English course, and consider as well their varying levels of interpretive competence, *Oroonoko* may offer crucial lessons. When I examined what was motivating my introductory students to enroll in English classes, I discovered that an approach that both acknowledges and accommodates *Oroonoko*'s plurality involves teaching interpretation itself.

A portion of the students attending my university in the metropolitan Detroit area are English concentrators because they have the unabashed wish to teach English and pursue a career in primary or secondary education. Since most students in my class will not teach at the collegiate level, I was forced to reevaluate how I taught *Oroonoko* because of their desire to teach literary interpretation to others and because of their diversity (generational, racial, and ethnic). Specialized knowledge about *Oroonoko*'s culture might help my students understand literature's relation to a specific historical period, but most would never teach a Restoration work in their classrooms: high-school English curricula cannot focus so intently on historical contextualization. Regardless of the material they will teach in their future classrooms, my teaching interpretation was a topic that could unite student and professor in a common goal.

The metropolitan Detroit area has a rich African American history but now also contains one of the largest Middle Eastern populations outside the Middle East. A twenty-year-old student wearing a hijab (head scarf) discusses *Oroonoko* beside an eighteen-year-old student wearing a fedora beside a fifty-year-old student wearing a baseball cap. What unites all three of these students is their desire to teach. Discussions about how Imoinda functions and whether the final paragraphs of *Oroonoko* promote slavery inevitably elicit a variety of perspectives; more important, the novel encourages readers to reflect on their unspoken standards of interpretation. Recognizing how Behn's work nurtures readerly self-consciousness, I now promote an approach that foregrounds the problem of *Oroonoko*'s multiplicity. My response, therefore, to choosing the most valuable interpretation of *Oroonoko* is not to choose. *Oroonoko* presents a lesson about the politics of interpretation that can benefit my students more than its Restoration emphasis on genre, gender, or society. I now teach *Oroonoko* to reveal to students exactly what is at stake in interpreting *Oroonoko* before a classroom audience.

For the future teachers of Detroit's diverse communities, what is at stake in teaching *Oroonoko* is critical self-consciousness. Its interwoven and almost inseparable identity categories (race, gender, religion, sexuality) do not need to be separated into lectures or frames for undergraduates to understand the value of the Restoration text. Instead, an approach that self-consciously reveals to them what each frame incorporates as well as what it ignores takes them backstage (into the very issue of why a handbook entitled *Approaches to Teaching* Oroonoko exists), showing them the political ramifications of interpreting Restoration literature in particular and any text in general. Introductory students should realize that even professors have blind spots when rendering a 1688 text intelligible to a modern audience.

If I am given two classes to teach *Oroonoko*, I begin the first by asking my students to identify what in the narrative strikes them as strange or foreign—traits or episodes that, when read with twenty-first-century expectations of what fiction should be, seem complicated, overwritten, or boring. Responses commonly include Behn's extended passages of description. My ice-breaking question shows students that they are not the only ones who question sections of text with which late-seventeenth-century readers would have been comfortable. Beginning to respect the formal otherness of a historically distant text, they can now consider how Behn's work may accomplish intellectual tasks that their assumptions at their first reading made them ignore. Concluding the first class, I ask students to suggest why Behn wrote the story, and their answers inevitably lead them to commit to a single theoretical lens. If a student's answer addresses abolition, I apply a historicist or postcolonial lens to clarify the complicated status of slavery during the Restoration. But I do not hide evidence, detailed mainly by Moira Ferguson, of how "*Oroonoko* does not sustain an emancipationist reading" ("*Oroonoko*" [Iwanisziw] 5). If a student's answer addresses Oroonoko's heroism, I apply a formalist lens to outline the generic conventions that readers expected to see in Behn. But I also review Behn's swerves toward generic novelty in these conventions, especially with reference to Imoinda. In other words, instead of ignoring the blind spots that must accompany each theoretical lens, I encourage students to identify the limitations of each. I try to leave them with their heads swimming from the messiness that teachers face when interpreting *Oroonoko* for any audience. I carry this self-conscious method of inquiry into the second class, demonstrating how we can read *Oroonoko* as an allegory of the Tory politics and the Glorious Revolution of Restoration England. For a course that provides a broad historical narrative of English literature, it is tempting to suggest that this allegory is what makes sense of the story. It is an attractive interpretation—one that tempts us to believe we have located the correct interpretation for an English course—linking Behn's global novelty back to England and creating a moment of Anglocentric truth. Students might feel relieved that interpretive certainty has been preserved. Yet Brown promotes "the African slave in Behn's novella not as a projection of colonialist discourse, contained or incorporated by a dominant power, but as an historical force in his own right and his own body" (*Ends* 63). I ask what we have lost by approaching the novel Anglocentrically. Students quickly see how this approach denies Oroonoko and Imoinda their blackness, how it strips them of their otherness, including their non-Christian alterity, and how it unconsciously privileges a certain race. Thus I have shown them how easy it is to perpetuate privileged strategies simply by interpreting a text for a class.

To strengthen this point about interpretive blind spots, I draw on the blackboard a large map of South America and Africa, carefully excluding England, since Behn's story does much the same. Finally, I stand on a chair and draw a smaller island, to scale, on the wall above the blackboard. The point I am making is that in Behn's narrative environment England is literally a marginal character. That students laugh or gasp when I draw directly on the wall makes the additional point that Behn's story breaks the stereotype of where English writing—or chalking—should take place. *Oroonoko* is English literature without a literal England, and the supposedly innocent act of representation, through words or maps, involves political choices. The specific perspective and politics that undergird the Anglocentric interpretation are no longer transparent. In the courses in which I teach *Oroonoko*, I do not deny its allegorical-Anglocentric resonance, but I want students to see that by teaching only that interpretation, an instructor silently promotes its political privileging of a specific race or sex. Future teachers should be as aware as possible of how teaching can replicate a politics that one would never consciously wish to convey.

Of course, any literary text can expose the limits of a theoretical lens. What makes *Oroonoko* exceptional is that Behn's self-conscious style draws our attention to the act of interpretation itself. Consider the narrator's first-person disclaimer extended over the initial paragraphs of the story: it details the editorial decisions that writers invariably make. Consider also how Behn draws attention to her narrative reasoning and enplotment: "Though this digression is a little from my Story, however since it contains some Proofs of the Curiosity and Daring of this great Man, I was content to omit nothing of his Character" (51). Finally, she unapologetically implicates the reader's interpretation as a constitutive part of Oroonoko's history: "Some have commended this Act, as brave, in the Captain; but I will spare my sense of it, and leave it to my Reader, to judge as he pleases" (31). Some of these self-conscious moments are self-contained paragraphs and become signposts that indicate that the writer's narration is inseparable from the reader's mediation. By highlighting what is and is not narrated, the narrator forces us to ponder the degree to which Behn's writing actually determines our interpretations. Similarly, to what extent have our own choices, identity categories, and politics shaped our interpretation?

The purpose of a self-conscious approach to *Oroonoko* is not to validate rampant subjectivity on the principle that everyone is right. Instead, it prompts us to ask, "If we constantly try to deny *Oroonoko* its otherness, then what does this interpretation say about us?" It has become a poststructuralist commonplace to propose that if interpreting literature cannot express a preexisting reality, then at least we can learn about our own contemporary preconceptions by reflecting on the claims and assumptions we make about that literature. In other words, interpreters learn as much about themselves as about the thing interpreted. Because Behn encourages such self-examination, *Oroonoko* might better be taught in introductions to literary theory or to secondary-school education than in period-specific English literature courses, in which professors are inclined to anchor a "Royal Slave's" story to England through Anglocentric metaphors, generic maneuvers, and curricula.

Imparting this self-consciousness to my students is not an abstract, graduate-level activity; rather, it constitutes a well-received and essential element to education, given that many of my students will become teachers who present curricular-assigned texts in their Detroit-based classrooms as political works. Students who are part of or who will teach a racially diverse audience quickly grasp this critical self-consciousness, as they are living the political consequences of interpretive decisions. This self-conscious approach not only offers a viable alternative to the lectures that typically frame an undergraduate's experience of *Oroonoko* (and Restoration literature in general) but also shows how *Oroonoko* may be taught as a text that speaks to the reality that all readers face when interpreting a text in a diverse classroom.

Oroonoko is a valuable text to teach to introductory students because Behn's self-conscious narration invites them to embrace the pluralistic nature of literary interpretation and to experience the political consequences that can result from teaching only one interpretation of a text. Especially in introductory survey classes, we might forget how we appear to students as we stand on the front stage of the classroom, presenting litanies of closely read evidence from printed texts, litanies that seem to promote one correct interpretation conducive to note-taking and memorization for the final exam. Maintaining a facade of unproblematic literary critique, we fail to introduce students to the current problems of the field, such as the polarizing binary of the political versus the aesthetic, the hermeneutics of suspicion, and the question of why literature is a separate discipline. This tempts us not only to ignore students who want to participate in as well as teach everything English literature has to offer but also to generate an unspoken rule that when students write about *Oroonoko* or any other work, they must produce a thesis that is the only true one and has no blind spots. It is therefore not surprising for students to attend our office hours and ask, "Is my interpretation correct?" By taking them backstage, into the politically messy and often chaotic decision-making process that attends literary criticism today, we can make them feel more confidently part of the process, part of the field. They can even begin to help us solve some of our problems. As a result, students grasp criticism's aim to be an ongoing dialogue and not, what Rita Felski deems, a "permanent diagnosis" that preserves the impression of quantitative certainty (1). Once students realize that an Anglocentric interpretation can dissolve Oroonoko's blackness, they begin to grasp the responsibility that attends teaching literature.

Finally, by acknowledging that in some of our classes students may be united by their desire to teach at the primary and secondary levels rather than at the collegiate level, we can use *Oroonoko* to teach a lesson that extends beyond English departments and disciplinary boundaries. From this perspective, *Oroonoko*'s messiness offers one of those rare moments that defy service-industry education by reminding both student and instructor that they are part of the same enterprise: a community of scholars learning from, becoming conscious of, each other's blind spots.

It is refreshing to realize that Behn's "messy" story, which implicates both narrator and reader in *Oroonoko*'s plot and Oroonoko's identity, can reach across three centuries and continue to destabilize complacent strategies of interpretation and unexamined authority, this time in our own classrooms.

COMPARATIVE CONTEXTS

Oroonoko's Cosmopolitans

Laura J. Rosenthal

Oroonoko is a remarkably resilient text, consistently appealing to students. I first taught it as part of a general introduction to the English major because of the interesting questions it raises about fictionality. I would have students read Behn's novel along with Ernest Bernbaum's 1913 essays ("Mrs. Behn's Biography" and "Mrs. Behn's *Oroonoko*"), in which Bernbaum claims that Behn fabricated her travels to Surinam. I suppose I used him as a bit of a straw man; his accusation, however, allowed students to explore the stakes of truth and fictionality, reenacting in some ways the early debates over the novel. Then *Oroonoko* became my starting point for courses on the eighteenth-century novel. It makes an excellent introduction to the problem of the novel's genre: one can point out and discuss the significance of the combination, as William C. Spengemann has discussed, of romance and realism, strands of literary form that can be pulled apart in *Oroonoko* in rather obvious ways (Africa as romance, Surinam as realism).

Since then, I have taught *Oroonoko* in several different special topics courses, graduate and undergraduate, that explored eighteenth-century constructions of race, gender, property, and political authority. These are issues central to the critical discussions of *Oroonoko* in eighteenth-century studies, and students find much compelling criticism to engage. More recently, I have been teaching an undergraduate survey of seventeenth- and eighteenth-century writing that prompted me to think about Behn's novel in some different ways. Teaching *Oroonoko* in the middle of a broader survey that includes John Milton's *Paradise Lost*, Margaret Cavendish's *The Description of a New World, Called the Blazing World*, and Francis Bacon's *New Atlantis* not only raises the possibility that Behn's narrative is the first novel in English but also shows that it is part of a seventeenth-century fascination with stories about venturing into unfamiliar worlds that may or may not exist. Behn was a playwright before she was a novelist, and while I do not have space in this survey course to include a heroic play, which would explain a lot to students about Oroonoko's character, I usually include William Wycherley's *The Country Wife* (1675), which also deals with characters venturing out of their familiar worlds, albeit over more limited geographic territory. At the heart of *The Country Wife* lies Horner's return from France and Margery's journey to the big city. *Oroonoko* not only looks forward to the realism and passion of novels and travel narratives but also participates in a cultural moment that raises questions about the Enlightenment, expansion, curiosity, and sophistication. Literary works as disparate as *The Blazing World*, *The New Atlantis*, *Paradise Lost*, *The Country Wife*, most of the period's heroic drama, and *Oroonoko* all express the seventeenth- and eighteenth-century fascination with the costs and benefits of becoming a citizen of the world.

Being a citizen of the world, of course, can mean many things. Behn's time and the elite circles in which she traveled, as Gerald Newman has shown, were defined by their cosmopolitan identity—what he calls, following E. P. Thompson, a "theater of greatness" (26), in which the elite used displays of elegance to distinguish themselves from the masses. Travel could help achieve this distinguishing: in the 1670s, elite families began sending their sons on the grand tour to form them into world citizens (Newman 42). Elites had long distinguished themselves through their manners, but in the late seventeenth century new opportunities for recreational and educational travel allowed a version of world citizenship to become part of this identity. Cosmopolitanism had other, intellectual components. Margaret C. Jacob shows how communities of scientists in the eighteenth century established cosmopolitan identities that crossed national boundaries. Many of these projects and networks were well under way in Behn's day. Behn was writing on the cusp of the Enlightenment, which professed, as Newman notes,

> a widespread faith in the power of human reason to penetrate nature, and a complementary conception of nature as a machinelike structure governed everywhere by fundamental laws, whether in celestial mechanics or terrestrial physics, anatomy or psychology, politics or international relations or history. The result was a generalizing, indeed a universalizing system of thought which emphasized the rationality of God, the regularity of natural processes, the oneness of humanity, the value of life and of intellectual freedom; and which implicitly opposed revealed religions, arbitrary government, national enthusiasms and war as artificial and costly barriers to human understanding and brotherhood. (5)

Cosmopolitanism, then, might be understood at this time in terms of scientific interest, personal sophistication, elegance, an interest beyond the local, a (perhaps qualified) tolerance of difference, intellectual curiosity, or a combination of these elements. It becomes a central issue in *Oroonoko*.

Although I hope to steer the class toward a consideration of the issue of cosmopolitanism, *Oroonoko* raises troubling questions that must be confronted at the outset. Twenty-first-century students inevitably want to discuss the entanglement of race, class, and gender in the novel. Many insightful critics have written about this entanglement, yet, as anyone who teaches this novel knows, there is a significant difference between the way students generally understand the terms *race*, *class*, and *gender* and the way various social hierarchies shaped Behn's narrative. There is always the decision to make at this point: How much time do I spend in class explaining the difference between *race* in the seventeenth century and *race* in the twenty-first century? How much time do I spend getting students to believe me? Often in graduate courses, we explore this problem in depth, consulting theoretical arguments, historical explorations, and other texts that raise similar issues. Graduate students generally assume the fluidity of race and gender through history; over the course of a seminar, we go into considerable detail about eighteenth-century distinctions among landed wealth, elite birth, and the moneyed class.

In my undergraduate survey, I frame the historical issues as best as I can in the time available. I have found, though, that a good way to move students to a more sophisticated understanding of them is to focus on *Oroonoko* as a literary work. With its claim to truth and autobiographical experience, the novel encourages an assumption of transparency that students would never make about *Paradise Lost* (although certainly the author makes his presence known there as well). I call their attention, then, to the distinction between the author and the narrator so we do not get caught up in unproductive debates about what Behn's personal feelings are. In my experience, students want to leap right into talking about the author, whom they generally do not, as least initially, separate from the narrator. It helps to talk about the recent biographical criticism. Janet Todd, who has collected all known information about Behn's life, argues that most likely Behn was the daughter of a barber and not the illegitimate child of an aristocrat (*Secret Life* 13–15), and surely not the daughter of a man who, as Behn's narrator puts it, "never arriv'd to possess the Honour" of being "Lieutenant-General of Six and thirty Islands, besides the Continent of *Surinam*" (43). Our discussion of what we know about Behn's life convinces students that while the novel might indeed be based on personal experience, the narrator cannot be read as identical to Behn. At the very least, time separates the two: the narrator nostalgically recalls events from a past when England possessed the colony of Surinam, which, the narrator of the present laments, is no longer the case. This separation of the historical Behn from the novel's narrator allows us to think about what we know about the character telling the story.

I try to redirect attention from what seems to be Behn's personal views and prejudices to how the text presents and reconciles (or fails to reconcile) the clash of different worlds. By the time students get to *Oroonoko*, they have already read several seventeenth-century narratives about alternative worlds. Oroonoko comes closer than *The Blazing World*, *Paradise Lost*, and *New Atlantis* do to referring to an actual geographic space. But like the other texts, it follows an anthropological impulse, describing the different ways in which societies can be organized. Later in the eighteenth century, Adam Smith, among others, would describe societal development in four stages: "hunting, pasturage, agriculture, and commerce" (30n21). For Enlightenment philosophers writing at a time when travel writing had become enormously popular and considerably more information about the rest of the globe had been gathered, this stadial theory offered an organized way of seeing all human beings as essentially similar though at different stages of development. But *Oroonoko* offers something different from the linear development implied by later travel narratives. Behn gives us three cultures: the Caribs, the Coramantiens, and the English, all fictionalized to various degrees. The Caribs are clearly represented as primitive and even brutal: they are appealing in their innocence and courage, but the self-mutilation of their leaders horrifies both the narrator and Oroonoko, who come from more sophisticated societies. Yet in the implied comparison between English commercialism and Coramantien absolutism, it is not entirely clear which is more "advanced." Both seem to have their profound weaknesses. For Behn, commercial activity is not clearly a step forward, as it is for Smith; it opens up opportunities for men like the English planters to squeeze profits from slave driving.

George Guffey, Laura Brown (*Ends* and "Romance"), and many critics since have pointed out parallels between Oroonoko's world and the world of the Stuarts, and indeed both Oroonoko and Charles I fell victim to a new system of commercial circulation. Comparing the English plantation and the Coramantien warrior culture, as Brown suggests, reveals a nostalgia in the narrative for a disappearing set of values. At the same time, the Coramantien way (and by extension the precommercial English world) is not idealized. Coramantien government in the novel depends on traditions passed on from one male ruler to the next. What happens in such a society when the ruler becomes impotent and self-indulgent? Clearly Oroonoko would have made a better king than his grandfather, but the structures that distinguish this society from the emerging commercial one prevent this transition. Behn and Milton might be at the opposite ends of the political spectrum, but neither *Paradise Lost* nor *Oroonoko* embraces absolutism. *Oroonoko* offers neither a model of inevitable progress, as does Smith, nor an uncomplicated model of simple nostalgia for a previous moment in English history. Instead, Behn organizes her story, as do Bacon and Cavendish, geographically rather than chronologically, inviting comparison without an unalloyed narrative of progress or decline.

Cavendish and Bacon focus on one figure who traverses different cultures while the other characters remain stationary and belong to a particular culture. Behn's novel, by contrast, presents a whole world of mobility: the English planters, the captain and crew of the slave ship, and the African slaves have all traveled, although under greatly different circumstances. Most of them travel in groups, but certain figures do not fit comfortably into any one community: Trefry remains at odds with the other settlers; Imoinda is thought to be dead in Africa, but in Surinam she stands apart from the other slaves; a Frenchman lives in Coramantien to tutor the prince. The two main figures at odds with their communities, of course, are Oroonoko and the narrator.

Students quickly recognize that Behn's Africa owes something to the period's idealized or fantasized spaces—Paradise, Atlantis, the Blazing World—instead of prefiguring, as does Surinam, the detailed realism of the novel. They also notice that Oroonoko is different from any of the other characters in the novel. I have never had a class that was not struck by his combination of Roman features and very dark skin. We register the troubling racial hierarchy implied by this physicality, but the anomaly of Oroonoko's position is also conveyed by the title: a slave himself, he nevertheless trades in slaves; he is captive to but also looks down on the Englishmen in Surinam. These paradoxes become central to his adventures in Surinam, in which men and women whom he may have sold into slavery now bow down before him as their leader and lack the military spirit that he admires. These paradoxes also define the strained friendship that develops between him and the young Englishwoman who accepts the job of entertaining the African prince to distract him from his bondage.

But even before his capture, Oroonoko lived an anomalous life. In a culture described as polygamous, he fell in love with one woman. This love defines the rest of the narrative and sets all his adventures in motion: it leads to his conflict with his grandfather, to his eventual capture and enslavement, to his rebellion against his captors, and to his gruesome death. Oroonoko is not just monogamous but heroically so. He could have selected several other wives in Coramantien, avoided conflict with this grandfather, and, presumably, eventually inherited the throne. Instead, he keeps his attention fixed on one woman, to his detriment. Imoinda also remains monogamous, even in ways that challenge plausibility. Students recognize the abusive master-slave relationship that Behn sets up in the New World; in *Oroonoko*, however, Imoinda, it seems, cannot be raped. She escapes sexual violation in Africa, when the grandfather who captures her proves impotent, and again in Surinam, when the slave drivers, despite their desire, show respect for her virtue and dignity.

Having spent several weeks on *Paradise Lost*, students recognize that in both Milton's and Behn's texts marriage is a central, defining feature of heroism and of culture. Adam and Eve in a sense invent marriage. At first enjoying a partnership without conflict, Adam has to decide whether he wants to follow Eve into mortality. Behn's narrative can be read as a feminist response: Imoinda never disobeys but falls from her African paradise anyway, which was already troubled by patriarchal abuse. Oroonoko follows unintentionally and unbeckoned. Why, then, does the author present him as so heroically monogamous? Students answer this question in different ways. Many qualities put the royal slave at odds with Coramantien culture. He excels in physical strength and military skill like his countrymen but differs from them not in just in rank but also in his intellectual curiosity: he knows all about the political situation in England, he "had heard of, and admir'd the *Romans*" (13), he has learned languages from his tutor. He befriends the English slave trader and ship's captain in part because he wants to exchange information about navigational technique. While another kind of narrative might have the hero tempted by women or money, here the Captain draws Oroonoko onboard through lively conversation and intellectual exchange. Oroonoko, in other words, has distinctly cosmopolitan inclinations.

Oroonoko's intellect parallels his Roman nose: we are told that his interest is in European rather than African royalty. Yet the hierarchy is not exactly racially aligned. In the new world of the English plantation system, Oroonoko finds greater limitation than he ever saw in Coramantien. As numerous scholars have observed and as students pick up right away, *Oroonoko* has no particular antislavery agenda, but neither does it depict colonialism in a flattering light. The outrage in the Surinam part of the novel is that a man of Oroonoko's stature should be held as a slave by—and thus as an abject inferior to—such unworthy men.

The overall idea that I am leading students to with this line of discussion is that although categories of difference familiar to us do not map onto *Oroonoko* in any easy way, Behn does make systematic distinctions. In this narrative about mobility, she distinguishes between those who are locally bound and those who have the cosmopolitan impulse. As we saw earlier in the class in Wycherley's *The Country Wife*, comedies at the time found considerable humor in the clashes between those who embodied the emergent sophisticated urban culture of London and those who did not fully understand it. Oroonoko's horrific enslavement is indeed part of the circumatlantic traffic that would later define the British Empire, but readers in the seventeenth century also had available to them, as a more immediate point of reference, numerous slave narratives, such as that of Joseph Pitts, that told stories of Europeans captured and enslaved in the Ottoman Empire. Behn's Africa seems suspiciously Ottoman, a point we often discuss as well. The practice of polygamy in particular was associated with the Ottoman Empire for seventeenth-century British readers. The custom of sending a veil does not to my knowledge appear in travel narratives of the Ottoman Empire, but certainly much is made by these writers of veiled women and harems. Behn transposes the erotics of the Ottoman baths, which rarely failed to attract the attention of European writers, onto the scene of the king's attempted seduction of Imoinda. With the king's impotence, we might even speculate that Behn combines the infamous figure of the eunuch with the Coramantien ruler. Later in the story, Jamoan wakes Oroonoko from his lethargy by telling tales of "Love and Gallantry" (29), a literary form associated with the Orient (as Ballaster has recently shown [*Fabulous Orients* 17]). Even certain elements of the setting suggest the Ottomans: Oroonoko's French tutor and the carpets that appear in the harem are more Ottoman than sub-Saharan. Carpets were a highly valued Ottoman import, and a French tutor would not have been unusual in the

Ottoman court. These associations further level the field between the English and Coramantien cultures in the novel, for the sophisticated Ottoman Empire was both frightening and enviable to seventeenth-century Europeans. Oroonoko and his countrymen are not benighted savages, as later racist apologists for the British slave trade would characterize Africans, but come from a society, not unlike English society in this respect, with varying levels of sophistication.

In *Oroonoko*, a small group of characters—the young narrator, Oroonoko, Trefry, and in some ways Imoinda—emerge as witty, educated, open-minded, literary, and curious about the world: they are cosmopolitans who transcend their specific national circumstances. Oroonoko loves one woman in a polygamous society, breaking both with his culture's tradition and with his grandfather, the king. To be sure, it is not so much monogamy that makes him cosmopolitan as his distinctiveness from the other characters in his culture. (Horner in *The Country Wife*, by contrast, stakes a claim to cosmopolitanism through a version of polygamy.) Oroonoko and the narrator, similarly curious, venture out to investigate the unknown tribes upriver. Just as he breaks with Coramantien conjugal custom and comes to disdain the Africans who do not share his outrage at enslavement, so she has nothing but contempt for the other English colonists, whom the novel represents as crude and self-serving. The English fail to recognize Oroonoko's royal status but in their provinciality also fail to appreciate the intellectual opportunity he could offer them. His greatness is partly a consequence of his royal blood but not entirely defined by it: after all, the figure of the Coramantien king suggests that it is possible to be dishonest, self-indulgent, lascivious, and impotent while having the same royal blood. Oroonoko is not so much an exception in a horde of barbarians as he is a member of a small group of world citizens who have more in common with one another than with provincials in various locations.

Like many seventeenth- and eighteenth-century texts we read in this survey, *Oroonoko* wrestles with the problem of cosmopolitanism. Critics have called attention to the synergy between the narrator and the royal slave, investigating their relationship from many angles. Whatever else draws them together, they share a vexed connection to cosmopolitanism. Oroonoko, understanding his status as transcendent, finds it puzzling that despite his nobility the English never free him. The narrator finds this puzzling as well. *Oroonoko* also contrasts the narrator with the other English people, who with the exception of an educated few reveal themselves as brutal and unscrupulous. One tragedy of this novel, then, lies in the failure of an English colonial society to be cosmopolitan despite the travels of its members. Its cosmopolitanism emerges only briefly and incompletely: the narrator feeds Oroonoko's intellectual curiosity and indulges her own, while at the same time knowing that her entertainment of the royal slave remains a trap to keep him from rebelling. Behn's vision of cosmopolitanism is pessimistic: travel and intellectual exploration lead to a sophistication that puts the narrator and Oroonoko at odds with their societies but does not give them the tools to form a new one.

Teaching *Oroonoko* with Milton and Dryden; or, Behn's Use of the Heroic

Laura L. Runge

The Female Quixote, published in 1752, centers on a debate over the durability of heroic values: "'But Custom,' said Arabella, 'cannot possibly change the Nature of Virtue or Vice: And since Virtue is the chief Characteristik of a Hero, a Hero in the last Age will be a Hero in this'" (Lennox 328). Defending the heroes that she alone admires, Arabella refers to the gap between late-seventeenth-century French romances and the middle eighteenth-century world she inhabits. The heroic romances that were immensely popular during Behn's lifetime fell out of favor by the middle of the following century, roughly about the same time that Behn's novels stopped being regularly reprinted. Arabella's optimism in the transcendent value of heroic virtue ultimately gives way to her rational acceptance of custom and Christian duty. The novel appears to reject the stoic self-sacrifice, bravado, and reckless violence of heroes motivated by extremes of love, honor, and glory—heroes who have a great deal in common with Behn's Oroonoko. The debate that Lennox's novel engages, therefore, has immediacy for those of us who teach Behn's story. First of all, it suggests the need to historicize the heroic character because it is tied to the mores of an age, and these are deeply connected to changing structures of gender, race, religion, and politics. Second, it asks us to consider the reader's position: How can we expect modern readers to appreciate the heroic nature of Behn's text if readers less than one hundred years later rejected it?

While much scholarship approaches *Oroonoko* as the start of a literary tradition, this essay demonstrates the importance of returning it to the contentious and idiosyncratic years of its production. The heroism with which Behn endues her character was the common stock of the Restoration. British admiration for the heroic, of course, drew from classical precedents, and Aristotle, Horace, and Longinus provided the critical terms on which the heroic genres were constructed. The unique conditions in Behn's England, however, added piquancy and personal investment to the meaning of heroic codes. A country divided in civil war, committed to a trial commonwealth, and then, in 1660, returned to a fragile monarchy knew about reversals of fortune and the price of martial valor. By 1688, when Behn put her narrative into print, England was on the eve of yet another political revolution, one that in the end was bloodless. Behn's writing, like much of her contemporaries', participated in explicit political endorsement (Zook; Kroll). Like the poet laureate, John Dryden, Behn supported the Stuart monarchy and the emerging Tory party. Her version of heroism celebrated Cavalier, inborn nobility consistent with kingship. Opposing voices, such as the republican John Milton, appealed to divine models for their versions of heroism, and *Paradise Lost*, originally published in 1667, was arguably the most important heroic poem in English. Both sides of the political spectrum claimed the heroic, as it was debated and revised by various participants.

The cultural conditions of the Restoration thus produced a flowering of generic experimentation in heroic modes. Heroic verse included the highly esteemed epic and tragedy, as well as panegyric and even satire; on stage, the heroic drama became something of a Restoration vogue. In prose, translations of French romances as well as homegrown heroic tales created a palate for extremes of love and honor, and the rising form of biography, such as was written by Lucy Hutchinson and Margaret Cavendish for their husbands, also qualified as heroic renderings (Staves 32–42). There are many possible reasons for this enthusiasm, from an ideological support for the restored monarchy to the influence of French tastes in the Stuart court to the psychological need of a populace wounded by civil war. This heroic outpouring gradually dried up after 1700, but it is important to see *Oroonoko* in the heady mix (Richardson).

Historicizing heroism, however, will not necessarily allow students comfortable access to Behn's hero. From beginning to end, Behn characterizes Oroonoko as exemplary, and the narrator indicates that she writes the novel for the sake of preserving her hero's memory. This consistency suggests a confidence in the heroic character that conveys in sentiment if not specifics. Students tend to agree that Oroonoko is heroic, but they respond in varying and confusing ways if asked why. Looking more closely at Behn's depiction of the heroic does not yield easy answers. As we historicize heroism and place Behn in conversation with other writers of her era, we confront the fact that the Restoration had many passionate and contradictory investments in the heroic. Drawing out the historical, literary, and cultural threads, one discovers that Behn's novel is a deeply ambivalent portrayal of masculine heroism. Yet, given the modern relevance of key factors in this depiction—religion, violence, gender, and race—an instructor could benefit from analyzing where the tensions lie and why.

The language of the heroic mode, which can be exaggerated and artificial, presents a fundamental challenge in reading *Oroonoko*. Behn adopts conventions of heroic romance and drama when Oroonoko speaks in phrases like, "*Whoever ye are that have the Boldness to attempt to approach this Apartment thus rudely, know, that I, the Prince* Oroonoko, *will revenge it with the certain Death of him that first enters*" (25). Restoration readers knew that this elevated diction signaled nobility of character while the message conveyed the fortitude requisite of heroes.

That being said, seventeenth-century authors held varying opinions on the right way to represent a hero, and representation was tied to a brand of heroic virtue. Milton, for example, offers in *Paradise Lost* a Christian heroism in contrast to classical: "argument / Not less but more Heroic than the wrath / Of stern *Achilles*" (9.13–15). He specifies new virtues

> Not sedulous by Nature to indite
> Wars, hitherto the only Argument

> Heroic deem'd, chief maistry to dissect
> With long and tedious havoc fabl'd Knights
> In Battles feign'd; the better fortitude
> Of Patience and Heroic Martyrdom
> Unsung. . . . (27–33)

Paradise Lost recognizes and parodies the conventions of the classical heroic in the figure of Satan while presenting an alternative hero, or set of heroes, in the figures of the Son of God, Adam, and perhaps Eve. The virtues of "Patience and Heroic Martyrdom" suggest a Christian alternative to warlike violence and an analogue for Puritans who died for their beliefs. As a further manifestation of religious and political difference, Milton, in a note on his verse, defends his use of blank verse as a true measure of "*English* Heroic Verse" in contradistinction to the rhyming lines of royalist heroic dramas—"the Invention of a barbarous Age, to set off wretched matter and lame Meter" (Introduction 210). Mercy, for Milton, is clothed in pure language.

Despite the political revolutions that changed his fate, Dryden had a lifelong commitment to classical heroic genres. In his preface to *Annus Mirabilis* (1667), he explains that "the most heroick Subject which any Poet could desire" is "a most just and necessary War" (1: 50). In the dedication to Mulgrave of his translation of Vergil's *Aeneid* (1697), he writes, "A heroick Poem, truly such, is undoubtedly the greatest Work which the Soul of Man is capable to perform. The Design of it, is to form the Mind to Heroick Virtue by Example." He follows Aristotle in demanding that the action be "always one, entire, and great." All elements must be "Grave, Majestical, and Sublime" (5: 267). With classical precedents to support them, these standards were widely accepted, and the heroic prose genres that developed in Behn's lifetime adopted the warlike subjects and sublime style, though they did not follow the unity of action.

Whereas classical heroism focused on war, seventeenth-century heroic genres appeared exceptionally concerned with conflicts of romantic love. This concern was especially true of the French romance and heroic drama and, unsurprisingly, *Oroonoko*. Dryden wrote in defense of his *Conquest of Granada*, "[A]n Heroick Play ought to be an imitation, in little of an Heroick Poem: and, consequently, that Love and Valour ought to be the Subject of it" (11: 10). Like Behn, he drew on the French romances that would become outdated a century later. But if he puts the heroic romance of La Calprenède and Scudéry in company with Homer and Tasso as models for his hero, he claims to be "more in love with *Achilles* and *Rinaldo*, than with *Cyrus* and *Oroondates*" (11: 16). Here and elsewhere Dryden offers a homosocial heroic love to offset the potentially feminizing effect of female relationships. In *An Essay of Dramatick Poesie*, he writes, "*Homer* describ'd his Heroes men of great appetites, lovers of beef broild upon the coals, and good fellows; contrary to the practice of the *French* Romances, whose Heroes neither eat, nor drink, nor sleep, for love" (17: 32). Behn's hero appears to have more in common with those across the channel.

Although his prowess on the battlefield earns Oroonoko initial honors, Behn suggests that the genuine source of his heroism lies in his character: "that real Greatness of Soul, those refin'd Notions of true Honour, that absolute Generosity, and that Softness that was capable of the highest Passions of Love and Gallantry" (12). More so than for Dryden or Milton, her hero's virtue is tied to his capacity for passionate, romantic love for a woman. In response to news of Imoinda's death, Oroonoko vows that "henceforth he wou'd never lift a Weapon, or draw a Bow; but abandon the small Remains of his Life to Sighs and Tears" (28), and he lies prostrate for two days refusing food and water. More important, Oroonoko is completely incapacitated by Imoinda's actual death, a point to which I will return.

Another controversy in heroic discourse centers on the morality of the hero. For ancient epics and French romances, vengeance and pride serve as laudatory motivations for heroic action, but Puritans identified vengeance and pride as principal human vices. Milton suggests an alternative model of heroism by opposing the classical heroics of Satan with the perfect moral nature of the Son of God (Steadman 254–55, 288). Dryden, in contrast, celebrates the exceptionality of traditional heroism: "[Poets] made their Hero's men of honour; but so, as not to divest them quite of humane passions, and frailties. They contented themselves to show you, what men of great spirits would certainly do, when they were provok'd, not what they were oblig'd to do by the strict rules of moral vertue" (11: 16). Violence, revenge, and fortitude, particularly fortitude in physical suffering, are hallmarks of the classical hero. Behn appears to side with Dryden, and she grants an exceptional morality to Oroonoko. His ability to kill is demonstrated throughout the novel. Certainly one of the text's greatest pedagogical difficulties lies in understanding his killing of Imoinda, but there are other questionable actions, such as selling Africans into slavery and later calling them, "Dogs, treacherous and cowardly, fit for such Masters" (56). Having the status as a hero may exempt Oroonoko from "the strict rules of moral vertue," but discussing this historical relativism in the classroom is likely to raise the point that heroic virtue has changed. Its change offers an opportunity to discuss current mores as tied to issues of violence, gender, religion, and race.

Much can be gained by focusing on the hero if one teaches *Oroonoko* after Milton's *Paradise Lost* and Dryden's *Absalom and Achitophel*. Although *Macflecknoe* is taught more frequently than *Absalom and Achitophel*, the latter offers more direct parallels both to *Paradise Lost* (Paulson 49) and to *Oroonoko*. The biblical parody and heroic couplets of *Absalom and Achitophel* make it accessible after a brief review of the politics of the Exclusion Crisis, and Dryden's work prepares students to see the less explicit political tensions in Behn's text (Kroll; Guffey). Rich comparisons can be drawn in terms of heroic style and allusion, the hero's moral character, the politics of his leadership, and more. Mindful of space, this essay takes up one particularly productive thread—the failed rebellion. Because of salient parallels, I highlight Milton's Satan as a heroic figure. As early as Dryden, readers recognized Satan as a hero. Dryden judged Milton's epic according to the classical standards he admired, failing to see the ways in which *Paradise Lost* would reshape the discourse surrounding heroic poetry. Yet Satan did not work as a hero for Dryden in part because he was defeated. His revenge on God the Father is undone by the self-sacrifice of the Son of God. Adam and Eve, though fallen from grace, have the promise of future salvation. Succeeding centuries have fully vetted the question of Satan's heroic status, and the important passages that yield diametrically opposed readings (Steadman; Carey). Like Oroonoko, Satan leads an insurrection that fails; like Oroonoko, he vows revenge, which also fails. Some critics, like Merritt Hughes, argue that Satan begins as a heroic character in the first two books of *Paradise Lost* and is degraded in his final scene in book 9. Others, notably Stanley Fish, maintain that Satan remains the same character throughout the poem; what changes is the reader's ability to perceive his flaws. Fish's insight that the text reads the reader is helpful here: if the Satan image forces the reader to question what heroic virtue is, then the poem engages students in an analysis they can carry over to the other works. Putting *Paradise Lost* into its Restoration context, some readers will find that it sets a Christian heroism of patience and martyrdom higher than classical bravery, vengeance, and war. Others may argue for the exceptional morality of Satan and see him justified in defiance of the Father's tyranny. As students note the similarities between Oroonoko and Milton's Satan, they can begin to question what revenge might mean in terms of heroic virtue.

Dryden's *Absalom* also centers on a failed rebellion in a poem with numerous and complicated connections to *Paradise Lost*. Dryden identifies one Miltonic echo, drawing a parallel in his dedication between Absalom, standing in for Monmouth, the king's illegitimate son, and Adam:

> *But, since the most excellent Natures are always the most easy; and, as being such, are the soonest perverted by ill Counsels, especially when baited with Fame and Glory; 'tis no more a wonder that he withstood not the temptations of* Achitophel, *than it was for* Adam, *not to have resisted the two Devils; the Serpent, and the Woman.* (2: 4 ["To the Reader"])

While the passage mitigates Monmouth's crime by disingenuously aligning Monmouth with Adam, it subtly redirects blame toward a woman. The poem realizes this misogynistic theme by the conspicuous absence of romantic values and female worth, an absence that contrasts sharply with the other examples. Instead the poem works out a series of paternal relationships and conflicting constructions of masculine virtue. Dryden represents Absalom as a rebel son, although he clearly makes him a pawn to Achitophel's Satan-like scheming. Yet the thirst for fame and glory animates the soul of Absalom and sets him on the path of doomed insurrection: "Desire of Greatness is a Godlike Sin" (2: 16 [line 372]). In contrast, Dryden characterizes David's (Charles II's) mildness as both a virtue and a weakness, associating the king with the mercy and patience of Milton's Son of God. The poem presents David's dignified authority at the end as a counter to the infection-like power of the mob supporting Absalom (28–29 [lines 753–810]). As the narrative moves from mistaken hero to certain hero—as in *Paradise Lost*—Dryden layers the heroic characterization in contrasting masculine values. He pits the "Manly Force" (16 [line 382]) of Absalom against the waning tolerance of David: "Beware the Fury of a Patient Man" (35 [line 1005]). Although Dryden leaves the ending uncertain, the insurrection is characterized as a failure, and David appears in godlike omnipotence in the closing lines. Dryden designs failure for Satan-like Absalom, but the complexity of the Miltonic parallels and gendered constructions leaves open the question of what heroic behavior is, particularly as fitting a man. For students today, the political agency of the rabble may in fact have heroic appeal, but the poem clearly favors tyranny when exercised by a mild patriarch. Dryden's political satire puts a great deal of stock in David's correct performance of masculine authority, impugning the rebellious son.

Students come to see that Oroonoko resembles both Satan and Absalom in his noble character and desire for sovereignty. Since Oroonoko is a prince tricked into slavery, however, the conditions of his subjection differ from those of the archangel and the bastard son. This comparison of fallen heroes thus offers an opportunity for students to discuss how conditions of race and the role of the African prince affect the representation of honor, bravery, and morality. For example, Oroonoko's speech to the male slaves provides an important contrast with the concluding arguments in book 2 of *Paradise Lost* and with Achitophel's seduction of Absalom. Each work presents a different rationale for rebellion that reflects the character's heroic standing. In the wake of defeat, Oroonoko, like Satan, vows himself to vengeance: "*I wou'd not kill my self, even after a Whipping, but will be content to live with that Infamy . . . till I have compleated my Revenge; and then you shall see that* Oroonoko *scorns to live with the Indignity that was put on* Caesar" (58). Ultimately, though, he fails to revenge his honor and restore his good name, and the key to this defeat is not the treachery of Byam or the institution of slavery but rather the effeminizing effects of love. The heroic code offers a justification for Oroonoko's decision to kill Imoinda; Oroonoko must seek revenge for his honor, and the expected consequence of that revenge is Imoinda's vulnerability to violence at the hands of the colonists. Yet Imoinda's valor and self-sacrifice in the death scene provide the opportunity for students to discuss how gender inflects the novel's codes of honor. Imoinda's self-sacrifice, as well as her service in the revolt, raises the possibility for a female heroism, which is distinct from Oroonoko's (Rose 85–112; Ortiz).

Having dispatched his beloved, Oroonoko is overcome by grief: "[H]e Tore, he Rav'd, he Roar'd, like some Monster of the Wood, calling on the lov'd Name of *Imoinda*" (61). He collapses and for eight days is unable to lift himself from the ground. This scene plays out the heroic conflict between love and honor, and love—translated into grief—triumphs. The immoral but heroic act of killing Imoinda is thus wasted in pathos, and this waste prefigures the literal emasculation of the hero several pages later. Behn, by having her hero defeated by the consequences of his own violent action, offers a serious challenge to the masculine heroic code.

But Behn gives Oroonoko the last word on honor in a religious critique that resonates back to Milton. Throughout the text, she puts Oroonoko in situations where his innate honesty is betrayed by the hypocrisy of Christian men, a failing that Tory writers associated with Puritan cant. After Byam tells him he will "Dye like a Dog," Oroonoko responds "that he was the only Man, of all the Whites, that ever he heard speak Truth" (64). While *Paradise Lost* suggests a Puritan ideal of martyrdom as an alternative to the classical heroic model, Behn's classical-romance hero is martyred speaking a biting indictment of Christian values.

Teaching *Oroonoko* in context with *Paradise Lost* and *Absalom and Achitophel* historicizes and complicates the idea of the heroic and thereby allows students better access to the complexity of Behn's character. None of these texts offers a simple model of heroism. Milton rejects the classical heroic model embodied in Satan but nonetheless offers a compelling portrait of its virtues; Dryden employs heroic parallels and gendered constructions to raise and ultimately discredit the rebel Whig, Monmouth; Behn borrows heavily from heroic genres to memorialize Oroonoko but in the end leaves the heroic code fractured. The comparison invites students to question whether the virtues of heroism translate into our age and to what extent custom has altered the construction of heroic masculinity. In what ways is violence, or mercy, or patience important to systems of religion and honor, then or now? How do constructions of race or gender factor in moral questions? Is the hero by definition exempt from the mores of other human beings? Instead of seeing Oroonoko's language and behavior as antiquated, this focus engages these questions as vital to every student.

Teaching *Oroonoko* with Early Modern Drama

Joyce Green MacDonald

Oroonoko teaches beautifully. I have taught it to undergraduates and to a mixed class of advanced undergraduates and graduates and always had a choice of topics to discuss. Students at both levels were intrigued by the mere fact of Behn's professional career, which unfolded during a period in which many of them assumed there were no women writers. They responded powerfully to the novel's portrait of life in Africa—even though that portrait is vaguely orientalized—before the advent of the Atlantic slave trade; they did not know of many texts that treated black Africans as independent subjects outside the framework of slavery. My female students especially were taken by Behn's Imoinda, whom they found independent, intelligent, and sexually assertive, freely acting on her desire for Oroonoko and resisting the lecherous old king. They enjoyed the manipulative Onahal and were amused, if slightly scandalized, by her fling with Aboan. Students of both genders would approach me as class ended to say they were convinced that the narrator wanted to "get with" Oroonoko; as one young man put it, "She's always talking about his body." Interestingly, they tended not to bring up this subject during class discussion.

My courses offered many avenues into the novel and into Behn's life and times. I was able to organize presentations on premodern women writers, on the pressure Behn's royalism put on the book's ideas of nobility, on the knowledge seventeenth-century Englishmen and women had of Africa and the New World. Still, I was nagged by the possibility that the quality and intensity of student responses were driven by what struck them as the novel's modernity. It was easy for them to grasp *Oroonoko* because it seemed obsessed by issues familiar to them in their own social experience: discussions of women's sexual autonomy, racial and cultural identity politics, the experience of race-based slavery for both slaves and masters. Combined with students' interest in the Behn phenomenon—a woman ahead of her time in building a professional identity for herself—*Oroonoko* rapidly closed the distance between its time and my students' present.

Its ready familiarity, however, is precisely what bothered me. *Oroonoko* may feel modern, yet it is emphatically not a modern work. One of my main pedagogical goals is making sure that students grasp not only the relevant elements of early modern culture as we read sixteenth- and seventeenth-century texts but also the considerable differences between early modernity and our time. That students respond to *Oroonoko* allows me to introduce them to important literary, social, and historical connections in the period, and it is versatile enough to fit comfortably into an undergraduate survey (its shortness is another blessing here) as well as into an upper-level special-topics course. But I wanted to make sure that students respected and understood its specific historicity before rushing with them to pull it into modernity.

My field is Shakespeare and Renaissance drama, and my first idea about how to help my upper-level students see what was distinctively unmodern about *Oroonoko* was to pair it with Behn's *Abdelazer*. This pairing led us to a deeper discussion of Behn's authorship, developing as the play does from the earlier *Lust's Dominion*, and it allowed me to give a swift kick to any lingering notions of her original genius. It introduced the subject of the breadth of her literary work: we did not read any of her poetry or her other plays, but it became clear to students that Behn was consciously working in several modes, building a career from the resources of the literary and theatrical past and not generating it entirely from her imagination. Thanks to *Abdelazer*, students saw that *Oroonoko* participated in a specifically early modern dialogue about race and masculinity. This realization complicated a too seamless connection with society today.

Abdelazer; or, The Moor's Revenge, Behn's only tragedy, is the feverish story of a Moorish prince taken to be raised in the Spanish court after his father is killed in battle by the king of Spain. Abdelazer is treated with honor and respect in the Spanish court, but as the play opens, he seethes with the desire for revenge against the royal family, largely because of the shame he feels as the queen's secret lover, subject to her demeaning sexual demands. The Spanish king's murder, at the hand of the queen in conspiracy with Abdelazer, creates the opportunity for Abdelazer to avenge himself not only against the queen but also against the entire royal family and the court. The queen's elder son, Ferdinand, has always loved Abdelazer's Spanish wife, Florella, while the younger son, Philip, despises Abdelazer and in concert with the cardinal, Mendozo, is briefly successful in having him exiled from court. The play follows Abdelazer's plot to destroy the royal family and install himself on the throne, a plot finally thwarted by Philip working with Florella's brother, Alonzo.

Abdelazer is quite theatrically self-aware. Behn draws on the technical resources of the Restoration stage to mount a climactic battle scene complete with movable painted scenery, while her antihero is dressed throughout in a "Moorish robe" (1.2.146), a property that visually announces his difference from the Spaniards among whom the play is set. The confidence with which Behn stages her big set scenes—for example, Isabella's murder of Florella (3.3.93) and the final crowded tableau in the last act, in which Abdelazer is killed—points to her skill in portraying action, a skill latent in the descriptions of life in Coramantien that my undergraduates found so intriguing. The scene of Oroonoko's death in Surinam has some of the same striking set-piece quality, as my students recognized; it distills the essence of his heroism and moral superiority into a single image of stoically borne martyrdom.

Abdelazer helped emphasize and clarify some of Behn's imaginative gifts, suggesting that they also shaped *Oroonoko*. But we found that *Abdelazer* departs from this shared norm in the way it makes explicit a deeply racialized sexual unease, which the novel chooses to mute. Isabella is so unbalanced by lust for her Moorish lover that she is willing to have Philip declared a bastard to further Abdelazer's search for vengeance—despite the damage to her reputation. In turn, Philip seems to regard the passive Florella, whom Ferdinand has fruitlessly desired for years, as a whore, simply because his brother wants her. Philip claims that Florella holds Ferdinand in "Chains," where he lies "drown'd in idle wanton Love" (2.1.47–48). Florella's marriage to Abdelazer is for Philip additional proof of her lasciviousness. As Abdelazer leads his wife from the banquet, Philip says everyone else may as well leave, since the Moor has taken away "[t]he fine gay play-thing, that made us all so merry" (2.117).

Both the exploitative Abdelazer-Isabella relationship and Philip's disgust with women's sexuality provided students with striking contrasts to Oroonoko and Imoinda's mutual loving desire. As we read *Oroonoko*, students were of two minds about the narrator's relation to and involvement in the events leading up to the deaths of Oroonoko and Imoinda. A vociferous faction asserted that the narrator was essentially playing dumb, that she was a member of Surinam's slaveholding society and profited from it despite her absence from the scene of Oroonoko's torture and death. Others insisted that as a woman she could not intervene in the slaveholders' revenge against the rebellious slaves and that her absence reflected her lack of authority in the colonial society. Remembering the privately expressed opinions of some undergraduates that the narrator was sexually interested in Oroonoko, I asked them to think about her silence and absence at this critical moment and to compare them with Philip's horror at his mother's willingness to abandon her "self, [her] honour, and [her] vows, / To wanton" in the arms of the "Sooty Leacher," Abdelazer (1.2.90–91). Philip calls Alonzo a "Pimp" (2.1.51) for having accepted Florella's marriage to Abdelazer, as though Abdelazer himself and not the old king had promoted it. Philip believes the impending marriage between Isabella and Abdelazer will somehow confirm Isabella's proclamation that Philip is "basely born" (4.1.63). Clearly, the idea that an interracial marriage can cast doubt about the circumstances surrounding one's previous conception and birth is completely illogical. But so is Isabella's willingness to have Philip excluded from the succession, since her lie about his legitimacy depends on her admission of infidelity to her late husband during his lifetime and thus opens her to the accusation of treason. In *Abdelazer*, female lust is so powerful that it can destroy a white woman's dignity and instinct for self-preservation and undermine orderly patrilineal descent. *Abdelazer*'s extremes provoked fuller discussion than *Oroonoko* did of interracial sex in early modern tales of cultural contact, and my undergraduates came away with a sense of how unusual for its period Behn's portrait is of the devotion between her African lovers.

Looking back at the narrator's absence from the climax of *Oroonoko* and using the unsatisfying end of *Abdelazer*—the single combat Philip desires never materializes, and Abdelazer is stabbed to death in the midst of a crowd, so we cannot know who is responsible for his death—I suggested to my upper-level students that we might be able to locate both works along a continuum of readiness to speak openly about the idea of race mixing in the seventeenth century. The motif connects the two works: Oroonoko's surprise at Trefry's reluctance to take by force the beautiful slave Trefry desires serves as an inversion of the queen's aggressively disordered desire for Abdelazer. It also connects them to Shakespeare's *Othello*. All three works share a domestic focus: the Oroonoko-Imoinda love story, *Abdelazer*'s sexual and marital intrigues, *Othello*'s runaway love match.

In *Abdelazer*, Abdelazer regards his wife as a possession, swearing to kill the new king, Ferdinand, for daring to desire her. Never fully accepted as an equal by the royal family, he cannot reconcile himself to life at the Spanish court despite the comfort of his circumstances there. The buried racial fears that Shakespeare's Iago recognizes and manipulates in order to destroy Othello are more fully articulated, much more explicitly acknowledged in Behn's play, as part of the characters' understanding of who the Moor is and of what place he can have in Spanish society.

Abdelazer, then, is a kind of mirror to both *Othello* and *Oroonoko*. It has no room for the romantic love that binds Oroonoko and Imoinda or (at least at first) Othello and Desdemona. It denies the possibility of peaceful integration of a black man into white society, even under the strictly delineated terms *Oroonoko* allows (for example, the planters can admire the African prince's nobility as long as he is securely kept in bondage). It rejects the possibility that a miscegenous bond can ever be anything but a matter of degradation and domination—first, as Abdelazer chafes under his sexual exploitation by the queen, then as he seizes on the idea of marrying her daughter as the surest way to gain the throne for himself (5.1.454–98). The complex love-hate relationship between him and Isabella provided students with a striking contrast to Oroonoko and Imoinda's trusting romantic and monogamous love, as well as to the deteriorating love between Othello and Desdemona. At the same time, Abdelazer's mechanistic use of marriage to avenge and usurp carries something of the horror Iago invokes as he tries to rouse Brabantio's disgust against his daughter's marriage: Desdemona will be "covered with a Barbary horse" (1.1.111). The fear, shame, and anger that Iago marshals as weapons in his private drive for power and revenge erupt into public life in *Abdelazer*.

If my undergraduates were unwilling to discuss in class the interracial sexual attraction in *Oroonoko*, my more advanced students engaged with the sexual elements in both Behn works. But I suspected that they were doing so more from their reading in American history and literature than from an early modern viewpoint. Premodern British discussions of race and modern American ones did not use the same tropes. I returned to my undergraduates' fascination with the character of Imoinda, therefore, and introduced a second Restoration play into our discussion, Thomas Southerne's 1695 dramatization of *Oroonoko*. Like *Abdelazer*, this play offered several ways of opening up discussion of *Oroonoko*. Its huge popularity in the eighteenth century placed Behn even more securely in her period's literary history, since it showed that she was not only a talented adapter of other works and modes but also the subject of others' adaptations. It suggested the continuing relevance of her portrait of slavery: Southerne's *Oroonoko* and its offshoots would speak passionately to the concerns of later abolitionists. Finally, Southerne's *Oroonoko*, with its Welldon sisters' marriage subplot, showed what sex, gender, and race had to do with one another in the colonial setting that Southerne borrowed from Behn.

Some of my *Oroonoko* students, having been in my Shakespeare classes, knew about the often weird history of Shakespearean adaptation, but even they were surprised to learn that an author went so far as to take a black character they admired and turn her into a white woman they found weak and uninteresting. They pointed out how Southerne's featuring a black hero with a white wife made *Oroonoko* look more like *Othello*. The substitution of a white Imoinda for Behn's black one also moved Atlantic slavery farther from the cultural context of her work. Instead of Behn's story of black love and black heroism—students loved the moment when Imoinda fights beside her husband in the slave rebellion—they were faced with a play that had lost all the features they found most compelling. Yet I needed to be sure that they were not so puzzled and disappointed by Southerne's *Oroonoko* that they would not want to read it on its own terms. The Welldon sisters came to my aid here: Charlot and Lucy's decision to use their wits to secure their financial futures and find sexual satisfaction along the way led us back to Behn's narrator and the fortunes that brought her to Surinam. Students pondered what courses of action were open to women in a colonial setting. In a play as popular as Southerne's was, in an England whose profitable sugar colonies in Barbados and Jamaica were already established, the comic marriage plot offered an indirect way of affirming the kind of position white women could occupy in the new social order.

Our considering Lucy and Charlot Welldon shed light on Behn's place in Restoration literary culture. Behn too was a woman trying to make her way in what my students thought of as a man's world. Yet she was able to imagine a love story that posed a direct threat to her world's acceptance of slavery and its accompanying racial ideologies. Instead of accepting from me Behn's originality without question, students discovered it for themselves by looking at other works related to the novel and seeing how those works treated the relation among race, sex, and slavery in the early colonial period.

I am again teaching a graduate seminar on race in early modern literature, where our texts include *Abdelazer*, possibly *Lust's Dominion*, and the two *Oroonokos*. Making primary documents available to students has been easier this time around because of my university's access to *Early English Books Online*. Before, we read photocopies of microfilmed pages, and I always wondered if this technological clumsiness was the reason for students' coolness toward Southerne. Modern printed editions will also simplify our comparative reading of texts surrounding *Oroonoko*. Derek Hughes's *Versions of Blackness* brings together his new editions of the two versions of *Oroonoko* as well as Henry Neville's *The Isle of Pines* and Behn's *Abdelazer*, and it is available in paperback. Going back and forth between modern editions and digitized images of seventeenth-century printed pages can offer visual affirmation of the difference and distance that underpin my approach to early modern materials.

Unbearable Theater: *Oroonoko*'s Sentimental Afterlife

Scott J. Juengel

Recall, again, the grisly end of Aphra Behn's *Oroonoko*. Or, rather, summon Oroonoko's impassive countenance in his final moments, once the fulfillment of heterogeneous fantasy—black, Roman, "Japan'd," and resembling the "Ancient *Picts*" (40)—now a mask of unblinking externality. As the relays between interiority and expression seem to short-circuit in Behn's concluding tableau, we are left with only the hero's blank resolution: "they cut his Ears, and his Nose, and burn'd them; he still Smoak'd on, as if nothing had touch'd him" (64). In the spectacular horrors of this scene, one might miss that humble phrase: "as if nothing had touch'd him." The touch in question flickers between flogging and feeling, between the hero's imperviousness in response to his tormentors' cruelty and his emotional retreat from the tragedy that bears his name. Why at the very limits of character does Behn resist the protocols of expression and, by extension, the grammar of sentimental identification? The answer appears simple: Oroonoko's stoic turn befits the noble ("Roman") bearing that has been on display since his first appearance in the narrative, a bearing that surpasses even "[t]he most famous Statuary" in figure and equipoise (13). Moreover, to suffer outwardly would be to cede the moment entirely to his torturers, who in capturing Oroonoko wish to possess him entirely, soul as well as body. Indeed, their desire to manage the signification of the event is made manifest when the hero's corpse is quartered and parceled to every corner of the countryside for the purposes of "Terrifying and Grieving [the slaves] with frightful Spectacles of a mangl'd King" (65).

But while steely resolve might safeguard his inborn nobility, much depends on our identification with Oroonoko as a feeling subject: as readers, we have witnessed him swoon with desire and loss, instruct with "the most tender, and most passionate Heart that ever lov'd" (20), and prove too trusting by half. Even the odd diversion with the electric eel seems especially designed to make a spectacle of our hero's all-too-human sensitivity. G. A. Starr saw in Behn's text the kernel of a pre-Shaftesburyian sentimental novel, noting that the eventual eighteenth-century man of feeling would resemble "an exotic and endangered species," as much the victim of a Hobbesian worldview as a philosophical answer to it (362–63).

I linger with our dying hero and the spectacle of his grim detachment in order to reflect on teaching *Oroonoko* through its relation to the sentimental theater that follows from it. Despite the unstageable nature of its gruesome end, *Oroonoko* possessed a popular theatrical afterlife in the eighteenth century, resurrected in plays by Thomas Southerne, John Hawkesworth, Francis Gentleman, John Ferriar, and others.[1] Because later theatrical versions improvised on Southerne more than on Behn, this essay considers how the problems of staging *Oroonoko* in 1696 lay bare a strategically half-realized sentimentality in Behn's original, while recasting the question that Behn's final scene makes so palpable: How much human suffering can one bear in literature?

I rarely teach one *Oroonoko* without the other now, in part because Southerne explicitly queries the relation between theatrical performance and prose fiction so central to Behn's novelistic turn, but also because the pairing reveals to students the political potential residing in, if sometimes obscured by, sentimentality. Without a doubt, the theatrical version is an ungainly affair (cringe-inducing in its own way, according to my twenty-first-century students), but the elusive politics of Behn's original, long a matter of critical contestation, paradoxically gains contour when read against the dramatic adaptation, an adaptation that historically nearly eclipsed the original.

In the dedicatory epistle to the duke of Devonshire that opens his 1696 *Oroonoko* (eds. Novak and Rodes), Southerne confesses his reliance on Behn for "the occasion of a most passionate distress in my last play," a reference to *The Fatal Marriage*, staged two years earlier, and now he "run[s] further into her debt" with his latest production (3). At the heart of Southerne's discomfort is a measure of incredulity, as he is unable to comprehend why Behn, a celebrated playwright herself, chose not to tell her African hero's story through performance:

> She had a great command of the stage, and I have often wondered that she would bury her favorite hero in a novel when she might have revived him in the scene. She thought either that no actor could represent him, or she could not bear him represented. And I believe the last when I remember what I have heard from a friend of hers, that she always told his story more feelingly than she writ it. Whatever happened to him in Surinam, he has mended his condition in England. He was born here under your Grace's influence, and that has carried his fortune farther into the world than all the poetical stars that I could have solicited for his success. (4)

Southerne's speculation regarding Behn's reluctance and his ensuing description of revivifying and repatriating *Oroonoko* for the English stage represent a complicated reading of both Behn's original narrative and the psychological and cultural politics that governed her choice of genre and medium. Countering *Oroonoko*'s interment in prose fiction with the hero's subsequent reanimation through theater, Southerne slyly returns the audience to the final scene of Behn's novel: instead of being torn asunder in Surinam, Oroonoko is now "mended" in England. Southerne's performative trope not only aspires to suture together what was so violently dismembered in his predecessor's text but, by reclaiming Oroonoko as English-reborn and fortunate, Southerne curiously transposes the entire racial ideology of the 1688 novel: the hero is figuratively rehabilitated as the English ward of the duke of Devonshire.

Of course, Southerne's galvanic metaphor is designed to suggest live bodies on real stages: more specifically, he recounts how the duke's tasteful judgment directed the playwright to John Verbruggen (4), the actor who would first play the part of Oroonoko. Verbruggen thus materializes what was unimaginable to Southerne's Behn. But what precisely is the source of the hero's unrepresentability and, by extension, Behn's arrested theatricality? His noble bearing? His "perfect Ebony" skin (13)? His grisly demise? Given my interest here in emotional elocution, Southerne's determination that *Oroonoko* is unbearable, or that the story elicits a superabundance of feeling, maps the expressive politics of the novel's ending—itself unbearable on numerous levels—back onto its author's psychic life. According to Southerne's scenario, the writing of *Oroonoko* in prose becomes either the bulwark against its misappropriation by others or the diverting of something otherwise too exquisite, or dreadful, into a less volatile medium.

So then how does Southerne reimagine Behn's tale to attenuate its psychological and political freight? What theatrical elements does he tease out of Behn's novel, and how does teaching his play alongside the original reveal for students the sentimental history that the original makes possible?

It is useful to follow Southerne's lead and consider the "mending" of the ending, particularly the manner in which Southerne sentimentalizes the racial violence that the original shuddered under. My students often struggle with or instinctively devalue the moments of heightened sentiment in Behn's text in their rush to determine where the novel stands on abolition. Southerne, on the other hand, actively resuscitates the dead melodrama of *Oroonoko*, creating a hero who persistently shrinks from the political quandaries of the novel, going so far as to capitulate to his own subjection. As he tells his incredulous comrade Aboan, their owners "bought us in an honest way of trade. . . . We ought not to complain . . ." (3.2.108, 119). Similarly, early in the play Oroonoko is accused of being "troublesome" by Captain Driver, the mercenary slaver who fears the African's mutinous nature (1.2.186). However, the term is notably blanched of its political force when Southerne's hero describes himself a scene or two later. "I am troublesome," Oroonoko laments, "My swoll'n heart / Bursts out its passage, and I must complain" (2.2.50–52). Such a shift in the semantics of distress—from sedition to surrender to sniveling complaint—surreptitiously emplots Southerne's general quietism, as his play routinely chooses pathos over politics.

But Behn's scenes of violence and dismemberment do not disappear entirely, for Southerne manages to encrypt her plot within his own. When Oroonoko first appears on stage, fettered and belittled by the cruel Driver, he announces his misfortune: "I am unfortunate, but not ashamed / Of being so" (1.2.241–42). Accepting the "slavish habit" he now wears, he envisions future cruelty that will not touch him: "Hard fare and whips and chains may overpow'r / The frailer flesh and bow my body down. / But there's another, nobler part of me, / Out of your reach, which you can never tame" (251–55).

Significantly, Oroonoko's gesture to his bowed and broken body initiates a pattern of imagery—what one might call torture in the subjunctive—that haunts his speeches throughout the drama. These iterative scenes embed the irreproducible ending of Behn's text in the play's rhetorical work, often in the form of sentimental flourish, as when Oroonoko tells Imoinda, "I have a heart; but if it could be false / To my first vows ever to love again, / These honest hands should tear it from my breast / And throw the traitor from me" (2.3.64–67). The telltale flinging of torn flesh, repeated throughout Behn's text—first by the tribal War Captains (50) and then by Oroonoko himself (62–63)—becomes a maudlin trope for inconstancy.

This form of intertextual disfiguring is deployed most poignantly and self-consciously as Oroonoko and Aboan suspect that Hottman, a blustering fellow slave, is a coward at heart. In order to expose Hottman's sham, Oroonoko asks Aboan to observe Hottman as Oroonoko seems to conjure up his own death:

> OROONOKO. (*aside to* Aboan). Observe him now.
> (*Aloud.*) I could die altogether, like a man,
> As you, and you, and all of us may do;
> But who can promise for his bravery
> Upon the rack, where fainting, weary life,
> Hunted through every limb, is forced to feel
> An agonizing death of all its parts?
> Who can bear this? Resolve to be impaled?
> His skin flayed off and roasted yet alive?
> The quivering flesh torn from his broken bones
> By burning pincers? Who can bear these pains?
> (3.4.68–76)

Hottman responds in confusion and fear, "They are not to be borne," but Oroonoko mocks him as a "man of mighty words," as one who "cannot hide his fear" (77–79).

Oroonoko's imaginative portrait of "agonizing death" follows Behn's graphic ending in brutal detail, but his insistent "Who can bear this?" sounds a question unspoken in the original: Hottman's exaggerated response to Oroonoko's recitation—his rolling eyes, evident fear, confusion—is clearly not the response of Behn's stoic hero, who did indeed "bear these pains" without so much as a grimace. Southerne's chiasmic displacement of Behn's violent tableau—real torture is borne impassively, imagined torture evokes exaggerated passions—allows the playwright to recognize the administrative terrors of the original without realizing them on stage, all the while tutoring his audience in the politics of empathy. The scene dramatizes the transitive and intransitive properties of *to suffer*, whereby the verb can signal a physical experience as such as well as its proxy (e.g., "to tolerate, permit, acknowledge"). Here Southerne recapitulates the end of Behn's novel but accesses what is unseen in the original: not only does Hottman's reaction demonstrate what is involved in suffering the thought of torture, it reflexively returns to the audience their own natural horror and the perils of sensitive identification.

Teaching Behn's text alongside Southerne's adaptation provides students access to a nearly contemporaneous interpretation of the 1688 *Oroonoko*, and the play's equivocations and attenuations frequently highlight moments of political and affective deliberation. Southerne cut the Coramantien episodes from the original, added a clumsy comic subplot involving two young Englishwomen "a-husband-hunting" in Surinam (1.1.4), converted Imoinda into a Desdemona-like European, and restyled the hero as a figure of accommodation who will not purchase his liberty "at the Christian price / Of black ingratitude" (3.2.102–03). When Aboan justifies revolt against their captors by "self-defense and natural liberty" (88), Oroonoko rejects the conspiracy, causing Aboan to plead, "O royal sir, remember who you are" (133). With this entreaty, Southerne's Aboan seeks to summon the intrepid side of Behn's hero rather than the swooning, submissive Oroonoko who, believing Imoinda dead, forsakes his bow and pledges to "abandon the small Remains of his Life to Sighs and Tears" (28). The more sentimental Oroonoko of Behn's must be roused to return to battle by his soldiers, who "fell on their Faces at the Foot of his Carpet . . . and besought him with earnest Prayers and Tears, to lead 'em forth to Battel, . . . and implor'd him to have regard to his Glory, and to the World" (28). Yet Southerne clearly fancies the prostrate hero, whose postures of grief here and in the woods beyond Parham theatrically concentrate the sentimental elements of the original. Indeed, Southerne's Oroonoko baldly petitions for compassion for the loss of Imoinda in Coramantien ("Do, pity me. / Pity's akin to love, and every thought / Of that soft kind is welcome to my soul. / I would be pitied here"), to which Blanford vows to bear what Behn and her narrator could not: "I dare promise to bear / A part in your distress, if not assist you" (2.2.57–60, 63–64).

Sentimental drama traffics in sad discourses and extraordinary melancholy, and Southerne's final scenes are prolonged exercises in pathos designed to render Oroonoko's irresolution spectacularly visible. Shortly after Aboan takes his own life, Oroonoko insists to Imoinda that "there is now no farther use of words" (5.5.106), yet what follows is a far cry from the stoic, pipe-smoking hero of Behn's original. For the next 170 lines, until Imoinda stabs herself, there are constant references to trembling, sighs, and weeping. Oroonoko exclaims that his "gushing eyes / Betray a weakness which they never knew" (129–30).

The final exchange with Imoinda about their suicide pact is excruciatingly protracted, a series of feints and stuttering half measures that follow from Oroonoko's insistent questions: "What can we do?" "Which is the way?" "[W]hat shall I do?" "Where shall I strike?" (155, 216, 225, 231). Handed the dagger to dispatch his willing wife, Oroonoko drops the weapon and, according to the stage directions, "throws himself on the ground" with the lament, "I cannot bear it" (249). His pusillanimity is most poignantly rendered when the weapon is returned to his hand and he must confront the horror of their preordained fate: "I'll turn my face away and do it so" (269).

Oroonoko's longing to turn away from the very tragedy he enacts onstage affectively captures and distills a desire that haunts both *Oroonoko* texts: the desire to not witness. When Oroonoko begins to appear a threat—because he seems "more retir'd and thoughtful"—Behn's narrator warns him that any resistance could "possibly compel us to treat him so as I shou'd be very loath to behold" (41). Later, when she fears that an enraged Oroonoko might "Cut all our Throats," the narrator retreats "down the River, to be secur'd." However, after the slave is recaptured and savagely beaten, she admits, "I suppose I had Authority and Interest enough there, had I suspected any such thing, to have prevented it" (57). Of course, she had suspected exactly such an insupportable episode, one she already knew she would not wish to abide or behold.

Clearly, Oroonoko's killing of Imoinda is fundamentally different from the spectacular brutality exacted by slavers, and when Oroonoko wishes to look away, we naturally read it as a sign of his faltering nerve. But then again, this is precisely the point. Southerne effectively erases the most extreme scenes of plantocratic violence, channeling their horrid efficiency into gestures of Romantic equivocation, a tactic consistent with Southerne's support for the amelioration of slave conditions (Rosenthal [Iwanisziw] 92–93). The play's amplified sentimentality thus imagines the continuance of the system of colonial slavery under softer forms of power. The tragedy of Oroonoko will not change with such reforms, however, for our sentimental hero makes clear that he is as much "a slave to love!" (5.5.1).

In other words, where Behn's *Oroonoko* could possibly be open to an ameliorist reading—although not an abolitionist one—in its portrait of sadistic and retributive violence, Southerne's *Oroonoko* presents the optimal conditions for sentimental drama. The playwright understands his decision to elide such violence as a means of mending what haunted Behn, therein providing the conditions by which the drama could be expressed "more feelingly" and thus returning us symbolically to the intimate scene of a story heard among friends. The raw power of the original *Oroonoko* has been effectively domesticated.

Of course, in the end, Southerne was right. The play was an enormous commercial success, and Southerne's redaction quickly became the definitive version of *Oroonoko* for the period—even as his comic plot was routinely maligned. Recognizing *Oroonoko*'s dramatic afterlife provides students with a historical case study in intertextual sentiment, and to teach Behn's novel in context is to acknowledge how pervasively the heroic slave was a theatrical incarnation, a figure of sentimentality mobilized in the service of a hard-edged political culture.

NOTE

[1] These and other manifestations of *Oroonoko* can be found in Iwanisziw, Oroonoko.

Two *Oroonokos*: Behn's and Bandele's

Jessica Munns

One of the first points to make to students reading Behn's novel and 'Biyi Bandele's play together is that Bandele's play, first performed by the Royal Shakespeare Company at The Other Place in June 1999, is not a direct adaptation of Behn's novel. His play is partly based on John Hawkesworth's 1760 adaptation of Thomas Southerne's 1696 adaptation of it. As such, Bandele's play takes its place in a long series of dramatic adaptations of Behn's *Oroonoko* that include late-eighteenth-century ameliorist and abolitionist dramas such as *The Benevolent Planters* (1789) and *The Prince of Angola* (1788).[1]

Bandele's *Aphra Behn's* Oroonoko *in a New Adaptation* divides into two parts, Coramantien in the first and Surinam in the second. The Surinam part, which derives from Hawkesworth, is shorter. Bandele concentrates on Africa in the early stages of white colonial trade as the slavers move in opportunistically to profit from internal power struggles. Unlike Behn, he is not much interested in Surinam. However, his play is more a meditation on than an adaptation of Behn's novel.

Bandele's play differs markedly from prior adaptations of *Oroonoko* and in some ways is closer to it. First, his is the only dramatic version that begins the story in Africa, as Behn's narrative does after a brief description of Surinam. Only in his play does one encounter Oroonoko and Imoinda as free people living in a lively and poetic, if violent, culture. Students should consider how this portrayal affects our response later to the enslaved couple. Second, although Behn's Oroonoko and Imoinda are Africans, natives of Coramantien, many stage adaptations made Imoinda European. Perhaps the presentation of the love of an African man and a European woman fascinated the audience, or perhaps they were simply used to such a relationship from Shakespeare's *Othello*. Bandele returns to Behn's conception of African lovers first thwarted by Oroonoko's great rival, the king of Coramantien, and then enslaved in the English colony of Surinam. Given that Bandele is closest to Behn in his setting and in the ethnicity of the major characters, discussion might begin by comparing their two versions of Africa and of Imoinda and Oroonoko.

Behn sets her novel in an African state that bears the name of a fort and trading post, not of a country. Her Africa, as Joanna Lipking has pointed out, "fits its seventeenth-century profile as a place of wealthy trader kings" (Preface xiii) and provides characteristics typical of seventeenth-century ideas about exotic places, such as the king's otan (harem). But the court of the king of Coramantien also echoes European courts as depicted in contemporary histories, plays, and novels, featuring jealous mistresses and scheming statesmen. Indeed, given the number of mistresses both Charles II and Louis XIV had, the otan in Coramantien suggests the court of London or Paris. Behn draws on classical sources when she describes Oroonoko as mourning the reported death of Imoinda Achilles-like in his tent while the tide of the battle turns against his army (27–29). The African part of Behn's novel thus draws on a range of contemporary sources—the popular and scandalous romans à clef, romance, classical traditions, and of course knowledge of the African slave trade in which England was engaged.

In contrast, Bandele's Coramantien is not an exoticized stand-in for a European court. Bandele has reset the African scenes in his native Nigeria, in the palaces and compounds of Yoruba nobles, where the Yoruba gods, such as Eshu, the trickster god, and Shango, the thunder god, are frequently invoked. In Kabiyesi, the king of Coramantien, Bandele has created a comic monster. Kabiyesi is a more fully drawn character than is Oroonoko's grandfather in Behn's novel, although like him he combines sexual appetite—particularly for Imoinda—with sexual impotence. His lack of priapic prowess is a comic theme throughout the first part. A former mistress, Lady Onola, scorns his abilities, while his praise singers stoutly rap about his sexual feats: "His Highness—long may he reign— / Fathered a child in Liverpool / While emptying his testicles / In Coramantien!" (29).

If Bandele's Oroonoko is no English gentleman, Behn's is. Behn grants her Oroonoko a European education, an innate horror at the execution of Charles I, and even hair that is styled to look like a periwig: "His Hair came down to his Shoulders, by the Aids of Art; which was, by pulling it out with a Quill, and keeping it comb'd; of which he took particular Care" (13–14). He is a Restoration dandy, his comb ever at hand. The episodes and descriptions of Oroonoko's interest in and knowledge of English and Continental culture are omitted from Bandele's play. What Oroonoko or any of the characters know of the wider world, they know only through their contacts with the white slave traders. Bandele's Oroonoko is at first a callow youth who enjoys playing traditional games and dancing with his friend Aboan (20–21). But he grows up fast as he faces war, love, betrayal, and loss. Bandele's kingdom is an imaginative historical reconstruction of a seventeenth-century African kingdom; it is also a modern place of slick politicians and strong-minded women, filled with anachronisms—such as references to raincoats. Throughout the first part, Bandele writes in an upbeat, often slangy style that mingles traditional invocations and chants, passages of eloquent poetry, and contemporary slang and clichés: "I scratch your back— / You scratch mine" (34). Is his mixture of styles equivalent to Behn's often breathless and hurried interjections such as, "I had forgot to tell you . . ." (40), combined with a *précieuse* language of the "Parley of the Eyes" (22)? Possibly, but the tonal mixing may be an independent result: both writers, deeply in tune with their times, tell a story that moves from high to low, from palace to slave shed, and from romance to tragedy, and the language follows the shifts.

On one level Behn's novel may refer to James II and his second wife, Mary of Modena. Like Oroonoko, James was often referred to as Caesar, and it is plausible that the name Imoinda is meant as a near anagram of Mary of Modena (Todd, *Secret Life* 418–19). Certainly the Eurocentric classical terms used to describe Imoinda and Oroonoko—"the beautiful *Black Venus*, to our young *Mars*" (14)—are similar to those Behn had employed to describe James and Mary in her Pindaric poem on James's coronation in 1685. But if her novel can be read in part as a political allegory, it was important for Behn to present Imoinda, even if improbably, as Oroonoko's virgin bride and thereafter his chaste and "Constant" wife (65). To that end, the king of Coramantien is impotent. He dares not kill her for fear of alienating his powerful grandson. Instead, he sells her into slavery and lies to Oroonoko that Imoinda is dead. In Surinam, the beauty of the renamed Clemene wins her admirers, including Trefry (38). When Imoinda's prior relationship with Oroonoko is revealed, the two are married with "much Magnificence" (40).

Imoinda, eulogized in the final lines of Behn's novel as "the Brave, the Beautiful, and the Constant *Imoinda*" (65), is all of these in Bandele's play, but in tune with his upbeat style, she is also occasionally caustic and witty. She is subject to horrific physical abuse while in Coramantien. After she stabs and presumably castrates Kabiyesi, Orombo, the king's scheming chief adviser, says, "Let's show her how real men do it" and "*lowers his trousers*" (63). Later, battered and chained, she is handed over by Orombo to the white slave traders. In Surinam, she is treated with respect, and the second part of the play opens with Stanmore and Trefry discussing Deputy Governor Byam's love for Clemene, a love that Byam confirms when he enters and admits he is "[e]very day more in love with her" (75). One result of fusing a shortened version of Hawkesworth's play, which is what we are seeing here, to Bandele's is that life can seem much more savage for free Africans in Africa than for enslaved Africans in Surinam.

In a talk at the Aphra Behn Society Conference in Denver in 2000, Bandele admitted that he was more interested in adapting the first part of Behn's novel, set in Africa, than in moving on to the part set in Surinam. Writing three hundred years after her death and from a postcolonial African rather than an English perspective, he had no interest in elaborating on life in a slave colony. Encouraged by the director, Gregory Doran, and the dramaturge, Simon Reade, he turned to Hawkesworth's version of Southerne's version of Behn's novel (Munns 190). Thus any comparison of Behn and Bandele must involve Hawkesworth, as Bandele's work is an amalgamation of these three different texts and styles. Bandele surely did not mean to represent Coramantien as savage, brutal, and vicious compared with Surinam, where slaves were worked to death, but is it possible that the mingling of texts produces this impression? The contrast is certainly strong between the colorful world of song, dance, and poetry in Coramantien and the drab world of slavery in Surinam, where the African captives' songs become laments. Since much of Behn's gruesome material, such as Imoinda's decapitation and Oroonoko's dismemberment, is omitted, does Bandele's Surinam seems safer than Coramantien?

Bandele, like all the dramatic adaptors, makes Oroonoko's death less horrific. After Imoinda welcomes her death at his hands, Oroonoko neatly breaks her neck, then forces Trefry to shoot him, thus dying rather cleanly at his friend's hand. In Behn's novel, Surinam is both a heaven and a hell: a garden of paradise and a place where dreadful events occur. Hawkesworth's Surinam is basically Southerne's without the humorous subplot, a place of pain for Oroonoko and Imoinda but also a dignified and civilized colony. Does Bandele's sudden move to a seventeenth-century English slave colony, where the English characters speak in the courtly dialogue of the times, heighten the sense of misery and the clash of cultures? Is the disjunction between the language and styles of the two parts of his play a way to convey the experience of capture and slavery? Is there both a gain and a loss in the abrupt change of styles?

Oroonoko's relationship with Imoinda in Behn's novel and in Bandele's play should be compared. In both, his struggle to protect her body, first from his grandfather and then from the colonists, concludes in the desperate solution of destroying her. Imoinda is a warrior princess, not only a good wife who fights beside Oroonoko; hers is the main voice urging him to revolt. In Behn, it can be argued that Oroonoko's strongest relationship is with the narrator, "whom he call'd his *Great Mistress*" and who converses with him seriously while somewhat dismissively teaching Imoinda "pretty Works" and telling her "Stories of Nuns" (41). In Bandele, Imoinda fades from the scene in the second part (where she is not depicted as pregnant), and there is no figure who corresponds to Behn's narrator. Instead of having strong relationships with two women, Bandele's hero has strong relationships with two men, Aboan and Trefry. Aboan admires Oroonoko, and Trefry seems more than half in love with him. Simon Reade has said that homoeroticism was "a conscious production sub-text" (Munns 191). Homoeroticism, sexual instability, and multivalence can, Jonathan Goldberg suggests, be found in Behn's *Oroonoko*, in terms of the relationship of the narrator and Oroonoko and the authority and authorship of the narrator. The narrator wields a "Female Pen" (36), standing in for Mr. Trefry, who meant to record the narrative, and Goldberg states that "[t]hrough gestures of distance and of identification, the position of the 'Female Pen' and the authority of Trefry are intertwined" (50). At times, as in the erotic description of Oroonoko and Imoinda consummating their love (24–25), Goldberg suggests that the narrator occupies all possible perspectives—she is both yielding maid and ardent lover (66), and one might add that she is aroused voyeur as well. In Bandele's play, Oroonoko's main relationship in Surinam is with his captors, in particular the compassionate Trefry, rather than with Imoinda, and Trefry, instead of numbering among Imoinda's admirers, is focused on Oroonoko. The final moments in which Oroonoko provokes Trefry into killing him, therefore, create a *Liebestod* finale, destroying two people, one on either side of the machinery of colonialism. By creating so strong and dramatic a relationship between Oroonoko and Trefry, Bandele restores an aspect of the earlier stage adaptations—a cross-racial love or friendship—hinted at in Behn's work in Oroonoko's admiration for his "*Great Mistress*."

Behn's Oroonoko and Imoinda are Eurocentric creations, and students can be encouraged to look for ways in which Bandele's hero and heroine are depicted in African terms—in relation, for instance, to language and customs. Is Oroonoko a weaker character in Bandele's play than in Behn's, and, if so, why? Was it less important for Bandele to depict a strong black hero than it was for Behn? In removing the narrator figure from his dramatic adaptation, is a powerful female presence also removed? Does Bandele's comic-horrific depiction of Kabiyesi relate to modern African states and add an apt political dimension that corresponds to Behn's political analogies to seventeenth-century England?

Is Behn's Imoinda, fighting beside her husband, as strong a, if not a stronger, depiction of a woman than Bandele's more passive heroine? What difference does our understanding of the development of the slave trade make to our reading of either text? Does Bandele's postcolonial text, which emphasizes the pain and cruelty of slavery, encourage one to read differently Behn's more courtly description of Oroonoko's and Imoinda's ordeal of captivity? Or is there a similarity between the earlier narrative, written at the dawn of English colonialism, and that by Bandele, written so much later?

There are many ways one can compare, contrast, and contextualize the novel and the play, since the pertinence of these two works to our current concerns with race, ethnicity, and gender makes their combined study both fascinating and important.

NOTE

[1] Editions of these plays, including Bandele's, are found in Iwanisziw's Oroonoko*: Adaptations and Offshoots*.

Representations of Race, Status, and Slavery in Behn's *Oroonoko* and Equiano's *Interesting Narrative*

Vincent Carretta

Nothing in *The Interesting Narrative of the Life of Olaudah Equiano; or, Gustavus Vassa, the African: Written by Himself* (1789) indicates that Olaudah Equiano had even heard of, let alone ever read, Aphra Behn's *Oroonoko; or, The Royal Slave* (1688). Yet Behn's fictional biography and Equiano's spiritual autobiography can usefully frame a course in representations of what we now call race. The assigned primary texts are organized chronologically to give the students the chance to watch history unfolding. Rather than lecturing to my students about the range of people classified as black or colored in the seventeenth and eighteenth centuries, I prefer to have them talk about how surprised they are to discover that range in the primary texts, a discovery that leads students to more theoretical concerns about race and nationality. Beginning a course with *Oroonoko* and ending with *The Interesting Narrative* enables us to reconstruct the evolution of such concepts as race, identity, status, slavery, and abolition during the long eighteenth century in writings by and about people of African descent.

Most of my students initially assume that the aforementioned concepts are synchronically stable, and they have already had some familiarity with nineteenth- and twentieth-century African American literature before they enter my classes. We spend the first day of class discussing their definitions of the concepts, which they often illustrate with references to the *Narrative of the Life of Frederick Douglass*. Then we move on to *Oroonoko*. Rather than telling my students that *Oroonoko* and other assigned readings will challenge their preconceptions, I simply ask them to note for class discussions anything in the texts that they find surprising or that seems historically inaccurate. They quickly discover from the works of Behn, Equiano, and others that the concepts they had agreed on at the beginning of the semester must be approached diachronically and are subject to change. In other words, time and place matter.

The theme of liberation found in *Oroonoko*, the *Interesting Narrative*, and other works in the course does not surprise students familiar with the nineteenth-century North American models of slavery, Africa, slave or escape narratives, and abolition. But they are startled by the diversity of the authors, subjects, and forms of the writings produced by and about people of African descent during the seventeenth and eighteenth centuries. The familiar nineteenth-century model includes tobacco or cotton plantations worked by Creole (i.e., American-born) slaves of African descent owned by Creole masters of European descent. Africa, when it appears at all, is a mythical past, a romanticized future, or the victim of present-day imperialist European powers. In the nineteenth-century model, slaves are all born in America and essentially undifferentiated from one another except by occupation. Slave owners and traders are all white, though in reality some free blacks owned black slaves in the United States (Berlin 38, 323), and the whole economic institution of slavery is defended by assertions of the racial inferiority of the enslaved.

The previous centuries present a far more varied picture. Enslaved people were imported throughout that period directly to the colonies from Africa, especially to the sugar-growing plantations of the West Indies, which included the setting of *Oroonoko*, where the very high mortality rate meant that the native slave population was not self-sustaining. By 1750, the majority of slaves in British North America, on the other hand, were native-born, with the population growing by natural increase (Berlin 83, 264). Europeans were dependent on Africans for the maintenance of the slave trade between the seventeenth and early nineteenth centuries because disease and local African political powers restricted Europeans to factories (trading posts) on the coast of Africa. Very few enslaved West Africans could have been exported to the Americas without the complicity of their fellow Africans. Much was made during the period of the differing suitability of the various African peoples for enslavement: some African nations were seen as too warlike, for example. Many slaves, and most in the West Indies, knew from their own African experience that being black was not synonymous with being enslaved. The fairly frequent West Indian slave revolts were consequently almost always led by non-Creole black Africans, for whom freedom was a memory of the recent past rather than a dream of the distant future. In the nineteenth-century model, North American slaves, however, were at least somewhat acculturated to slavery, having been born into it and knowing no other way of life.

Slavery was perceived primarily as an economic concern rather than a moral problem before the last decades of the eighteenth century. The initial basis of African slavery was predominantly political and financial rather than racial. Since we tend to see what we expect to see, most of my students initially read *Oroonoko* superficially as an account of race-based slavery with an abolitionist message. They assume that race is always defined by phenotype and that any objection or resistance to being enslaved must be based on the emancipationist premise that slavery is an evil and easily defined institution. But, inevitably, some students notice immediately that Behn uses race in ways that seem odd to them, and never quite in the way they expected. By looking more closely at the text, all the students recognize without my having to tell them that references to Imoinda as her father's "only Daughter left of his Race" (14), the African king's "having no Sons of all his Race remaining alive" (26), and Oroonoko as being "the last of his Great Race" (40) cannot possibly mean race in the sense they are accustomed to. Race can only mean lineage, or a genealogical line, in these contexts. The closest Behn comes in *Oroonoko* to using race in a way familiar to my students is when Oroonoko denounces his white oppressors as members of "*such a degenerate Race*" (53).

Once my students' fundamental preconception about race has been unsettled by the textual evidence, they become more open to having their other assumptions interrogated. Recognition of the equation of race and lineage in *Oroonoko* helps them understand why Behn devotes more than a third of her text to Oroonoko's life in Africa. Behn's oxymoronic subtitle—*The Royal Slave*—begins to make sense to them: to Behn's readers who share her belief that societies are naturally hierarchical, Oroonoko's African lineage, or race, grants him a status that should render him above the condition of a slave. We discuss Aristotle's distinction between natural slaves and natural masters (1989–92), as well as contemporaneous seventeenth-century arguments justifying the enslavement of prisoners of war (Loomba and Burton 44–45), as background to appreciating Oroonoko's appeal to his countrymen to revolt:

> *And why,* said he, *my dear Friends and Fellow-sufferers, shou'd we be Slaves to an unknown People? Have they Vanquish'd us Nobly in Fight? Have they Won us in Honourable Battel? And are we, by the chance of War, become their Slaves? This wou'd not anger a Noble Heart, this wou'd not animate a Souldiers Soul; no, but we are Bought and Sold like Apes, or Monkeys, to be the Sport of Women, Fools and Cowards; and the Support of Rogues, Runagades, that have abandon'd their own Countries, for Rapin, Murders, Thefts and Villanies. . . .* (52)

When Oroonoko's fellow enslaved Africans fail to follow his lead in rebelling against their white masters, he admits to being "asham'd of what he had done, in endeavoring to make those Free, who were by Nature *Slaves*" (56).

Social status supersedes race as a defining category not only in Behn's *Oroonoko* but also in Thomas Southerne's 1696 play, *Oroonoko*, which was based on Behn's novel and performed repeatedly during the eighteenth century. The 1776 frontispiece to Southerne's *Oroonoko* illustrates the complexity of complexion and status during the seventeenth and eighteenth centuries. Charles Grignion's print, after a painting by John James Barralet, shows that Southerne saw no reason not to represent Behn's enslaved African heroine, Imoinda, as the enslaved white wife of Oroonoko. As the costumes they wear in the frontispiece suggest, Imoinda and Oroonoko should *own* slaves, not *be* them. The pathos of the play is not caused by the institution of slavery but rather by the inappropriate enslavement of those who should, by right of birth, be at the top of the social order (Carretta 285).

The concept of the African too inherently noble to be enslaved was not restricted to fictional accounts. In two separate historical cases during the first half of the eighteenth century, Africans who were thought to have been wrongfully enslaved were ransomed into freedom when their situations became publicly known. Job Ben Solomon and William Ansah Sessarakoo were enslaved in Africa and taken, respectively, to Maryland and the West Indies. When their fates became known in London, the Royal African Company redeemed Ben Solomon, and the British government bought Sessarakoo's freedom. Both men, slave owners themselves in their native lands, were repatriated to Africa (285–88).

My students' predictable questions about Behn's references to "*Indian Slaves*" (51) and white "*Slaves* for Four Years, that Inhabited among the *Negro* Houses" in Surinam (51–52) allow me to introduce the historical context of unfree labor in which *Oroonoko* is embedded. Slavery was not strictly defined by white ownership of black workers during the period framed by *Oroonoko* and the *Interesting Narrative*. Writers remarked on the existence of white slaves, especially in eastern Europe, and the word *slave* itself comes from the word *Slav*. Slavery was not abolished in Muscovy (Russia) until 1723, when it was superseded by serfdom. The enslavement of Christian Europeans by Muslim African whites on the Barbary Coast or by Muslim Turks in Asia was a major concern during the period, getting more treatment in print before 1770 than did the condition of black African slaves. Britain was not able to force North African Muslims to abolish the enslavement of European Christians until 1816, nearly a decade after it had abolished its own trade in black Africans.

Various forms of coerced labor existed in Britain itself, some of which were introduced into the American colonies. Coerced labor of whites in Britain and its colonies included indentured servants (and even apprentices), who signed away their freedom for a specified amount of time in exchange for room and board and a guaranteed job (or job training), in effect becoming voluntary slaves. At least fifty thousand convicts were transported at the government's expense from Britain to the colonies to be sold as servants to work out their sentences following the Transportation Act of 1718 (Ekirch 1).

Perhaps the most significant of the many improbabilities my students notice in *Oroonoko* is the deference shown to Imoinda and Oroonoko by virtually everyone in Surinam. But having discussed the notion of natural hierarchy, they understand why Imoinda is not raped by white men who have power over her but whom she outranks. And the welcome Oroonoko receives from fellow Africans he had conquered in war and enslaved becomes understandable in light of Behn's royalist ideology. Consequently, he "was receiv'd more like a Governor, than a Slave." Not surprisingly, Oroonoko "was infinitely glad to find his Grandure confirm'd by the Adoration of all the Slaves" (37).

Oroonoko ultimately rebels not because he is mistreated but because he suffers status dissonance as a "Royal Slave" whose inappropriate condition would be passed on to his unborn child. Oroonoko is by genealogical descent a member of a naturally superior race in Behn's Surinam. But although he resists his own enslavement and unsuccessfully leads a slave revolt to assert his proper status, Oroonoko is an abolitionist neither in the pre-nineteenth-century sense of being opposed to the transatlantic slave trade nor in the nineteenth-century sense of opposing the institution of slavery. For example, Oroonoko unhesitatingly offers to buy his and Imoinda's freedom with "either Gold, or a vast quantity of Slaves" (40–41), because he has no objection in principle to the institution of slavery. Indeed, *Oroonoko* endorses slavery even as it denounces the improper enslavement of its hero.

A century after *Oroonoko*, the irony of fighting for the freedom to enslave was highlighted in June 1772, when the lord chief justice of the King's bench, Lord Mansfield, declared in the case of James Somerset that Somerset's owner could not legally force his slave to return from England to the West Indies. Although Mansfield's ruling was technically limited to the question of the legality of forcibly removing someone in England to colonial slavery, it was immediately misinterpreted to mean that slaves were free as soon as they set foot on English soil. Advertisements for sales of slaves, notices of runaway slaves, and attempts to enforce colonial slave laws in Britain—all already rare in England—disappeared after the Mansfield ruling. Colonial newspapers advised their slave-owning readers not to bring their human property to England.

The political status of people of African descent became a subject for public argument in the ideological conflict during the American Revolution. The Americans' victory in the civil war that we now call the American Revolution led to a visible increase after 1783 in the numbers of free blacks accompanying their loyalist former masters as they left the former thirteen colonies for Canada and London, along with the many slaves who had emancipated themselves by joining the British forces in the war. The sight of unemployed and impoverished blacks in London prompted the formation in 1786 of the Committee for the Relief of the Black Poor, which promoted the project for resettlement in Sierra Leone, in which Equiano played a major role. According to a report in the newspaper the *Public Advertiser* in 1787, sympathy for the black poor was so widespread that white beggars disguised themselves as blacks to increase their incomes (Report).

The aftermath of the defeat by the colonists was a time for national reassessment in Britain, a time well suited for the potentially spiritually regenerating moral crusade against Britain's dominant role in the transatlantic slave trade. The Committee for Effecting the Abolition of the Slave Trade, most of whose members were Quakers, was created in London in 1787 and began distributing anti-slave-trade pamphlets throughout the country at the peak of the African slave trade. The late-eighteenth-century crusade to end British involvement in the transatlantic slave trade prompted defenders of the trade to challenge the status of enslaved people of African descent as human beings. Scores of publications were produced by both sides in the national debate.

Against this background, Equiano published his *Interesting Narrative*, the first full account of the slave trade and slavery published by a former African slave. Equiano's work, which went through nine British editions between 1789 and 1794, is the longest and most significant publication by an African Briton in the century. Equiano asserted his British identity by placing himself centrally in the context of eighteenth-century writings against the slave trade by whites. He structured his *Interesting Narrative* as a petition against the trade, beginning with an address to the members of both houses of Parliament and virtually ending with a petition to Queen Charlotte. More significantly, Equiano offered his *Interesting Narrative* as the account of the slave trade from the African victim's perspective that its opponents needed.

My students are well prepared by the time we consider the *Interesting Narrative* to notice the many ways in which Equiano also challenges their preconceptions. Like the fictional Oroonoko a century earlier, Equiano is highborn, his father an Igbo tribal elder, one of the *embrenché* or scarified decision makers (Carretta 9), and so his enslaved condition is as oxymoronic as the notion of Oroonoko, "the royal slave." *Oroonoko* is the tale of a tragic figure who fails to regain the noble status denied him by enslavement. The *Interesting Narrative* is Equiano's account of the successful recovery of his status. Equiano asserts his identity as a Briton more fully than any of his predecessors of African descent.

British and American identities were political constructions invented in the eighteenth century rather than the traditional ethnic or religious categories, which they subsumed. Thus after the Union of 1707 one could be a Scots Briton, a Welsh Briton, as well as an English Briton. Or an African Briton. Claiming to be African by birth despite evidence to the contrary in his baptismal and naval records, Equiano represents himself as British by acculturation and choice (Carretta 80–81, 89, 147–49, 324). He can, of course, never be English, in the ethnic sense in which that word was used during the period, as his white wife is English. He adopts, however, the cultural, political, religious, and social values that enable him to be accepted as British. Yet he always retains his perspective as an African who has been deracinated and thus has the advantage of knowing his adopted British culture from both the inside and the outside, a perspective that W. E. B. DuBois calls the double consciousness of the black person in a predominantly white society (364–65). This double consciousness is reflected in the use of dual identities by Olaudah Equiano / Gustavus Vassa. Once he became free in 1766, the man who first publicly identified himself in 1789 as Olaudah Equiano continued to use the name imposed on him in slavery as his legal name, as well as in private and public correspondence. Hence the dual names he retains in the title of his autobiography. The absence of Oroonoko's slave name, Caesar, in Behn's title reflects her hero's ultimate rejection of the English society and the status it had tried to impose upon him.

Equiano's encounter with a black boy on the Isle of Wight during the 1750s indicates that he may not be fully comfortable in his position on the border between African and European identities. Although he calls the encounter "a trifling incident," it is a telling example of how quickly he had become acculturated into his new self and at the same time readily defined by others as still African (85). Confronted by the black boy, in effect his own mirror image, he initially turned away from him before embracing his African side. A question the prince of the Musquito Indians asks Equiano in chapter 11 of the *Interesting Narrative* subtly reminds us just how far Equiano has come in the process of his British acculturation: "At last he asked me, 'How comes it that all the white men on board, who can read and write, observe the sun, and know all things, yet swear, lie, and get drunk, only excepting yourself?'" (Interesting Narrative 204). In the eyes of another non-European who has encountered the Old World, Equiano appears to be morally whiter than whites.

Equiano offers the transformation of his own attitude toward the varieties of eighteenth-century slavery as a model for the moral progress of his readers as individuals and of the society he now shares with them. By claiming personal experience and direct observation, Equiano becomes an expert on the institution of slavery as well as on the effects of the African slave trade. Most students are surprised to discover that eighteenth-century slavery was not a monolithic institution, simply divided into white owners and black chattels. Equiano's initial encounter with slavery is reportedly in Africa, where slavery is domestic in its native African form. Slaves are treated almost like members of their owners' families because of close personal contact. Thus African slavery seems benign, and not obviously dehumanizing. Slavery there is neither racially based nor hereditary. Equiano's description of African slavery would have reminded his more educated readers of ancient classical slavery. Slavery is simply one of the many levels that constitute the apparently healthy social order in which Equiano finds himself near the top. But the European slave trade with Africa has gradually spread like an infectious disease farther inland until it destroys even the tranquility of Equiano's homeland. He tells us that his first owners are fellow Africans, and his treatment becomes increasingly more dehumanizing as he approaches the English ships on the coast, the source of the infection. And when he finally encounters the financial cause of the disease, he remarks, "[T]he white people looked and acted, as I thought, in so savage a manner; for I had never seen among any people such instances of brutal cruelty; and this not only shewn towards us blacks, but also to some of the whites themselves" (56–57). The trade corrupts everyone.

Equiano does not, however, condemn slavery; he condemns some kinds of slavery. He experiences the other side of slavery in fact when, as a free man, he effectively supports the African slave trade, buying his fellow countrymen and becoming their overseer for Dr. Irving's Central American plantation. Priding himself on being an exemplary slave driver, he resigns because of the immoral behavior of his associates, not because he rejects slavery. Only after he returns to Old England, the land of liberty, "where [his] heart had always been," does he come to see that the trade must be abolished because it cannot be ameliorated (147). And he leaves his readers with little choice but to conclude that the institution of slavery must be abolished too.

At the end of the course we look again at the students' initial definitions of concepts such as race, identity, status, slavery, and abolition. In light of the readings by Behn and Equiano, no one in the class any longer questions that the definitions of these terms must be historically and geographically contingent.

The Early Modern Body in Behn's Poetry and *Oroonoko*

Roberta C. Martin

Like many both inside and outside the academy, my students tend to read anachronistically. They view early modern minds and bodies entirely from a twenty-first-century perspective, and the idea not only that social and cultural environments in the early modern period might have differed radically from theirs but also that bodies might have been experienced far differently makes them skeptical if not queasy. For my current students, nothing is more naturalized than their male or female bodies.

Consequently, investigating the early modern humoral body is useful preparation both for Behn's slyly gendered amatory poetry and for the peculiar "body language" of *Oroonoko*. Understanding the uncertainties of early modern embodiment offers students a way to grasp the seemingly extravagant language and behavior displayed in *Oroonoko*, and the disturbing trope of self-demonstrating anatomy brings coherence to the darker side of Behn's complex achievement.

Before turning to the ambiguously gendered bodies in Behn's poetry and the excessively dramatic ones in *Oroonoko*, my students and I indulge in humor—four of them: black bile, yellow bile, blood, and phlegm. These substances constituted the physiology and psychology of early modern persons (Lindemann 69). If the humors were unbalanced by inner swellings or external environmental forces, illness occurred; when they were stopped up—when these fluids could not move freely within the body or pass easily in and out of it—such blockages caused distress to mind and body. From the time of Hippocrates (c. 450–c. 370 BCE) and Galen (129–c. 200 CE) until the seventeenth century and beyond, a mixture of what Mary Lindemann calls "*environmentalism* and *humoralism*" (9) conditioned perceptions of the body and its health. This complex and layered Hippocratic-Galenic tradition descended from the Greek physicians and Aristotle and was then altered by Arab physicians, through whose manuscripts it was passed on. Changing and developing through the centuries, these humoral and corporeal perceptions determined the physiological well-being and the psychological health of most of the Western world (Nutton).

Emotions not only were dependent on the body's humoral balance but also were thought to flow. Ulinka Rublack observes that the classical humanist education taught that a proper balance of emotion necessitated both "relativizing" and "expressing feelings" (3). Like Sigmund Freud three centuries later, Francis Bacon felt that repressed emotions were unhealthy. In fact, in "Of Friendship," he writes, "A principal fruit of friendship is the ease and discharge of the fullness and swellings of the heart" (*Essays* 139). Mind and body were materially interrelated. If feelings "swelled the heart," then such a literal enlargement was physically and mentally dangerous unless relieved by "verbal transmission," as Rublack notes (3).

Interdependence of mind and body seems remarkably modern, but when we imagine the body's interior today, we most likely think of organs, not fluids. If jaundiced and aching, we probably think it's the kidney or liver, not bile, and when an invading organism attacks, we boot the alien body out of our own and return to normal health. In the early modern period, there was no such thing as normal health. Degrees of physical well-being depended on how well a person balanced the fluid humors and managed those external influences that determined the degree of one's sickness or health. As Lindemann observes, "Standard therapies . . . depended on readjusting perceived imbalances either by siphoning off a humor that had grown too strong or become corrupt, or by bleeding, purging, [or] vomiting" (10).

Today we see and feel our skins as impermeable protective barriers between our inner organs and the outside world. The early modern body, however, was not a self-contained and enclosed entity but a leaky bag of fluids. Influences and vapors flowed in at will, altering the health and attitudes of the body; humors, juices, and, in extremis, vital spirits flowed out. Bodily organs were important but only in relation to the fluids on which they depended. The heart sank or trembled, and blood froze not metaphorically but literally. Further, most of my students firmly believe that "male" and "female" are genitally defined, ahistorical, and essentialized physical categories. They are not entirely happy to learn that, as Thomas Laqueur observes,

> sex is a shaky foundation. Changes in corporeal structures, or the discovery that things were not as they seemed at first, could push a body from one juridical category (female) to another (male). These categories were based on gender distinctions—active/passive, hot/cold, formed/

> unformed, informing/formable—of which an external or an internal penis was only the diagnostic sign. (135)

In effect, sexual category in the seventeenth century was determined not primarily by organs but by the heat and dryness characteristic of the male body or by the coolness and dampness that determined the sex of the female body.

Once early modern bodies have been historicized and genders destabilized, we can turn to Behn's amatory poetry to see how our informed corporeal understanding affects interpretation. Her "imperfect enjoyment" poem "The Disappointment" (*Works* [Todd] 1: 65–69), possibly composed as part of a group competition that included John Wilmot, earl of Rochester, reconceives Rochester's "Imperfect Enjoyment" poem by capitalizing on one of the worst libertine embarrassments and, using the traditional characteristics of males and females as outlined in humoral theory, reverses the genders of the participants.

A libertine shepherd, Lysander, propelled perhaps by the urge to rebalance his bodily fluids, "[s]urpriz'd fair *Cloris*" in a "Thicket" (lines 3, 11). Cloris "[p]ermits his Force" (14), while seeming also to resist. When Lysander persists, Cloris ambiguously faints away. Lysander, so overwhelmed by the sight of her body through her "loose thin *Robes*" (63), is unfortunately "too transported" (72) to rise to the occasion.

Since, according to humoral theory, the difference between men and women lies in their body heat and moisture, the hot, dry, masculine Lysander presses his "burning trembling Hand" (line 36) to the moist Cloris's "Snowy Brest" (37)—cool as well as white. Her eyes cast a "Humid Light" (56), and love's "Altar" is a "Fountain where Delight still flows" (45, 49). While Cloris is the epitome of moist, early modern womanhood, the overheated Lysander suffers from extreme humoral imbalance. With the fluid flow of his emotion blocked, his ardor decidedly dampens as his "Insensible" falls "weeping in his Hand" (90). Cloris, returning from the convenient faint, reaches for "that Fabulous *Priapas*, / That Potent God" (105–06) but finds "that God of her Desires / Disarm'd of all his Awful Fires, / And Cold as Flow'rs bath'd in the Morning-Dew" (112–13). Not only is Lysander cold and damp, but Cloris suddenly heats up with "Confusion" (115): "The Blood forsook the hinder Place, / And strew'd with Blushes all her Face" (116–17). Cloris leaves Lysander cursing, in usual libertine fashion, "the *Shepherdess*'s Charms" (139). He is cold, limp, damp, and faint—in short, he is female. The lovers have switched sexes. Behn evokes the Hippocratic-Galenic anatomical understanding of male and female while exploiting Restoration uncertainty about sexual categories.[1]

The early modern period marked a crucial transition from Hippocratic-Galenic perceptions of the body to what we consider modern views of physiology and anatomy. Vesalius's *De humani corporis fabrica libri septem* (1543), strikingly illustrated with self-demonstrating anatomical figures, was foundational to a new, empirical anatomy, as were William Harvey's observations of blood circulation.[2] Critical to this change in corporeal understanding were the remarkable early modern anatomy theaters of Europe and Britain. These anatomical displays became so fashionable that there arose, as Jonathan Sawday points out, a "culture of dissection" that involved a "network of practices, social structures, and rituals surrounding [the] production of fragmented bodies" (2).

The way people experienced their bodies changed slowly. Harvey himself, despite revolutionizing the early modern understanding of the cardiovascular system, was in fact theoretically as traditional in his notions about the body and its humoral composition as were most anatomists and physicians of the Restoration. Like paradigms of sexual difference, old and new epistemologies of the body existed together well into the nineteenth century. The resourceful Behn, therefore, might plausibly have deployed the extant paradigms of medical knowledge to present in her works both humoral and anatomical embodiment and, more darkly, vivisective dismemberment. Richard Sugg observes in a discussion of vivisection that no one in the Renaissance advocated human vivisection, but "various figures seemed ready to believe that the practice might be carried out by their contemporaries" (164). Indeed, if Behn was seeking a way to represent the violence and horror that she claims to have witnessed in Surinam, the new anatomy texts, with their brilliantly executed figures of live dissected figures holding apart incisions that cut deep into the interior walls of abdomen, bowels, and brain, offered her examples.[3]

But before my students and I encounter the desperate and demoralized Prince Oroonoko "severing" the face from his dead wife's body (61), we meet him as he becomes, in the language of the traditional, humoral paradigm, increasingly blocked and unbalanced. Internal imbalance and social and cultural impotence plunge him into what Noga Arikha describes as a "[h]ypochondriac" disease caused by "excessive black bile" and, "by definition, melancholic" (114). Oroonoko has shown early signs of this disorder. His first excessive display of emotion and the increasingly violent ones that follow demonstrate the effects of stoppages that block the healthy discharge of black bile and thus cause attacks of melancholia.

His first humoral blockage occurs at seventeen, when his mentor, the "old General," dies saving his life by taking an arrow through the eye, and the prince, a lifelong warrior, must assume leadership of his country's army "afflicted as [he] was" (12). Then, blissful over Imoinda, Oroonoko returns to court "with quite another Humour than before" (15). However, he must hide—stop up—his feelings, because his grandfather also desires Imoinda, and she must comply, becoming part of his grandfather's harem. Imoinda and the prince continue to stop up their passion until Imoinda, flooded with moist, gender-appropriate grief, dissolves in humoral tears as she is led against her will to the royal (and ironically appropriate) ceremonial bath by the impotent old king, who in turn is unbalanced by disproportionate "new Sparks of Love" (16). To my students, Behn's seemingly excessive descriptions in *Oroonoko* begin to make ominous, rhetorical sense. Despite the ironic complexities at work in the text, the extreme responses of these characters and the hyperbole Behn deliberately deploys at first seem bizarre to our modern, semidisembodied understanding of emotion. For the early modern Behn, however, these emotional responses and psychological behaviors are directly instantiated by the physiological imbalance of the humoral body.

Oroonoko, hearing of Imoinda's alleged death as he is about to engage the enemy, immediately vows that "henceforth he wou'd never lift a Weapon, or draw a Bow; but abandon the small Remains of his Life to Sighs and Tears and the continual Thoughts of what his Lord and Grand-father had thought good to send out of the World" (28). Sunk in depression and awash in black bile, he tells his troops that they should "*behold* Oroonoko, *the most wretched, and abandon'd by Fortune, of all the Creation of the Gods*" (28). He finally rouses himself to regain the field, but his prior shockingly feminized and unmilitary behavior marks the end of the amatory phase of his physioemotional devolution.

Since raging passions occur even before Oroonoko and Imoinda are forced into foreign circumstances, where can melancholic language turn for the representational resources to express the vivisectional violence ahead? The vocabulary of traditional natural philosophy was adequate, perhaps, for the turbulent vicissitudes of romance in both poetry and prose, but in Surinam Behn's noble victims face the lethally comprehensive cruelty of racism and betrayal. In 1688, when an older Behn, personally and politically disenchanted, published *Oroonoko*, her disillusioned imagination may have recognized in the empirical but startlingly transgressive practices of dissection, and, implicitly, of vivisection, a violent lexicon of tropes that exploited the harsh and intrusive implications that lurked just beneath the skin of the new science.

Indeed, in her discursive choices, the ill and aging author might have profoundly identified not only with her younger self but also with the colonialized, ambiguously noble, but ultimately powerless Oroonoko, who in the end controlled nothing but Imoinda's death and mutilation and the dissection of his own body. Behn's account of his self-mutilation after he kills Imoinda is infused with a phantasmagoric violence that is a qualitative leap beyond her previous humoral tropes.

His revolt a failure, his wife and unborn child dead, he lies prostrate, enfeebled by grief, for eight days beside Imoinda's corpse (61–62). But any lofty sentiment or nobility lurking in the language or circumstances of the scene is obliterated, because Imoinda's body, like the dismembered parts on a dissection table, has begun to stink of decomposition (62). When the unbalanced prince is overtaken by the English, who, their own violence notwithstanding, are horrified at his, he tries but fails to explain his act. Mere words are not enough. Transmogrified quite literally into a tragic figure of anatomical demonstration, he raises his knife against the English in defiant scorn: "*Look ye, ye faithless Crew*, said he, *'tis not Life I seek, nor am I afraid of Dying*; and, at that Word, cut a piece of Flesh from his own Throat, and threw it at 'em" (62–63).

In part, Oroonoko invokes the bizarre heroism of the war captains of Surinam, who before an engagement vied for the generalship by hacking off parts of their own faces in a demonstration of self-dissection designed to reveal not their corporeal interiors but their "passive Valour" (50). A well-balanced Oroonoko once considered this "a sort of Courage too Brutal to be applauded" but "express'd his Esteem of 'em" (50). Now a general no more, he appropriates their indigenous qualities. To elevate his status above the "*shameful Whip*" (63), he eviscerates himself in a tortured display of self-demonstrating dissection.

Back at Parham, a "Chirugeon" attempts to reassemble the nearly departed hero, but Oroonoko appears to the narrating Behn "like a Death's Head black'd over; nothing but Teeth, and Eyeholes" (63). This starkly complex image unites the Renaissance *vanitas* emblem with the accurately illustrative, skeletal images from the anatomies, under color of slavery, to produce a newly constructed and ghastly representation of blind rage and racial subjugation. Oroonoko in his vivisectional orgy eloquently carves into his own flesh the hieroglyphics of his pride and humiliation. Behn's intense and repugnant drama of the "Death's Head" displaces and effaces Oroonoko's own faceless victim, his spousal possession, whom according to the customs of his country he has the right to kill as an expression of love (61). The narratorial Behn seems to ask us to practice a kind of cultural relativism by identifying with the betrayed and enslaved "Caesar," whose child, as a slave, would belong not to him but to the slave owners. He is driven to destroy his unborn child to preserve not the object of his passion—but his own paternity.

As we reach Oroonoko's final, "pyre-rrhic" moment, while we recognize that execution is the classic punishment for all traitors to the English crown, we must also recognize another morbid, autoptic parody in the outrageous dissective dismemberment and immolation that accompanies Oroonoko's execution (64). In this scene, satirist Behn has given us a fully realized, self-demonstrating "live anatomy" inside out: "Caesar" stands calmly with a pipe instead of a knife, demonstrating not his dissected anatomy but the vivisection itself. His organs, instead of being exposed, disappear one by one into the fire. Instead of revealing a more exact anatomy, he is rendered limb by limb corporeally invisible, revealing the repellent anatomy of slavery and social brutality. At the beginning of her account, the narratorial Behn hails Oroonoko as a nobly attractive hero, but at the conclusion of his story, the authorial Behn leaves him a uxoricide without even a body to stand in.

In her poetry, Behn slyly manipulates traditional humoral theories to undermine sexual difference and satirize conventional attitudes and amatory rituals. In the classroom, the unbalanced humors of bodies in love offer playful trajectories of meaning that students are quick to appreciate. In *Oroonoko*, in addition to conventional romance motifs, Behn is concerned with issues of violence, race, gender, and political injustice. For these darker, more dangerous issues, she turns, perhaps, to the new physiology for the more violent tropes generated by the intrusions of dissection and by the brutality of vivisection. Student readers, now familiar with the play of humors in her poetry, are prepared to appreciate this disturbing representational transformation. They more readily understand how the body of the noble prince, constructed in a theory of humors, is then dismembered and destroyed by racism, betrayal, and bitterness. The language of Romantic excess that puzzles students is more understandable in the context of a historical and social violence expressed through dissective and vivisectional tropes taken from the discourse of the new science.

Intractable ambiguities about both narratorial and authorial attitudes remain in *Oroonoko*: humoral theory, anatomy, and dissection may have lent themselves to a parody that is now hard to determine. But approaching this complex work first through Behn's poetry and then through both the traditional humoral body and the new science offers us additional, culturally relevant ways to read *Oroonoko*.

NOTES

[1] Many other Behn poems play on the unstable nature of sex and gender categories. See "On a Juniper-Tree, Cut Down to Make Busks," "To the Fair Clarinda, Who Made Love to Me, Imagin'd more than Woman," "Song (I Led My Silvia to a Grove)," "A Letter to a Brother of the Pen in Tribulation," "Verses Designed by Mrs. A. Behn, to Be Sent to a Fair Lady, That Desir'd She Would Absent Herself, to Cure Her Love: Left Unfinished," "To Amintas, upon Reading the Lives of Some of the Romans," "Ovid to Julia: A Letter," "Song (While, Iris, I at Distance Gaze)," and "Song: Love Arm'd" (all in *Works* [Todd] 1).

[2] The original Latin text of *De Motu Cordis* was published in 1628 and the Latin text of *De Circulatione Sanguinis* in 1649. The first English translation of both was published in 1653.

[3] For this self-demonstrating figure and a gallery of other medical and anatomical images, including Vesalius's famous muscle men, see the Wellcome Institute image collection online (http://images.wellcome.ac.uk/). Additionally, the Anatomia Collection at the University of Toronto has hundreds of easily accessed plates online (http://link.library.utoronto.ca/anatomia/application/index.cfm). Illustrations for some of the new anatomy texts were done by artists like Michelangelo and Albrecht Dürer, and these illustrations were available to the literate English person when Behn was writing *Oroonoko*. Three print sources for images from the history of anatomy and physiology are J. B. deC. M. Saunders and Charles D. O'Malley, *The Illustrations from the Works of Andreas Vesalius of Brussels*; Robert Beverly Hale and Terrence Coyle, *Albinus on Anatomy with Eighty Original Albinus Plates*; and Martin Kemp and Marina Wallace, *Spectacular Bodies: The Art and Science of the Human Body from Leonardo to Now*.

Oroonoko and the Problem of Teaching Novelty

Emily Hodgson Anderson

Eighteenth-century novels activate a question common to all forms of pedagogy: How can the unfamiliar be made accessible to readers or students? "Nothing odd will do long," Samuel Johnson famously (albeit mistakenly) claimed of *Tristram Shandy* (Boswell 696), and if oddity transcends all frames of reference, a text or topic will certainly vanish without a trace. Our job as teachers is to use what students do know to get them to learn something about what they do not. This is an old dance, and students and teachers both know the steps; the assumption behind any syllabus is that it will introduce something new. But the choreography creates problems of its own: because of this assumption, students find it hard to distinguish between novelty bred of their unfamiliarity with the topic at hand and novelty intrinsic to the topic.

When I taught *Oroonoko* as the lead-off text in a survey-of-the-novel course, I discovered two things. First, it was a text so different from what students expected of novels that they did not quite know how to read it. Second, without knowing more about prose fiction of the late seventeenth century, they tended to dismiss its differences as symptomatic of the era. Yet *Oroonoko* is a consciously innovative text, one meant to be recognized by its contemporary readers as new and different and one devoted to analyzing the epistemological challenges of novelty itself.

In my prior work, I have approached these issues by discussing how Behn's treatment of novelty in *Oroonoko* can illuminate our strategies in teaching the text (E. Anderson). In this essay, I describe why, after a few frustrating experiences in my survey, I now teach *Oroonoko* in the company of other examples of Behn's short fiction. These literary contexts, I have found, delimit a space from which we may productively teach this novel and what is novel about it. In particular, I have had success teaching *Oroonoko* after *The Fair Jilt* and *The History of the Nun*.

When students read these additional examples of Behn's short fiction, they start to recognize a sense of conscious experimentation that links all Behn's prose; her fascination with novelty becomes itself a connecting theme. Behn's commitment to experimentation is evident in the thematic treatments of innovation shared among these texts: her interest in inconstancy, her use of the truth claim, and her focus on vow breaking. These narrative and sexual behaviors are fueled by a search for the new and different, and we discuss how the heroines who devote themselves to that search come to emblematize their creator's experimental pursuits.

Behn devoted much of her writing to encouraging readers to make these connections. As Margaret Ferguson puts it, she "invited her contemporary readers and spectators to perceive authorial self-references and to enjoy the titillating pleasures of decoding those allusions, recognizing 'likenesses' in the texts to the shape-shifting public character known variously as 'A.' or 'Astrea' or 'Aphra' Behn" ("Authorial Ciphers" 226). The "authorial ciphers" that Ferguson describes are littered throughout Behn's writing—textual moments that urge readers to note connections among various texts by Behn and between Behn and the characters she creates. Yet Behn is also known for her enigmatic persona, and debates about her biography have dogged Behn scholarship for decades. These "authorial ciphers," then, do not lead readers to some final, pat solution about their author but prompt readerly acts of decoding, and the "likenesses" in Behn's prose have produced many conflicting critical accounts.

Just so, critics like Robert Chibka find evidence for Behn's authorial persona by tracing chameleon tendencies in her characters. The title of his well-known essay comes from a statement in *Oroonoko* by Onahal to Aboan—"*Oh! Do not fear a Woman's Invention*" (23)—that Chibka sees as equally applicable to the authorial Behn. The pattern, by which the dissembling female character stands in for her author, is perpetuated in Miranda in *The Fair Jilt*, who exhibits both invention and narrative flexibility in her attempts to woo a lover. With her sights set on the priest Father Henrick, Miranda "ceas'd not to pursue him with Letters, varying her Style; sometimes all wanton . . . sometimes feigning a Virgin-Modesty" (20). As in Chibka's example, acts of female inventiveness or dissembling are linked to acts of authorship, and the practice of authorship is itself cast as an act of disguise.

The one constant of these author-figures is inconstancy, a characteristic for which they suffer. The narrative innovations of Miranda confirm her as a character "naturally Amorous, but extreamly Inconstant" (11). Her ever new and different writing style reflects her "fickle Humor" and foreshadows her ultimate inability to be "confin'd to one Man" (11). This temperament leads her to pursue priests, pages, and princes; it moves her to attempt the murder of her sister, and finally, in perhaps the most fickle shift of all, to reform (48). Her actions result in her ridicule and imprisonment, an outcome suggesting that her search for the new and different leads to bad ends.

And yet, inconstancy is required to produce and preserve that which is novel, which, given Behn's penchant for experimentation, seems to be her authorial goal. Why would an author who embraces innovation critique the characteristic she herself exhibits? Doing so is itself inconsistent, and Behn's views on inconstancy—whether it is a characteristic to be criticized or applauded—are remarkably, and appropriately, unstable. These shifting views are revealed in our classroom segue from *The Fair Jilt* to *The History of the Nun*, a tale that begins with a celebration of constant women and an exhortation against broken vows. Behn dedicates her tale, however, to the duchess of Mazarine, Hortense Mancini, a woman renowned for her independent spirit, the abandonment of her husband, and her many lovers—among them Charles II. If anyone could be characterized as a "fair vow-breaker" (Behn's subtitle), it was Mazarine, and, by lauding her, Behn contrasts the sentiment of her dedication and the promises of her tale. The frame of this piece destabilizes how we read the moral—"Never break a vow"—stated within it.

Even without the frame, it is hard to determine the moral focus of this tale, as the opening exhortation against vow breaking quickly shifts to the narrator's analysis of the causes that move women to break vows in the first place. We are told that "without all dispute, Women are by Nature more Constant and Just, than Men, and did not their first Lovers teach them the trick of Change, they would be *Doves*, that would never quit their Mate" (211). The onus would then seem to be on men, or at least on the social behaviors women learn from them. But our prior discussion of Miranda, whose fickle nature nearly destroys a (possibly sham) prince, makes a problematic context for this conclusion, not just because Miranda is inconstant but also because she did not learn her inconstancy from a former lover. Neither does Isabella in *The History of the Nun*: her first husband, Henault, is faithful to her through seven years of postwar slavery. It is she who is inconstant when, supposing him dead, she marries again. Isabella's unintentional bigamy leads her to the far worse crime of double murder and finally to her public execution, which she prefaces with the now familiar, yet now more complicated exhortation, "never to break a Vow" (257).

More complicated, because Isabella's closing tribute to constancy has been consistently undermined by her conduct during life. Students often read this tale as preaching not against vow breaking but against the unrealistic vows that society, religion, and even narrative demand. "I could wish," states the narrator, "that Nunneries and Marriages were not to be enter'd into, 'till the Maid, so destin'd, were of a mature Age to make her own Choices" (213). The narrator illustrates, through her textual examples as well as through her shifting attitudes toward them, that it is unrealistic and unnatural to expect fidelity in a person, and that such expectation actually produces the opposite effect. So although this tale opens with a tribute to naturally constant women, the "*Indian* Wives" who "would leap alive into the Graves of their deceased Lovers and be buried quick with 'em" (211–12), students are led to question the extent to which that constancy can ever be a natural trait.

The opening tribute to constancy in *The History of the Nun* can also jar when students get to *Oroonoko* and read of the nameless "*Indian* woman, [Byam's] Mistress," who sucks the venom from the evil Byam's wound (55), or the description of "the Brave, the Beautiful, and the Constant *Imoinda*" (65), whose fidelity, like Isabella's faithlessness, leads to death. Two women who meet the same end, Isabella and Imoinda are heroines whom students first read as diametrically opposed. One woman dies at the hand of her husband; one woman kills hers. One is an example of constancy; one of broken vows. Imoinda's execution stands as a testament to her marital commitment; Isabella's is a punishment for the deviations she made from hers. Yet there are disturbing similarities between the two women, which lead savvy readers to question how much, if at all, Imoinda's constancy is a virtue for which she should be lauded or which she can ever attain.

So, for example, Imoinda is the "Heroick Wife" who pleads for death with eyes "Smiling with Joy" (60). Isabella likewise receives her death sentence "joyfully" and fulfills it under the terms of marriage, dying "Chearful as a Bride" (257). But the simile is suspect: Isabella is a widow twice over, and her ill-fated marriages, and indeed her choice of the matrimonial vow over the religious one, lead to her death. Her fate casts a shadow over Imoinda's vows, one only intensified by the fact that for both heroines the volitional commitment of love is circumscribed by enslavement (Henault's and Oroonoko's). That constancy and inconstancy in marriage both seem subject to external constraints may explain why the fair vow breaker Isabella and the constant Imoinda meet death in the same way: Isabella's executioner "sever'd her Beautiful Head from her Delicate Body" (258), and Oroonoko severs "[Imoinda's] yet Smiling Face" from her "Delicate Body" (61).

The description of Imoinda's death echoes eerily with students, who read it after discussing Isabella's death in *The History of the Nun*. The disorientation they experience from noting parallels between two seemingly opposite characters shows them how textual parallels can both echo and contradict. The refrain "Never break a vow" registers differently when they reach the end of *The History of the Nun*, differently again when they read *Oroonoko*. The claim of Behn's narrator in *History of the Nun* that "[t]he Resolution, we promise, and believe we shall maintain, is not in our power" (212) applies to character and narrative alike.

Thus, just as the faithless libertine (and there are many of them in Behn's works) can be characterized by his repeated exhortations of undying love, the truth claim that prefaces each of these early prose narratives can become both a source and a sign of fiction. A narrative protestation of fidelity, the truth claim binds these stories to a veracity based on faithful repetition. These claims characterize the narratives that follow as real-world exemplars, and the narratives base their didactic potential on the necessity of examples to the epistemic process. Yet the same examples that should encourage emulation and breed familiarity come to teach us, in Behn's world, a lesson about novelty, about inconstancy itself.

So when Behn references her own tales as examples, the decision takes on an added significance. Charged with the task of occupying Oroonoko and Imoinda during threats of a mutiny, the narrator engages Imoinda by "teaching her all the pretty Works that I was Mistress of; and telling her Stories of Nuns" (41). This reference, as Paul Salzman notes in his edition of Behn's works, reflects on her "stories of nuns" (Oroonoko *and Other Writings* 271n45) and specifically the stories we have just discussed. This intertextual allusion creates its own kind of repetition, as readers (both Restoration and today's) are encouraged to recall, even reread, these alternate tales. As one of Ferguson's "authorial ciphers," the reference creates connections among Behn's disparate authorial voices. Like other female protagonists, the narrator becomes an emblem for the author, even as the acts of authorship invoked display a highly critical attitude toward fidelity, religious or otherwise.

Oroonoko is thus rightfully read as providing an "education in skepticism" (Chibka, "Oh!" 515). When Behn's royal slave finally concludes that "there was no Faith in the White Men, or the Gods they Ador'd" (56), the text would have us believe that he is right—and bemoan the credulity that made this lesson so long in coming. Similarly, we as readers are encouraged to be more skeptical of the narrator's assertions and to be attuned to her characteristic shifts and changes. But these tales, when studied together, teach more than incredulity. They teach us about the very workings of novelty and inconstancy, about "the trick of Change" (211) in an epistemological, if not an emulative, sense.

Novelty, as *Oroonoko* makes clear, will otherwise have a vexed relation to knowledge. "[W]here there is no Novelty, there can be no Curiosity," claims the narrator early on (9). Yet curiosity is a debatable good, since the learning gained through it is often fatal. It leads Oroonoko to fish for the "*Numb Eel*" that almost kills him (46–47); it leads the narrator to her protagonist and thus to her tragic tale. *Oroonoko*'s dedication praises Lord Maitland as reading "not Vainly for the gust of Novelty, but Knowledge, excellent Knowledge" (6), forcing a distinction between the terms. Novelty in this context suggests readers who are unable to see past the glamour of innovation or who become enamored solely and superficially with the new. Better in this context to be like *The History of the Nun*'s stoic Isabella, with her "evenness of Mind" so that "nothing created wonder in her, tho' never so strange and Novel" (216).

Yet, only pages later, Isabella reframes her conduct as replete with the "Sins of Curiosity" (218). Just as novelty is inevitable, Behn presents curiosity as an inevitable human state. The challenge then becomes how to make the quest for newness into a productive epistemological experience, and in *Oroonoko* productive curiosity is hard to find. The entire colonial expedition ends disastrously, the British being ousted by the Dutch, the Dutch in turn being brutalized by the natives. The quest for new adventures in the New World remains "oftentimes Fatal and at least Dangerous" (43).

At the same time, *Oroonoko* contrasts the exploration of Surinam with the narrating of this exploration; it posits the difference between a novelty experienced and a novelty recalled. In writing this tale decades after her supposed journey, Behn acknowledges to Maitland that she at once depicts the "New and Strange" and reflects on the challenge of such depictions, adding that "these Countries do, in all things, so far differ from ours, that they produce unconceivable Wonders" (7), and she often finds herself relating that which "possibly will find no Credit among Men" (46). Her story is thus as much a reflection on how to make the novel credible as it is an account of novelty as lived. The product of such reflections, her text stands as the generative result of her tragic encounters and the more analytic response to the curiosity that prompted them.

By focusing on the intellectual challenges posed by novelty and by locating these discussions in an innovative textual medium, *Oroonoko* re-creates this same tension for its readers: we are caught between the experience of novelty and a productive analysis of it. *Oroonoko* challenges us not only to perceive but also to analyze the text itself as "new and strange" (8). As I hope my students realize, both the content and the context of Behn's other fiction provide a model for how this challenge may be engaged. Read together, these works of fiction allow us to explore both the risks that novelty poses to its audience and the boundaries that make it recognizable: they show us how lessons in how to read Behn's texts are encoded in the texts themselves. Our job is to make these texts and lessons available, to show how Behn's oeuvre can be used to expose the innovative nature of the texts within it.

Transatlantic Crossing: Teaching *Oroonoko* with *The Widdow Ranter*

Jane Milling and Cynthia Richards

The connections between the novel *Oroonoko* (1688) and the play *The Widdow Ranter* (1689) are many and well documented. Both works were readied for publication during the last months of Aphra Behn's life. Both evoke a nostalgic turn to her early years as a young able traveler when she is no longer young or able. Both are set in the New World, *Oroonoko* in Surinam and *The Widdow Ranter* in the North American colony of Virginia. Both feature heroes who lead failed insurrections against provisional governments viewed as corrupt, and both heroes die tragically. Both portray colonial councils that violate precepts of honor and suggest a New World order in disorder, with little hint of the virtues soon to be associated with New World experiments in democracy. Finally, both point, at least obliquely, to the role of women in the New World and to the suggestion of greater, if provisional, powers for women in colonial spaces from which patriarchs are noticeably absent.

Still, pairing these texts in the classroom can give instructors pause. Their differences are significant and can obscure the importance of *Oroonoko*. Behn's novel is her most celebrated work and certainly secures her place in the development of a prose tradition. By contrast, *The Widdow Ranter* has long been viewed as one of her least successful plays and has only recently attracted sustained critical debate. The comic tenor of the play, moreover, would appear to undercut the more serious criticism that the novel levels against colonial councils, and Bacon as a hero connected with Oroonoko does little for Oroonoko's reputation. Both the historical and the fictionalized Bacon of Behn's play appear as less than noble, and the comparison of their deaths can make Oroonoko's seem more pathetic than tragic. If we read *Oroonoko* as at least partially a bid by Behn to establish the fame of her female pen, poignantly at a time her hand has grown "lame," as she reports to Abigail Waller (O'Donnell, "Aphra Behn" 8), the comparison with *The Widdow Ranter* can jeopardize that bid. We need look no further than Thomas Southerne's dramatic adaptation of *Oroonoko* and his incorporation of a comic subplot with similarities to the plot of *The Widdow Ranter* to see how easily the farcical representation of women can undermine Behn's writerly ambition.

Yet the benefits of pairing these texts far outweigh the risks. This discovery led the two of us, after meeting at a conference and spending time together in an airport during a weather delay, to throw our lots together and pair not only Behn's two transatlantic texts but our two classes as well. As individual instructors, we may never have been willing to take on this challenge; together, we found ourselves embarking on a rather ambitious (and possibly foolhardy) transatlantic crossing of our own. We both taught *Oroonoko* but in very different contexts, and so we commenced a month-long electronic linkage of our courses, one a first-year drama course at the University of Exeter, in England, the other an upper-level literature course at Wittenberg University, a liberal arts college in Ohio. We would have our students engage in e-mail exchanges with one another about Behn's *Oroonoko* and *The Widdow Ranter* along with Southerne's *Oroonoko* (for mediation), and then we would ask each class to perform for the other a scene selected from the novel or the play, their performances to be exchanged via the Internet.

Since Behn's two works and Southerne's adaptation complicated issues of race and gender, showed instability and rebellion in the emerging capitalist colonies of the New World, focused on a radical reshaping of national identity and personal allegiance, we were particularly interested in encouraging our students to reflect on what it means to perform a national identity. These three works, written as American identity was taking shape and as English aristocratic tradition was coming into conflict with the emerging mercantile ethos of the New World, seemed ideal for helping our students historicize and complicate those identities.

Moreover, the combination of a prose work and two plays demonstrated to our students that a performance component lies in all written scripts, including the supposedly transparent account of the life and death of an African prince.

Our students performed their national identities with vigor. Regardless of their ethnic background, they assumed a straightforward national identity when they played the role of either American class or British class in this electronic transatlantic crossing. The vigor was more striking in the British classroom, because a third of the students were of Indian descent or from another European country. It was less surprising in the American classroom, where most were white Ohioans. (Diversity in the Ohio classroom was limited to one African American student and one with Native American ancestry.) The irony that ethnic diversity alone complicated stereotypes of British and American identity was not lost on us as instructors, but it did not lessen the enthusiasm with which both our classrooms assumed their stereotypic roles.

Students identified characters as British or American and promoted those who stood for the respective national values, but then students were unsettled to see the other class either criticizing those values or identifying them as their own. In addition, the exercise left few heroes intact, including, as we had feared, Oroonoko. Read against *The Widdow Ranter* and Southerne's theatrical adaptation, Oroonoko emerged as at best a compromised hero, powerless against the politics of the New World, a mere pawn in a largely ideological battle between Old World honor and New World expediency. Yet what he lost in grandeur, he gained in pathos. Students felt his loss in ways we had not anticipated. From viewing Oroonoko's death in the context of Bacon's ignoble death, they found Oroonoko less heroic but more human. His death was no longer just a horrific account of a martyr's preordained fate but rather the result of human choices and even foolish mistakes. Thus, when they saw the Oroonoko of Southerne's theatrical adaptation achieve a more classically heroic end, they mourned the human Oroonoko of the novel. But as Oroonoko lost heroic stature, Imoinda surprisingly gained it. Both sides of the Atlantic agreed on her heroism and, through her representation, on the significance of what Behn had to say. In Imoinda's wake, national identities finally evaporated.

The class began along divided lines. The Ohio students were quick to find national value in the figures of the Virginia council in *The Widdow Ranter.* Tradesmen, former indentured servants, convicted felons were all types familiar to them from their high school history books. Although these characters are given such unflattering names as Dullman, Timorous, Whiff, and Whimsey, the students saw much in them to appreciate. Compared with the melodramatic Bacon, the council seemed a more capable lot. The council's lower-born members are a consistent source of comic relief in the play but rarely the explicit object of a joke. That fate—the students thought—falls to naive arrivals to the New World, in particular Hazard and, more obliquely, Bacon, who continues to rely on outmoded practices of honor when pragmatism is the new model. The Ohio students, even when made aware of the historical roots of Behn's play and told that the actual Bacon staged a revolt against Governor Berkeley to protect the interests of plantation owners against English economic policies, remained unmoved in their reading of Bacon. They saw him as a creature of the Old World, too class-bound and classically trained to represent the fluid figure they considered central to a New World vision. More challenging to their positive reading of colonial governance was the way the ragtag council of *The Widdow Ranter* is ironically reflected in *Oroonoko*, in the brutal expediency with which the Surinam council orders Oroonoko's torture and execution. The comic traps that Whiff and Whimsey set for the unsuspecting Bacon are no longer funny when juxtaposed against the treachery of Deputy Governor Byam, who promises Oroonoko forbearance after the revolt but delivers instead a brutal whipping. As a result, the Ohio students in their choice of scene to perform tended to steer away from *Oroonoko*, unwilling to play the more unflattering parts scripted for them there. Implicitly at least, they acknowledged more the complicity of the narrator in Oroonoko's fate. Their unquestioning faith in democratic councils was ultimately shaken by what unfolded in *Oroonoko*, and they refused to reproduce the narrator's politics by representing a scene from this text.

By contrast, the Exeter students found little identifiable Americanness in the works at first, reading them mainly as critical commentary on English colonial activities, much as early critics of *The Widdow Ranter* had done. For these students, most of the English settlers reflected a recognizable English class anxiety, including the relentless worry about social class, inheritance, and due process of law, along with the depiction of a hard-drinking culture. In searching for American identity, they found Bacon to be an American hero, embodying the complexity of colonial engagement—he is fighting a native population yet is in love with their queen. Although Bacon defends a plantation economy, he resists the Old World power of England and its disreputable proxy in the council. What troubled the Exeter students is that Byam could be read as a parallel to Bacon: Byam is aided by an Indian lover; defends the plantation economy, particularly the recovery of human capital in the form of the slaves; and in the execution of Oroonoko acts independently of the lord governor. Yet Byam is an English villain for whom Behn's narrator has nothing but contempt. Trefry, one of the novel's few moral voices, describes him as a tyrannical abuser of authority who dismisses moderating voices, relying on his ironically dubbed "wise Council" for support and for the execution of his will (59). In fact, if Byam has a parallel in *The Widdow Ranter*, it is in the figure of Wellman, the vacillating and self-interested deputy governor of Virginia. So just as the Ohio students found their faith in colonial councils shaken, the Exeter students found British authority in disarray and few characters to claim happily as their own.

Moreover, Oroonoko's death is contaminated when it is read against Bacon's death. Bodies litter the landscape of *Oroonoko*, and the threat of death hangs over the narrative, but the only deaths that matter are those of the leading characters. The body count of Oroonoko's army slain in their tents (28); the mother, her children, and the footman massacred by Caribs (47); and the deaths of council members hanged by the Dutch (59) are not meaningful or symbolic. But neither is death an unlucky consequence of "bloody flux and lice," as it is for the Bacon of the historical record (Pulsipher 45). Like Oroonoko, Bacon is deemed "above the Common Rank," as one "studying the Lives of the Romans" (1.1.113, 115), and his death, like Oroonoko's, is intended to matter. But our students, reading the texts against each other, found a surprising sense of dislocation between their own idea of a heroic death and the depiction of the deaths of both Oroonoko and Bacon, who despite their tragic status, die in complicated and contaminated ways. Oroonoko fails to revenge himself on the deputy governor, and our students read the lingering excesses of his torture as failure. Bacon's failure is worse, his Roman suicide a premature response to a tough battle ultimately won. Our students read the death of neither as heroic. They did not consider Oroonoko's to be martyrdom, as Laura Brown ([Nussbaum and Brown] 38–41) and Ros Ballaster ("New Hystericism" 290) do, but something closer to Joseph Roach's notion of "sacrificial expenditure" (41, 158). For them, the deaths of both Oroonoko and Bacon appeared simply a waste.

Only Southerne's adaptation normalized for them Behn's dangerous complexity into heroic form, allowing Oroonoko to kill the governor and stab himself twelve lines before the end of the play. Southerne replaced the uncomfortable "sacrificial expenditure" of Oroonoko's death in Behn's text with a less challenging vision of revenge and heroic self-determination and avoided facing his execution, as Susan Iwanisziw puts it, "as an indicator of the colonial malfeasance that transformed this African prince into a dead slave" ("Behn's Novel Investment" 81). By contrast, the parallel with Bacon's death in *The Widdow Ranter* revealed that suicide, and even revenge, was just another cost of colonial occupation. In the midst of battle and on the verge of victory against the deputy governor, Bacon mistakenly kills his beloved Native American princess,

Semernia, and then, intentionally, himself. The threat of both assimilation and revolt is thus removed by his haste to take the heroic path. Reading these texts together, our students saw how the heroics of self-determination proved futile against the realities of colonial life, where human life was measured in productivity rather than in noble action. Only when divorced from this context could an individual's death become meaningful—as a rendering of Imoinda's death performed by the Exeter students revealed. Delivered in a wordless, gestic style, their dramatic performance of Behn's prose account made the Ohio students see for the first time the pathos of a death in which Oroonoko and Imoinda lack the freedom to write their own fate and so must act it out instead.

The pairing of *Oroonoko* and *The Widdow Ranter* drew students' attention also to the performative aspects of the novel's narration. It helped them make sense of the physicalization of emotion in *Oroonoko*, shown by the success of the Exeter students' symbolic mime of Imoinda's death. The swooning, falling, and lingering looks that characterize the highly emotional behavior of the characters echo accepted theatrical conventions of tragedy and tragicomedy on the Restoration stage. Comparing the novel and the play did not undercut the novel's significance; instead, it revealed to our students just how innovative Behn was.

With the male characters morally compromised, the Ohio students increasingly found refuge in the female characters. In particular, the "rags to riches" story of the Widow Ranter appealed to them. Initially a white slave, "a Woman bought from the Ship by Old Colonel *Ranter*," she marries and outlives her master, and by the time we encounter her, she possesses "Fifty thousand Pounds Sterling" and a "Generous" reputation (1.1.79–85). Her home serves as a kind of New World trading post, where colonial women freely discuss their desires and seek the men they love while the Widow Ranter distracts and disarms her male visitors with punch and tobacco. When she avows that "we rich Widdows are the best Commodity this Country affords," we hear neither protest nor despair, only opportunity (3.83–84). That she pursues her dreams by dressing as a man; fighting for the object of her desire, Daring; and then fighting at his side only increases her appeal. Cross-dressing here is neither a gimmick nor an outmoded theatrical convention but a true mark of Ranter's masculine American character. As Daring concedes, "I never lik'd thee half so well in Petticoats" (4.2.282). For the Ohio students, only the women in Behn's two works merited the designation of heroic or represented the fluid ideologies of the New World. As Shannon Ross explains, "Within the new comic space of the post-Bacon New World, Ranter holds discursive sway" (86). Disenfranchised, kept from political power, and left with only their wits to defend them, the female characters offer a safe harbor in the embattled space of colonial politics—and in the heated e-mail exchanges of the students' transatlantic classroom.

Yet Behn's promise of female heroics, as Margaret Ferguson cautions ("News"), comes at a cost: the sacrifice of the racially other female to the aspirations of her white female counterpart. The plots of both texts support Ferguson's reading. Like the widow, Semernia cross-dresses and heads into battle, but her lover fails to recognize her, and she dies mistakenly by his sword. Like the female narrator, Imoinda professes great respect for Oroonoko, but that respect silences rather than authorizes her voice; it even renders her compliant in her own beheading. Semernia, in the Ohio classroom, emerged as just such a foil, quickly dismissed as less interesting than Ranter because she is more vulnerable. Imoinda, however, escaped such an easy opposition. The pairing furthered a rereading of her not as a sacrificial victim but as the heroine Behn's narrator insists she is. For both the Ohio and the Exeter students, Imoinda in America no longer resembled the younger Imoinda of Coramantien or, for that matter, the Native American Semernia. No longer a young girl trapped in a king's court, helplessly communicating in sighs and signs, she becomes in the New World a frequent visitor in the narrator's home and "a sharer in all our Adventures" (51). Like Ranter, she takes readily to the battlefield, fighting at Oroonoko's side, and "having a Bow, and a Quiver full of poyson'd Arrows . . . [she] wounded several, and shot the *Governor* into the Shoulder" (55). Students were intrigued to find that she holds, as Ross terms it, "discursive sway," with her story of slavery shaping the future of her "Infant yet Unborn" and inspiring Oroonoko's insurrection (51).

That Imoinda holds such discursive power in the New World is first attested to by Trefry, who reports to a shocked Oroonoko that Clemene, Imoinda's New World incarnation, can keep his sexual advances in check through her self-representation alone (38). By contrast with Imoinda, the female narrator looks weak, "possess'd with extream Fear" and "fly[ing] down the River" when the rebellion unfolds (57), acting more like the cowardly council members Whiff and Whimsey than the bold Ranter. Not until the final line of the novel, when Behn's narrator makes Imoinda's name nearly as central to this narrative as Oroonoko's, does the narrator, and by proxy Behn herself, begin to act like the New World woman our students wanted her to be.

The differences between the white slave Ranter and the black slave Imoinda prove greater than their similarities as the tragic history of the transatlantic slave trade unfolds. Both Ranter and Imoinda may be bought from a ship, but only Ranter is free to change her state. She may boast of being the country's "best Commodity," but Imoinda knows that she herself will be defined by economic value. Ranter represents her own interests; Imoinda cannot. But any oversimplification of what makes both female figures heroic finds its antidote in the pairing of the play and novel. Two groups of Ohio students who chose to stage scenes that featured the Widow Ranter made her heroic, and one even cast a male student in her role to emphasize her masculine glory. Imagine, then, their shock when they saw mirrored across the Atlantic the Widow Ranter portrayed by their Exeter counterparts not as the play's comic trickster but as its satiric object. Having read the play in the context of an introduction to drama class, the Exeter students found Ranter to be not a New World woman but a theatrical type—the female rake. As such, the Widow Ranter did not hold "discursive sway"; instead she was easily written off. For both groups of students, it became clear that no vision of these female figures could exist independent of the transatlantic connections that forged them and that continued to operate powerfully in the interactions between the classes. Students began to realize the provisionality of their own national identities.

Teaching these works together was not without its dangers. Students did identify more with the comic characters of Behn's play and find in them greater national virtue than they did with the characters in *Oroonoko*, which carried harsher truths. They also saw Oroonoko's death in a more compromised light. The classic concept of honor as a sustaining virtue suffered when these works were read together. Moreover, our experiment in asking students to perform their national identities in this context at first led to a greater entrenchment of the roles representing those identities. Yet the rewards ultimately outweighed the risks. Initial national identifications faded as students came to know the texts better and saw their interpretations performed transatlantically. Reading these works together, they experienced more viscerally the loss of Oroonoko and the complicity in his fate of their own democratic narratives. Finally, it brought to the forefront what Behn's narrator claims as one of her chief concerns: the "surviv[al] to all Ages" of not only the name of Oroonoko but also that "of the Brave, the Beautiful, and the Constant *Imoinda*" (65).

Since 2002, we have not taught these texts transatlantically—time and distance make that experiment difficult to continue—but we nearly always teach these works together in our separate classrooms, often without Southerne's text to buffer them. Remarkably, we find that even without a transatlantic classroom setting, both British and American students experience these same insights. In studying these works together, they recognize the instability of national narratives, the complicity of a New World narrative in the death of the noble hero, and the role of performance in the structuring of a prose account.

Most of all, students realize the significance of Imoinda and, through her, of Behn in defining heroism in a world where heroism seems to have lost its traditional moorings.

Behn and the Canon

Jane Spencer

The publication of a book on teaching *Oroonoko* — the present volume — is one indication of how far Aphra Behn has traveled since the 1970s. Back then, when I was an undergraduate, she was not part of the canon of university-studied literary works. Still, universities harbored a few forward-thinking enthusiasts for her writing. None of her works was set reading for my university course in English literature, but I was introduced to her because my tutor, James Booth, included an optional lecture on her in a course on seventeenth-century literature. This was about the time that Maureen Duffy's biography sparked new interest in Behn, fostered by the growth of women's literature courses. Over the next few decades, Behn had a remarkable revival on the stage, in print, and in the academy, where she was increasingly taught, usually as a pioneering female writer: the first woman professional writer, an early woman dramatist, an early woman novelist. In 1986, Mary Ann O'Donnell, introducing the first edition of her Behn bibliography, urged us to study her "not because she is a woman writer, but because she is an important writer" (*Aphra Behn* 11). How have we responded?

Behn is certainly a major presence in the more diverse and dispersed canon of early-twenty-first century university courses. A brief survey of Web sites indicates that in the academic year 2009–10, undergraduates were studying her in many places and under many headings. At the University of Pennsylvania, they might read her alongside Rochester, Wycherley, Cleland, and Boswell in Literary Erotics in the Eighteenth Century or with Rowe, Richardson, and Burney as part of Epistolary Fiction; at Loughborough University, they might choose an optional module devoted to her. At McGill University, they would encounter her first in an introductory Survey of English Literature I; then, represented by *Oroonoko*, in the intermediate course titled The Earlier Eighteenth-Century Novel; then, represented by *The Rover*, in the advanced course Studies in Drama: Comedy; and again in the advanced undergraduate or master's course Literary Forms: Travel and the Transformation of Knowledge. She is taught at Miami University, Ohio, as the culminating writer in the course British Women Writers: Medieval, Renaissance, and Restoration Women and as the inaugural writer of English fiction in English Fiction before 1832 at Toronto. She is taught in courses devoted to women's writing, to drama, to fiction, to early modern writing, to Restoration writing, to travel writing, to race and literature. At the University of Exeter, *The Rover* figured for some years in an introductory undergraduate course, Past and Present, making Behn the first female writer our students encountered in terms of literary-historical chronology and their undergraduate classes. *Oroonoko* and *The Rover* are the Behn texts most frequently included in university courses, but her other fiction and plays along with selections of her poetry also appear on course lists. She is both canonized and made the occasion for interrogating the canon: a long-running Open University course in the United Kingdom introduces issues of canon formation in Shakespeare, Aphra Behn and the Canon, which is also the title of an Open University book (Owens and Goodman) and of a module offered at Sim University in Singapore.

These repeated acts of inclusion in university courses along with the new editions and criticisms that accompany a place on the syllabus are, according to Barbara Herrnstein Smith's relativist theory of literary value, powerful "institutional acts" that bring "the work into the orbit of attention of a population of potential readers," making it "more likely both that the work will be experienced at all and also that it will be experienced as valuable" (46). Behn's canonical value continues to increase. We experience her, of course, in the light of our own and our time's preoccupations: "the conjunction of cultural studies and feminism," as Janet Todd puts it, has made her new critical prominence safe (*Critical Fortunes* 129). The feminist criticism of the 1970s and 1980s was behind the revival of Behn, and judging by her current appearance on women's studies programs and in many courses devoted to women's writing, her gender remains an important aspect of our concern, suggesting that Behn as an important writer is still entangled with Behn as a woman writer in our approaches to her. But if she entered the modern university as a woman writer, her place there has been consolidated by *Oroonoko*'s ability to lend itself to the discussions of race, colonialism, imperialism, and slavery that have been so important a part of literary and cultural criticism over the last thirty years. This state of affairs has caused anxiety among some critics that historical understanding of Behn's most famous work might be lost in a presentist focus on issues that, however important in themselves, are arguably not central to it (D. Hughes, "*Oroonoko*" 154).

But *Oroonoko* invites plural readings. It does bear on questions of race, colonialism, imperialism, and slavery, if in a specifically seventeenth-century way, and the eighteenth century's construction of the "*Oroonoko* legend" (Sypher 108), whereby Behn's story fed an antislavery argument that was far removed from her intentions, is part of the novel's larger significance. At the same time, it rewards study of the occasion of its composition at a time of Stuart crisis (Guffey) and of its complex engagement with memories of the time of its setting (Todd, *Gender* 43–49). Indeed it serves, as many teachers have found, as a good stage for introducing debate about how we read the texts of the past.

What might Behn have made of the question of her place in today's canon? A literary canon was certainly in the process of conscious construction in her time, as writers laid claim to a place in ancient lineages and publishers brought out collected editions of significant writers complete with prefatory biographies. Behn, with her expressed hope to be remembered with Sappho, and her editors, who tried out the innovative form of a collected edition of her fiction a few years after her death, were at the forefront of this development. Behn came more and more in her later years to care about her claims on posterity. In the preface to one of her early comedies, *The Dutch Lover* (1673), she defended plays as entertainments that had no need of learning: "*I think a Play the best divertisement that wise men have; but I do also think them nothing so, who do discourse so formallie about the rules of it, as if 'twere the grand affair of humane life*" (*Works* [Todd] 5: 162). But in her final years she turned not against entertainment (she was as dependent on it as ever) but toward a way of conceiving of her entertaining work as part of an ancient and honorable tradition. Defending *The Luckey Chance* (1687) against criticisms of indecency, she appealed not only to its popularity ("I found by my Receipts it was not thought so Criminal") but also to its rights to the ancient freedoms of poets: "All I ask, is the Priviledge for my Masculine Part the Poet in me, (if any such you will allow me) to tread in those successful Paths my Predecessors have so long thriv'd in, to take those Measures that both the Ancient and Modern writers have set me, and by which they have pleas'd the World so well." Threatening (idly enough, since she could not afford to carry it out) to give up writing without proper appreciation, she continued: "I value Fame as much as if I had been born a *Hero*; and if you rob me of that, I can retire from the ungrateful World, and scorn its fickle Favours" (7: 217). Here she brings the concerns of heroic literature—the hero's concern for his reputation—into the question of a writer's reception. She reconceives the writer, even the modern writer working for bread, as hero.

Elsewhere Behn treats the writer, more conventionally, as the guardian of others' fame. In her later work, she repeatedly examines the idea of the writer's job of immortalizing the hero—a central theme of *Oroonoko*, with its ambiguous relation between the royal slave of the title and his eventual historian. The narrator is dazzled by Oroonoko/Caesar, considering him the heroic ideal come to life, a great warrior, great lover, and "Royal Youth" whose quality impresses itself on all beholders even in slavery: "his Eyes insensibly commanded Respect, and his Behaviour insinuated it into every Soul" (36). Her task is to record the gallantry and bravery that the world has lost with his death, with a strict adherence to the "Truth" (8) that her hero has always honored and that his enemies, from the treacherous slaving captain to Deputy Governor Byam, have always violated. But Oroonoko's heroic deeds in Coramantien have to be taken on the trust of his tale, and his actions in Surinam call his heroism into question. His fine deeds of tiger killing and of wrestling with numb eels amount to little more than diverting, and being diverted by, the deceptively friendly colonists, while his killing of Imoinda provokes open debate: is it tragic necessity or horrible example of husbandly prerogative taken too far? Meanwhile, the narrator herself, spying on her hero on behalf of the mistrustful colonists, then bewailing her inability to save him, is at least partly implicated in the faithlessness that destroys the truthful Oroonoko. Her pen is invoked at the end to solve the problems its work has revealed and to enable Oroonoko/Caesar's "Glorious Name to survive to all Ages" (65).

The parallels that have been noted between James II and Oroonoko make this examination of heroism also an ambiguous tribute and perhaps, as Todd has suggested, a warning to the king (*Secret Life* 418). In her poems, Behn treats

James more simply. Her late Pindarics take on the task of insistent celebration of the increasingly unpopular Stuart monarchy. In her *Congratulatory Poem to the King's Most Sacred Majesty, on the Happy Birth of the Prince of Wales* (1688), she claims the role of loyal and successful prophet: "Long with *Prophetick Fire*, Resolv'd and Bold, / Your *Glorious FATE* and *FORTUNE* I foretold" (*Works* [Todd] 1: 297 [lines 7–8]), but her rhetorically necessary poetic humility ("My *Pleasure*'s too Extream for *Thought* or *Wit*" [line 62]) also seems consistent with the clichés and hyperboles of the verse. More poetically interesting is her response to political reversal shortly afterward, when James fled, William and Mary arrived, and the Williamite Gilbert Burnet apparently asked her to turn her hand to celebrating the new regime. *A Pindaric Poem to the Reverend Doctor Burnet on the Honour He Did Me of Enquiring after Me and My Muse* refuses the request with great care. At first, the poet appears about to agree to it. Claiming to have been nothing but an unambitious pastoral poet before, she is roused by Burnet's praise to aspire to the "more exalted" thoughts of heroes and kings (308 [line 40]). But then her "stubborn Muse" refuses to obey:

> My Muse that would endeavour fain to glide
> With the fair prosperous Gale, and the full driving Tide
> But Loyalty commands with Pious Force,
>   That stops me in the thriving Course.
> The Brieze that wafts the Crowding Nations o're,
>   Leaves me unpity'd far behind
>   On the Forsaken Barren Shore,
> To sigh with Echo, and the Murmuring Wind.
> (lines 49–56)

The image of the lonely loyalist replaces that of the triumphant poet. In the light of James's exile, the role of the successful writer whose claim to immortality rests on celebrating the fame of others has been rejected. In this context, praise of Burnet's powerful writing becomes slyly ironic:

> 'Tis to your Pen, Great Sir, the Nation owes
> For all the Good this Mighty Change has wrought;
> 'Twas that the wondrous Method did dispose,
> E're the vast Work was to Perfection brought.
> Oh strange Effect of a Seraphick Quill!
>   That can by unperceptable degrees
> Change every Notion, every Principle
>   To any Form, its Great Dictator please.
> (lines 66–73)

She accuses him, politely, of twisting the truth in support of the new king and queen. The ending dismisses while pretending to praise both William and Burnet: "And great *NASSAU* shall in your Annals live / To all Futurity" (lines 100–01). In Burnet's annals—not in Behn's.

At the end of her life, Behn could see plenty of reason for the fame she valued to fall into obscurity. She had seen her plays attacked for indecency, and, in her preface to *The Luckey Chance*, she had complained about a lack of support from her "Brothers of the Pen" (7: 217). She was convinced that her reputation as a writer of comedy would have stood much higher had her plays come out under a man's name (216–17). She was on the losing side in what the Whiggish thinkers she despised were to call the Glorious Revolution, and she had no intention of joining "[t]he Man that chang'd his Note, / And he who has turn'd his Coat" (1: 359 [lines 12–13 of "The Complaint of the Poor *Cavaliers*"]). In her late poems, she took a longer view, looking to a poetic immortality that she hoped to be granted when the political wheel turned again. In her 1688 elegy on Edmund Waller's death, she entered—yet again—what had been a mainly male tradition, that of forging one's place in the literary line by honoring a dead fellow poet: "Eternal, as thy own Almighty Verse, / Should be those *Trophies* that adorn thy *Hearse*" (289 [lines 16–17]). Under the conventional self-deprecation that names her verses "Transitory *Flowers*" (line 21) is the equally conventional claim to have inherited the dead poet's mantle: "Such *Tributes* are, like *Tenures*, only fit / To shew from whom we hold our *Right* to *Wit*" (23–24). Waller, Behn claims, first "Nurst" her "Infant *Muse*" (26), and he taught poets "how to *Love*, and how to *Write*" (45), that combination for which Behn herself was famous. When she portrays him as neglected in his late years, "Scorning th'unthinking *Crowd*" (63), and quitting "the Stage," the parallel with her position holds. Implicitly, the poem expresses a hope that the "*Circulary Course*" (52) of the sun, with whose beams Waller's poetic power is compared, will bring a renewal of his fame and her own.

Among Behn's contemporaries, it was not Waller but John Milton whose sun was to rise decisively in the next century, but neither in politics nor in style could Behn have been one of Milton's daughters. She placed herself, always, with royalists. Translating the sixth book of Abraham Cowley's *Of Plants*, she followed Cowley to claim the bays only in secondary position, "after Monarchs," who have first title to their garlands (1: 325 [line 586]). But when "*The Translatress in her own Person speaks*," she adds the bolder and now famous claim that she has a "double right" to those bays because she shares Daphne's sex and Apollo's power, and she places herself in a female line "with *Sappho* and *Orinda*," claiming immortality for her verses along with theirs (590–94). Her association with these two famous women poets was to be strengthened in eighteenth-century disscusions of women's writing. It was not a connection that necessarily helped her in the age of feminine delicacy: she was tainted with Sappho's reputation for warmth and looseness and compared unfavorably to the pure and matchless Orinda. But a later age would rediscover her, partly because of a feminist fascination with the female lines of the past. We have learned, as this volume among many others shows, to find her important for other reasons too, if not always the ones she would have expected.

Behn would have been glad to know that her comedies received the praise she always thought they deserved. She probably expected her poetry, especially her translation of Cowley and her Stuart panegyrics, to carry her fame forward rather than a short piece of rapidly written fiction like *Oroonoko*. "I writ it in a few Hours" she explains in her "Epistle Dedicatory" to Lord Maitland, excusing its "Faults of Connexion; for I never rested my Pen a Moment for Thought" (7). She exaggerates her carelessness, perhaps, but the fact remains that what she presents as a lightweight piece has become her most canonical, its "Faults of Connexion" carefully pondered by a generation of critics who have used it to forge connections of their own.

If Behn hoped that a further restoration of the Stuarts would one day bring honor to their loyal poet, she was of course wrong. But our abiding interest in other aspects of the literary world she belonged to—its tentative moves toward freethinking, its experiments with fiction, its command of the stage, its fascination with the new world of the colonies, and its response to the growing slave trade—provides many other reasons for reading and remembering her work. She would no doubt have been startled, but I am sure she would have been pleased to know that 320 years after her death at least one university (Waterloo, Ontario) would be inviting students to encounter writers such as Dryden, Etherege, Rochester, and Wycherley by enrolling in a course entitled The Age of Aphra Behn: Restoration Literature.

NOTES ON CONTRIBUTORS

Sharon Alker, associate professor of English and general studies at Whitman College, is the author of numerous essays on the literature of the long eighteenth century and a co-founder of the Defoe Society. With Holly Faith Nelson she has written on Shakespeare's treatment of the Scot in *Macbeth* and edited collections of essays on James Hogg and Robert Burns.

Emily Hodgson Anderson, associate professor of English at the University of Southern California, is the author of *Eighteenth-Century Authorship and the Play of Fiction: Novels and the Theater, Haywood to Austen* as well as recent articles on Maria Edgeworth and Charles Macklin's Shylock. Her current work investigates how eighteenth-century novelists appropriated Shakespearean characters and themes.

Srinivas Aravamudan is professor of English and dean of humanities at Duke University. He is the author of *Enlightenment Orientalism: Resisting the Rise of the Novel* and *Guru English: South Asian Religion in a Cosmopolitan Language* and also editor of William Earle's *Obi; or, The History of Three-Fingered Jack*. His *Tropicopolitans* won the outstanding first book prize of the MLA.

Ana de Freitas Boe, associate professor at Baldwin-Wallace College, has written on Mary Wollstonecraft and Hannah More and is currently coediting the collection of essays *Heteronormativity in Eighteenth-Century Literature and Culture*.

Erik Bond, associate professor of English literature at the University of Michigan, Dearborn, has written on James Boswell, the Great Fire of London, Frances Burney, and Dickens. He is the author of *Reading London: Urban Speculation and Imaginative Government in Eighteenth-Century Literature*.

Keith M. Botelho, associate professor of English at Kennesaw State University, is the author of *Renaissance Earwitnesses: Rumor and Early Modern Masculinity*. He is currently completing a book tentatively titled "Little Beasts: Bees, Man, and the Renaissance Culture of the Hive."

Vincent Carretta, professor of English at the University of Maryland, is the editor of works by Olaudah Equiano, Ignatius Sancho, Ottobah Cugoano, Phillis Wheatley, Philip Quaque, and other eighteenth-century transatlantic authors of African descent. His monographs include biographies of Equiano and Wheatley.

Ashley Cross, professor of English, Manhattan College, has written on Mary Darby Robinson, Anna Seward, Charlotte Dacre, Mary Shelley, and Percy Shelley. She is the author of the forthcoming *Mary Robinson and the Genesis of Romanticism: Literary Dialogues and Debts, 1784–1821*.

Laura Doyle, professor of English at the University of Massachusetts, received the Perkins Award Book Prize for her *Bordering on the Body: The Racial Matrix of Modern Fiction and Culture*. Her most recent book is *Freedom's Empire: Race and the Rise of the Novel in Atlantic Modernity, 1640–1940*.

Karen Gevirtz, associate professor of English at Seton Hall University, has written a number of articles on seventeenth-century women, including Behn, and on the eighteenth-century novel. She is the author of *Life after Death: Widows and the English Novel, Defoe to Austen* and coeditor, with Mona Narain, of *Gender and Space in British Literature, 1660–1820*.

Derek Hughes, professor emeritus of English at the University of Aberdeen, is the author of *Dryden's Heroic Plays*; *English Drama, 1660–1700*; *The Theatre of Aphra Behn*; and *Culture and Sacrifice: Ritual Death in Literature and Opera*. He recently edited *Oroonoko* among other works in *Versions of Blackness* and with Janet Todd edited *The Cambridge Companion to Aphra Behn*.

Scott J. Juengel, senior lecturer at Vanderbilt University, has written on *Fanny Hill*, *Frankenstein*, and the early novel and catastrophe. He is finishing an edition of Defoe's *Journal of the Plague Year* and working on the relation between modern constructions of race and mimetic theories and practices between 1650 and 1839.

Thomas W. Krise, professor of English and president of Pacific Lutheran University, is the editor of *Caribbeana: An Anthology of English Literature of the West Indies, 1657–1777*. His publications and research interests focus on early Caribbean, British seventeenth- and eighteenth-century, and early American literature.

Joyce Green MacDonald, associate professor of English at the University of Kentucky, is the author of *Women and Race in Early Modern Texts* and essays on race and performance in Renaissance drama. Her current project is a book on how Shakespearean texts and genres have been transformed in American contexts.

Roberta C. Martin, associate professor emerita of English at East Carolina University, has written on Milton and on the destabilization of sexual categories in Aphra Behn. Her current projects include a full-length study of Behn and self-demonstrating anatomy.

Shawn Lisa Maurer, associate professor of English at the College of the Holy Cross, is the author of *Proposing Men: Dialectics of Gender and Class in the Eighteenth-Century English Periodical* and the editor of Elizabeth Inchbald's *Nature and Art*. She has published widely on Restoration and eighteenth-century literature, especially drama and theater. Her current book project studies adolescence and the novel in the eighteenth century.

Jane Milling, senior lecturer at the University of Exeter, is the editor of Susanna Centlivre's *The Basset Table*, coauthor of *Devising Performance: A Critical History*, coeditor of the first volume of the *Cambridge History of British Theatre*, and the author of essays on Restoration actors and women dramatists.

Jessica Munns, professor of English literature at the University of Denver, is the editor of *Restoration and Eighteenth-Century Theatre Research* and author and coeditor of many books, articles, and chapters on Restoration and eighteenth-century literature.

Holly Faith Nelson, professor and chair of English and codirector of the Gender Studies Institute at Trinity Western University, is the coeditor of *The Broadview Anthology of Seventeenth-Century Verse and Prose*; *Of Paradise and Light: Essays on Henry Vaughan and John Milton*; and *Digital Defoe: Studies in Defoe and His Contemporaries*.

Mary Ann O'Donnell, professor emerita of English and former dean of the School of Arts at Manhattan College, teaches in the Marymount Manhattan College Program at the Bedford Hills Correctional Facility. Among her publications on Behn is the primary and secondary bibliography of Behn's works.

Bill Overton was professor of literary studies at Loughborough University at the time of his death in 2012. He is the author of *Fictions of Female Adultery, 1684–1890: Theories and Circumtexts*, of *The Eighteenth-Century British Verse Epistle*, and of a wide range of essays, including "Aphra Behn and the Verse Epistle" and "Aphra Behn and Versification."

Cynthia Richards, professor and chair of the English department at Wittenberg University, is the editor of Wollstonecraft's *The Wrongs of Woman; or, Maria* and the author of articles on Aphra Behn, Eliza Haywood, Mary Wollstonecraft, and Mary Hays.

Leslie Richardson taught for eight years at Xavier University of Louisiana, the only Catholic HBCU in the United States. Now director of the Center for the Advancement of Teaching at Florida International University, she is the author of "Leaving Her Father's House: Locke, Astell, and Clarissa's Body Politic" and "'Who Shall Restore My Lost Credit?': Rape, Reputation, and the Marriage Market."

Laura J. Rosenthal, professor of English at the University of Maryland, is the author of *Infamous Commerce: Prostitution in Eighteenth-Century British Literature and Culture* and coeditor of *Monstrous Dreams of Reason: Body, Self, and Other in the Enlightenment*.

Margarete Rubik, professor of English literature at the University of Vienna, is the author of *Early Women Dramatists, 1550–1800* and the editor of *Aphra Behn and Her Female Successors*.

Laura L. Runge, university professor of English at the University of South Florida, is the author of *Gender and Language in British Literary Criticism, 1660–1790* and editor of *Aphra Behn Online: Interactive Journal for Women in the Arts, 1640–1830*.

Jane Spencer, professor of English literature at the University of Exeter, is the author of *The Rise of the Woman Novelist*; *Aphra Behn's Afterlife*; and *Literary Relations: Kinship and the Canon, 1660–1830*. Her current work focuses on animals in the Enlightenment.

Laura M. Stevens, associate professor of English at the University of Tulsa, is the author of *The Poor Indians: British Missionaries, Native Americans, and Colonial Sensibility* and editor of *Tulsa Studies in Women's Literature*. She is writing a book on eighteenth-century British missionary fantasies.

James Grantham Turner, James D. Hart Professor of English at the University of California, Berkeley, has written on literature and art from the Renaissance to the eighteenth-century. He is the author of *Schooling Sex: Libertine Literature and Erotic Education in Italy, France, and England, 1534–1685*.

Rose Zimbardo retired from Stony Brook University as distinguished professor in 1997 and is now an adjunct professor at the University of San Francisco. She has written four books, the most recent of which is *The Conceptual Design in Shakespeare's Comedies* (2012) and many articles on subjects varying from Chaucer to Aphra Behn.

SURVEY PARTICIPANTS

As we prepared this volume, we had as our guide the combined wisdom of many scholars who shared with us their experiences and sometimes their frustrations in teaching Aphra Behn's *Oroonoko*. For their generosity in filling out the survey questionnaire and for their many insights, we are most grateful.

Sharon Alker, *Whitman College*
Emily Hodgson Anderson, *University of Southern California*
Srinivas Aravamudan, *Duke University*
Carolyn Jursa Ayers, *Saint Mary's University, Minnesota*
Ana de Freitas Boe, *Baldwin-Wallace College*
Erik Bond, *University of Michigan, Dearborn*
Keith M. Botelho, *Kennesaw State University*
Yolanda Caballero Aceituno, *Universidad de Jaén*
Ann Campbell, *Boise State University*
Elizabeth Child, *Trinity College, Washington DC*
Pilar Cuder-Dominguez, *Universidad de Huelva*
Tammy L. Durant, *Metropolitan State University*
Jorge Figueroa-Dorrego, *Universidad de Vigo*
Karen Gevirtz, *Seton Hall University*
Lisa Gim, *Fitchburg State University*
George Haggerty, *University of California, Riverside*
Pamela S. Hardman, *Cuyahoga Community College*
Lucy Kelly Hayden, *Eastern Michigan University*
Howard V. Hendrix, *California State University, Fresno*
Oddvar Holmesland, *Agder University*
Aleksondra Hultquist, *University of Illinois, Urbana*
Scott J. Juengel, *Vanderbilt University*
Thomas W. Krise, *Pacific Lutheran University*
Richard Kroll, *University of California, Irvine*
Joanna Lipking, *Northwestern University*
Paula Loscocco, *Sarah Lawrence College*
Roberta C. Martin, *Eastern Carolina University*
Shawn Lisa Maurer, *College of the Holy Cross*
Katherine Montwieler, *University of North Carolina, Wilmington*
Holly Faith Nelson, *Trinity Western University*
Felicity Nussbaum, *University of California, Los Angeles*
Bill Overton, *Loughborough University*
Patricia Pender, *Pace University*
Keith Peterson, *Brigham Young University, Hawai'i*
Heather Powers, *Indiana University of Pennsylvania*
Martha Rainbolt, *DePauw University*
Leslie Richardson, *Xavier University of Louisiana*
Margarete Rubik, *University of Vienna*

Kathryn Rummell, *California Polytechnic State University*
Laura L. Runge, *University of South Florida*
Laura M. Stevens, *University of Tulsa*
Dennis Todd, *Georgetown University*
James Grantham Turner, *University of California, Berkeley*
Melora Vandersluis, *Azusa Pacific University*
Joanne van der Woude, *Harvard University*
Sonia Villegas-López, *Universidad de Huelva*
Elizabeth A. Way, *Wake Forest University*
Rose Zimbardo, *University of San Francisco*
Madhvi Zutshi, *Rutgers University, New Brunswick*

WORKS CITED

Abrams, M. H., et al., eds. *The Norton Anthology of English Literature*. 2 vols. 6th ed. New York: Norton, 1993. Print.

Addison, Joseph. "*Spectator* No. 69." Damrosch et al. 1C: 2330–32.

Albert, Pamela J. *Transatlantic Engagements with the British Eighteenth Century*. New York: Routledge, 2008. Print.

Anderson, Emily Hodgson. "Novelty in Novels: A Look at What's New in Aphra Behn's *Oroonoko*." *Studies in the Novel* 39.1 (2007): 1–16. Print.

Anderson, Fred. *Crucible of War: The Seven Years' War and the Fate of Empire in British North America, 1754–1766*. New York: Vintage, 2000. Print.

Andrade, Susan Z. "White Skin, Black Masks: Colonialism and the Sexual Politics of *Oroonoko*." *Cultural Critique* 27 (1994): 189–214. Print.

Aravamudan, Srinivas. "Petting Oroonoko." *Tropicopolitans: Colonialism and Agency, 1688–1804*. Durham: Duke UP, 1999. 29–70. Print.

Archer, John Michael. *Old Worlds: Egypt, Southwest Asia, India, and Russia in Early Modern English Writing*. Stanford: Stanford UP, 2001. Print.

Arikha, Noga. *Passions and Tempers: A History of the Humours*. New York: Harper, 2007. Print.

Aristotle. *Politics*. *The Complete Works of Aristotle*. Vol. 2. Ed. Jonathan Barnes. Princeton: Princeton UP, 1984. 1986–2129. Print. Bollingen Ser.

Astell, Mary. *Reflections upon Marriage: The Third Edition: To Which Is Added a Preface, in Answer to Some Objections*. London, 1706. *Women Writers Online*. Web. 13 Feb. 2010.

Athey, Stephanie, and Daniel Cooper Alarcón. "*Oroonoko*'s Gendered Economies of Honor/Horror: Reframing Colonial Discourse Studies in the Americas." *American Literature* 65.3 (1993): 415–43. *EBSCO*. Web. 7 July 2009.

Aughterson, Kate. *Aphra Behn: The Comedies*. New York: Palgrave, 2003. Print.

Bacon, Francis. *The Essays*. Ed. John Pitcher. Harmondsworth: Penguin, 1985. Print.

———. *New Atlantis*. *Essays and* New Atlantis. Ed. Gordon S. Haight. New York: Black, 1942. 243–302. Print.

Ballaster, Ros. "'A Devil on't, the Woman Damns the Poet': Aphra Behn's Fictions of Feminine Identity." *Seductive Forms: Women's Amatory Fiction from 1684–1740*. Oxford: Oxford UP, 1992. 69–113. Print.

———. *Fabulous Orients: Fictions of the East in England, 1662–1785*. Oxford: Oxford UP, 2005. Print.

———. "New Hystericism: Aphra Behn's *Oroonoko*: The Body, the Text, and the Feminist Critic." *New Feminist Discourses: Critical Essays on Theories and Texts*. Ed. Isobel Armstrong. London: Routledge, 1992. 283–95. Print.

Bandele, 'Biyi. *Aphra Behn's* Oroonoko *in a New Adaptation*. Charlbury: Amber Lane, 1999. Print.

Bannet, Eve Tavor. *Empire of Letters: Letter Manuals and Transatlantic Correspondence, 1680–1820*. Cambridge: Cambridge UP, 2005. Print.

Beckles, Hilary, and Verene Shepherd. *Caribbean Slavery in the Atlantic World: A Student Reader*. Kingston: Randle, 2000. Print.

Behn, Aphra. *Abdelazer; or, The Moor's Revenge: A Tragedy*. London, 1677. *EEBO*. Web. 28 May 2010.

———. "The Disappointment." 1680. Damrosch et al. 1C: 2126–29.

———. *The Fair Jilt*. Behn, *Works* [Todd] 3: 1–48.

———. *The Histories and Novels of the Late Ingenious Mrs. Behn*. London, 1696. *EEBO*. Web. 26 Oct. 2009.

———. *The History of the Nun*. Behn, *Works* [Todd] 3: 205–58.

———. *Oroonoko*. Introd. Lore Metzger. New York: Norton, 1973. Print.

———. *Oroonoko*. Ed. Janet Todd. London: Penguin, 2003. Print.

———. *Oroonoko*. D. Hughes, *Versions* 117–89.

———. Oroonoko *and Other Stories*. Ed. Maureen Duffy. London: Methuen, 1986. Print.

———. Oroonoko *and Other Writings*. Ed. Paul Salzman. Oxford: Oxford UP, 1994. Print. World's Classics.

———. *Oroonoko; or, The Royal Slave*. Ed. Joanna Lipking. New York: Norton, 1997. Print. Norton Critical Ed.

———. *Oroonoko; or, The Royal Slave*. Ed. Catherine Gallagher. New York: Bedford–St. Martin's, 2000. Print.

———. *Oroonoko; or, The Royal Slave*. Read by Elizabeth Klett. *Internet Archive*. Internet Archive, 26 Aug. 2009. Web. 11 July 2011. LibriVox Free Audiobook Collection.

———. *Oroonoko; or, The Royal Slave: A True History*. London, 1688. *EEBO*. Web. 15 Oct. 2009.

———. *Oroonoko; or, The Royal Slave: A True History* [transcription]. London, 1688. *Chadwyck-Healey*. Web. 15 Oct. 2009.

———. Oroonoko, The Rover, *and Other Works*. Ed. Janet Todd. London: Penguin, 1992. Print.

———. *A Pindarick Poem on the Happy Coronation of His Most Sacred Majesty James II*. London, 1685. Print.

———. *The Widdow Ranter*. 1690. Behn, *Works* [Todd] 7: 285–354.

———. *The Works of Aphra Behn*. Ed. Montague Summers. 6 vols. 1915. New York: Phaeton, 1967. Print.

———. *The Works of Aphra Behn*. Ed. Janet Todd. 7 vols. London: Pickering; Columbus: Ohio State UP, 1992–96. Print.

Berkhofer, Robert F., Jr. *The White Man's Indian: Images of the American Indian from Columbus to the Present*. New York: Knopf, 1978. Print.

Berlin, Ira. *Many Thousands Gone: The First Two Centuries of Slavery in North America*. Cambridge: Harvard UP, 1998. Print.

Bernbaum, Ernest. "Mrs. Behn's Biography a Fiction." *PMLA* 28.3 (1913): 432–53. Print.

———. "Mrs. Behn's *Oroonoko*." *Anniversary Papers by Colleagues and Pupils of George Lyman Kittredge*. Boston: Ginn, 1913. 419–35. Print.

Black, Joseph, et al., eds. *The Broadview Anthology of British Literature: The Restoration and Eighteenth Century.* Peterborough: Broadview, 2006. Print.

Blake, William. "Little Black Boy." 1789. Damrosch et al. 2A: 167–68.

Boswell, James. *The Life of Johnson.* Ed. R. W. Chapman. 1904. New York: Oxford UP, 1998. Print. Oxford World's Classics.

Bowers, Jennifer, and Peggy Keeran. *Literary Research and the British Renaissance and Early Modern Period: Strategies and Sources.* Lanham: Scarecrow, 2010. Print.

Brenner, Robert. *Merchants and Revolution: Commercial Change, Political Conflict, and London's Overseas Traders, 1550–1653.* Princeton: Princeton UP, 1993. Print.

Brontë, Charlotte. *Jane Eyre.* 1847. Ed. Richard A. Dunne. 3rd ed. New York: Norton, 2000. Print. Norton Critical Ed.

Brown, Laura. *Ends of Empire: Women and Ideology in Early-Eighteenth Century Literature.* Ithaca: Cornell UP, 1993. Print.

———. "The Romance of Empire: *Oroonoko* and the Trade in Slaves." *The New Eighteenth Century: Theory, Politics, and English Literature.* Ed. Felicity Nussbaum and Laura Brown. New York: Methuen, 1987. 41–61. Print.

Browning, Elizabeth Barrett. *Aurora Leigh.* 1856. Damrosch et al. 2B: 1203–26.

Burney, Frances. *Evelina; or, The History of a Young Lady's Entrance into the World.* Ed. Kristina Straub. Boston: Bedford, 1997. Print.

Burns, Robert. "Man Was Made to Mourn: A Dirge." *Robert Burns: Selected Poems.* Ed. Carol McGuirk. London: Penguin, 1993. 54–56. Print.

Cabeza de Vaca, Alvar Núñez. *Chronicle of the Narváez Expedition.* 1542. Trans. Fanny Bandelier. Rev. Harold Augenbraum. New York: Penguin, 2002. Print.

Cameron, W. J. *New Light on Aphra Behn.* 1961. Darby: Arden Lib., 1978. Print.

Campbell, Mary Baine. *Wonder and Science: Imagining Worlds in Early Modern Europe.* Ithaca: Cornell UP, 1999. Print.

Carey, John. "Milton's Satan." *The Cambridge Companion to Milton.* Ed. Dennis Danielson. 2nd ed. Cambridge: Cambridge UP, 1999. 160–74. Print.

Carlton, Charles. *Going to the Wars: The Experience of the British Civil Wars, 1638–1651.* London: Routledge, 1992. Print.

Carnell, Rachel K. "Subverting Tragic Conventions: Aphra Behn's Turn to the Novel." *Studies in the Novel* 31.2 (1999): 133–51. *EBSCO.* Web. 7 July 2009.

Carretta, Vincent. *Equiano, the African: Biography of a Self-Made Man.* Athens: U of Georgia P, 2005. New York: Penguin, 2006. Print.

Cavendish, Margaret. "Assaulted and Pursued Chastity." Cavendish, Blazing World 45–118.

———. *Bell in Campo. Bell in Campo [and] The Sociable Companions.* Ed. Alexandra G. Bennett. Peterborough: Broadview, 2002. 23–120. Print.

———. The Blazing World *and Other Writings.* Ed. Kate Lilley. New York: Penguin, 2004. Print.

———. *The Description of a New World, Called the Blazing World: Observations upon Experimental Philosophy: To Which Is Added, the Description of a New Blazing World.* London, 1666. *EEBO.* Web. 23 Jan. 2010.

———. "A Description of the Battle in Fight." Cavendish, *Poems* 173–77.

———. "An Elegy on My Brother, Kill'd in These Unhappy Warres." Cavendish, *Poems* 196.

———. *Poems and Fancies*. London, 1653. *EEBO*. Web. 18 June 2013.

Chibka, Robert L. "'Oh! Do Not Fear a Woman's Invention': Truth, Falsehood, and Fiction in Aphra Behn's *Oroonoko*." *Texas Studies in Language and Literature* 30.4 (1988): 510–37. Print.

———. "Truth, Falsehood, and Fiction in *Oroonoko*." Behn, *Oroonoko; or, The Royal Slave* [Lipking] 220–32.

Clarendon, Edward Hyde, earl of. *The History of the Rebellion and Civil Wars in England, together with an Historical View of the Affairs in Ireland*. 7 vols. Oxford: Oxford UP, 1849. Print.

Coleridge, Samuel Taylor. "Kubla Khan." 1816. Damrosch et al. 2A: 602–04.

Colonial House. Ed. Sallie Clement and Kathryn Walker. PBS Home Video, 2004. DVD.

Columbus, Christopher. *Select Letters of Christopher Columbus: With Other Original Documents, Relating to His Four Voyages to the New World*. Trans. and ed. R. H. Major. 2nd ed. London: Hakluyt Soc., 1870. *Google Books*. Web. 17 Aug. 2009.

Conrad, Joseph. *Heart of Darkness*. 1899. Damrosch et al. 2C: 1954–2010.

Cook, James. *An Account of the Voyages Undertaken by the Order of His Present Majesty for Making Discoveries in the Southern Hemisphere*. 3 vols. Ed. John Hawkesworth. London, 1773. *South Seas: Voyaging and Cross-Cultural Encounters in the Pacific, 1760–1800*. Web. 23 Apr. 2013.

Cowley, Abraham. "To the Royal Society." *A History of the Royal Society*. By Thomas Sprat. London, 1668. B1r–B3v. *Google Books*. Web. 16 Jan. 2010.

Craton, Michael. *Empire, Enslavement, and Freedom in the Caribbean*. Kingston: Randle, 1997. Print.

Cunningham, Richard L. "The Biological Impacts of 1492." *The Indigenous People of the Caribbean*. Ed. Samuel M. Wilson. Gainesville: UP of Florida, 1997. 31–35. Print.

Damrosch, David, et al., eds. *The Longman Anthology of British Literature*. 4th ed. 2 vols. New York: Longman, 2010. Print.

Davis, David Brion, and Steven Mintz. *The Boisterous Sea of Liberty: A Documentary History of America from Discovery through the Civil War*. New York: Oxford UP, 1998. Print.

Davis, Natalie Zemon. "Maria Sibylla Merian." *Women on the Margins: Three Seventeenth-Century Lives*. Cambridge: Harvard UP, 1995. 140–202. Print.

Defoe, Daniel. *Moll Flanders*. Ed. Albert J. Rivero. New York: Norton, 2004. Print. Norton Critical Ed.

———. *Robinson Crusoe*. 1719. *Project Gutenberg*. Web. 17 Aug. 2009.

DeMaria, Robert, Jr., ed. *British Literature, 1640–1789: An Anthology*. Oxford: Blackwell, 1996. Print.

Díaz del Castillo, Bernal. *The True History of the Conquest of New Spain*. Trans. Alfred Percival Maudslay. 5 vols. London: Hakluyt Soc., 1908–16. Print.

Dooley, Brendan. Introduction. *The Politics of Information in Early Modern Europe*. Ed. Dooley and Sabrina A. Baron. London: Routledge, 2001. 1–16. Print.

Douglass, Frederick. *Narrative of the Life of Frederick Douglass, an American Slave: Written by Himself*. Boston, 1845. Print.

Doyle, Laura. *Freedom's Empire: Race and the Rise of the Novel in Atlantic Modernity, 1640–1940*. Durham: Duke UP, 2008. Print.

Dryden, John. *Works*. Ed. Edward Niles Hooker, H. T. Swedenberg, Jr., and Vinton Dearing. 20 vols. Berkeley: U of California P, 1956–89. Print.

DuBois, W. E. B. *The Souls of Black Folk*. *Writings*. Ed. Nathan Huggins. New York: Lit. Classics of the United States, 1986. 357–547. Print.

Duffy, Maureen. *The Passionate Shepherdess: Aphra Behn, 1640–89*. London: Cape, 1977. Print.

Du Tertre, Jean-Baptiste. *Histoire générale des Antilles habitées par les François*. 4 vols. Paris, 1667–71. Print.

Egerton, Douglas R., et al. *The Atlantic World: A History, 1400–1888*. Wheeling: Davidson, 2007. Print.

Ekirch, A. Roger. *Bound for America: The Transportation of British Convicts to the Colonies, 1718–1775*. New York: Oxford UP, 1987. Print.

Eltis, David, and David Richardson. *Atlas of the Transatlantic Slave Trade*. New Haven: Yale UP, 2010. Print.

Equiano, Olaudah. The Interesting Narrative *and Other Writings*. Ed. Vincent Carretta. 1995. New York: Penguin, 2003. Print.

———. "The Interesting Narrative of the Life of Olaudah Equiano." Excerpt. Damrosch et al. 2A: 216–24.

Fabian, Johannes. *Time and the Other: How Anthropology Makes Its Object*. New York: Columbia UP, 1983. Print.

Felsenstein, Frank. *English Trader, Indian Maid: Representing Gender, Race, and Slavery in the New World: An Inkle and Yarico Reader*. Baltimore: Johns Hopkins UP, 1999. Print.

Felski, Rita. *Uses of Literature*. Malden: Blackwell, 2008. Print.

Ferguson, Margaret. "The Authorial Ciphers of Aphra Behn." *The Cambridge Companion to English Literature, 1650–1740*. Ed. Steven N. Zwicker. Cambridge: Cambridge UP, 1998. 225–49. Print.

———. "Juggling the Categories of Race, Class, and Gender: Aphra Behn's *Oroonoko*." *Women's Studies* 19 (1991): 159–81. Print.

———. "Juggling the Categories of Race, Class, and Gender: Aphra Behn's *Oroonoko*." Hendricks and Parker 209–24.

———. "News from the New World: Miscegenous Romance in Aphra Behn's *Oroonoko* and *The Widow Ranter*." *The Production of English Renaissance Culture*. Ed. David Lee Miller, Sharon O'Dair, and Harold Weber. Ithaca: Cornell UP, 1994. 151–89. Print.

Ferguson, Moira. "*Oroonoko:* Birth of a Paradigm." *New Literary History* 23.2 (1992): 339–59. Print.

———. "*Oroonoko*: Birth of a Paradigm." Iwanisziw, *Troping* 1–15.

———. *Subject to Others: British Women Writers and Colonial Slavery, 1670–1834.* New York: Routledge, 1992. Print.

Fish, Stanley. *Surprised by Sin: The Reader in* Paradise Lost. 2nd ed. Cambridge: Harvard UP, 1997. Print.

Foster, Shirley. *Across New Worlds: Nineteenth-Century Women Travellers and Their Writings*. New York: Harvester, 1990. Print.

Frangos, Jennifer, and Cristobal Silva, eds. *Teaching the Transatlantic Eighteenth Century*. Cambridge: Cambridge Scholars, 2010. Print.

Frohock, Richard. *Heroes of Empire: The British Imperial Protagonist in America, 1596–1764*. Newark: U of Delaware P, 2004. Print.

———. "Violence and Awe: The Foundations of Government in Aphra Behn's New World Settings." *Eighteenth-Century Fiction* 8.4 (1996): 437–52. Print.

Gale, Theophilus. *Of Philologie*. 2nd ed. London: Thomas Gilbert, 1672. *EEBO*. Web. 18 Jan. 2010. Part 1 of *The Court of the Gentiles*.

Gallagher, Catherine. "The Author-Monarch and the Royal Slave: *Oroonoko* and the Blackness of Representation." Gallagher, *Nobody's Story* 49–87.

———. "Colonial Life in Suriname." Behn, *Oroonoko* [Gallagher] 337–41.

———. Introduction. Behn, *Oroonoko* [Gallagher] 3–25.

———. *Nobody's Story: The Vanishing Acts of Women Writers in the Marketplace, 1670 to 1820*. Berkeley: U of California P, 1994. Print.

———. "Who Was That Masked Woman? The Prostitute and the Playwright in the Plays of Aphra Behn." Gallagher, *Nobody's Story* 1–48.

Gautier, Gary. "Slavery and the Fashioning of Race in *Oroonoko*, *Robinson Crusoe*, and Equiano's *Life*." *Eighteenth Century: Theory and Interpretation* 42.2 (2001): 161–79. Print.

Gay, John. *The Beggar's Opera*. Damrosch et al. 1C: 2557–603.

Genette, Gérard. *Narrative Discourse: An Essay in Method*. Trans. Jane E. Lewin. Ithaca: Cornell UP, 1980. Print.

Gevirtz, Karen Bloom. *Life after Death: Widows and the English Novel, Defoe to Austen*. Newark: U of Delaware P, 2005. Print.

Gilbert, Sandra M., and Susan Gubar, eds. *The Norton Anthology of Literature by Women*. 3rd ed. 2 vols. New York: Norton, 2007. Print.

Giles, Paul. *Transatlantic Insurrections: British Culture and the Formation of American Literature, 1730–1860*. Philadelphia: U of Pennsylvania P, 2001. Print.

Godwyn, Morgan. *The Negro's and Indians Advocate*. London, 1680. Print.

Goldberg, Jonathan. *Desiring Women Writing: English Renaissance Examples*. Stanford: Stanford UP, 1997. Print.

Goreau, Angeline. *Reconstructing Aphra: A Social Biography of Aphra Behn*. New York: Dial, 1980. Print.

Gray, Thomas. "Elegy Written in a Churchyard." 1751. Damrosch et al. 1C: 2670–73.

Greenblatt, Stephen. *Marvelous Possessions: The Wonder of the New World*. Oxford: Clarendon, 1991. Print.

Greenblatt, Stephen, and M. H. Abrams, eds. *The Norton Anthology of English Literature*. 8th ed. 2 vols. New York: Norton, 2006. Print.

Greer, Germaine. "Aphra Behn." *Teaching Tudor and Stuart Women Writers*. Ed. Susanne Woods and Margaret P. Hannay. New York: MLA, 2000. 204–13. Print. Options for Teaching.

Grignion, Charles. Frontispiece. *Oroonoko: A Tragedy*. By Thomas Southerne. London, 1776. Print.

Grotius, Hugo. *The Rights of War and Peace*. 1625. Ed. Richard Tuck. Indianapolis: Liberty Fund, 2005. Print.

Guffey, George. "Aphra Behn's *Oroonoko*: Occasion and Accomplishment." *Two English Novelists: Aphra Behn and Anthony Trollope: Papers Read at a Clark Library Seminar, May 11, 1974*. Los Angeles: William Andrews Clark Memorial Lib., 1975. 3–41. Print.

Hainsworth, Roger, and Christine Churches. *The Anglo-Dutch Naval Wars, 1652–1674*. Stroud: Sutton, 1998. Print.

Hale, Robert Beverly, and Terrence Coyle. *Albinus on Anatomy with Eighty Original Albinus Plates*. 1979. New York: Dover, 1988. Print.

Hall, Kim. *Things of Darkness: Economies of Race and Gender in Early Modern England*. Ithaca: Cornell UP, 1995. Print.

Harriot, Thomas. *A Briefe and True Report of the New Found Land of Virginia*. Frankfurt: 1590. Introd. Paul Hulton. New York: Dover, 1972. Print.

Hartley, L. P. *The Go-Between*. 1953. Ed. Colm Tóibín. New York: New York Rev. of Books, 2002. Print.

Hemans, Felicia. "The Wife of Asdrubal." 1819. Damrosch et al. 2A: 836–38.

Hendricks, Margo. "Alliance and Exile: Aphra Behn's Racial Identity." *Maids and Mistresses, Cousins and Queens: Women's Alliances in Early Modern England*. Ed. Susan Frye and Karen Robertson. Oxford: Oxford UP, 1999. 259–73. Print.

———. "Civility, Barbarism, and Aphra Behn's *The Widow Ranter*." Hendricks and Parker 225–39.

Hendricks, Margo, and Patricia Parker, eds. *Women, "Race," and Writing in the Early Modern Period*. London: Routledge, 1994. Print.

Hickeringill, Edmund. "From *Jamaica Viewed* (1661)." Krise 31–50.

Hodes, Martha, ed. *Sex, Love, Race: Crossing Boundaries in North American History*. New York: New York UP, 1999. Print.

Hoegberg, David E. "Caesar's Toils: Allusion and Rebellion in *Oroonoko*." *Eighteenth-Century Fiction* 7.3 (1995): 239–58. Print.

Hogarth, William. *The Rake's Progress*. Damrosch et al. 1C: 2603–12.

Holmesland, Oddvar. "Aphra Behn's *Oroonoko*: Cultural Dialectics and the Novel." *ELH* 68.1 (2001): 57–79. Print.

Homer. *The Odyssey*. Trans. Richmond Lattimore. New York: Harper, 1967. Print.

Horsman, Reginald. *Race and Manifest Destiny: The Origins of American Racial Anglo-Saxonism*. Cambridge: Harvard UP, 1981. Print.

Hudson, Nicholas. "From 'Nation' to 'Race': The Origin of Racial Classification in Eighteenth-Century Thought." *Eighteenth-Century Studies* 29.3 (1996): 247–64. Print.

Hughes, Derek. "*Oroonoko*: The Editor and the Marketplace." O'Donnell and Dhuicq 154–61.

———. "Race, Gender, and Scholarly Practice: Aphra Behn's *Oroonoko*." *Essays in Criticism* 52.1 (2002): 1–22. Print.

———. *The Theatre of Aphra Behn*. Basingstoke: Palgrave, 2001. Print.

———, ed. *Versions of Blackness: Key Texts on Slavery from the Seventeenth Century*. Cambridge: Cambridge UP, 2007. Print.

Hughes, Derek, and Janet Todd, eds. *The Cambridge Companion to Aphra Behn*. Cambridge: Cambridge UP, 2004. Print.

Hughes, Merritt Y. "Satan Hero?" Introduction. Milton, *Paradise Lost* 177–79.

Hutchinson, Lucy. *Memoirs of the Life of Colonel Hutchinson: With a Fragment of Autobiography*. Ed. N. H. Keeble. London: Dent, 1995. Print.

Hutner, Heidi, ed. *Rereading Aphra Behn: History, Theory, and Criticism*. Charlottesville: UP of Virginia, 1993. Print.

Iwanisziw, Susan B. "Behn's Novel Investment in *Oroonoko*: Kingship, Slavery, and Tobacco in English Colonialism." *South Atlantic Review* 63.2 (1998): 75–98. Print.

———, ed. Oroonoko*: Adaptations and Offshoots*. Aldershot: Ashgate, 2006. Print.

———, ed. *Troping* Oroonoko *from Behn to Bandele*. Aldershot: Ashgate, 2004. Print.

Jacob, Margaret C. *Strangers Nowhere in the World: The Rise of Cosmopolitanism in Early Modern Europe*. Philadelphia: U of Pennsylvania P, 2006. Print.

Jefferson, Thomas. *Notes on the State of Virginia*. 1785. *Thomas Jefferson: Writings*. Ed. Merrill D. Peterson. New York: Lib. of Amer., 1984. Print.

Jehlen, Myra, and Michael Warner, eds. *The English Literatures of America, 1500–1800*. New York: Routledge, 1997. Print.

Jones, J. R. *The Anglo-Dutch Wars of the Seventeenth Century*. London: Longman, 1996. Print.

Joyce, James. "Eveline." 1914. Damrosch et al. 2C: 2222–25.

Keats, John. "La belle dame sans merci." 1819; 1848. Damrosch et al. 2A: 904–06.

Kemp, Martin, and Marina Wallace. *Spectacular Bodies: The Art and Science of the Human Body from Leonardo to Now*. London: Hayward Gallery; Berkeley: U of California P, 2000. Print.

Kipling, Rudyard. "Gunga Din." 1890. Damrosch et al. 2B: 1742–43.

———. "White Man's Burden." 1899. Damrosch et al. 2B: 1777–78.

Knight, Sarah Kemble. *The Journal of Madame Knight*. Introd. George Parker Winship. 1920. Whitefish: Kessinger, 2004. Print.

Kowaleski-Wallace, Elizabeth. *The British Slave Trade and Public Memory*. New York: Columbia UP, 2006. Print.

———. "Transnationalism and Performance in 'Biyi Bandele's *Oroonoko*." *PMLA* 119.2 (2004): 265–81. Print.

Kreis-Schinck, Annette. *Women, Writing, and the Theater in the Early Modern Period: The Plays of Aphra Behn and Suzanne Centlivre*. Madison: Fairleigh Dickinson UP; London: Assoc. UPs, 2001. Print.

Krise, Thomas W., ed. *Caribbeana: An Anthology of English Literature of the West Indies, 1657–1777*. Chicago: U of Chicago P, 1999. Print.

Kroll, Richard. "'Tales of Love and Gallantry': The Politics of *Oroonoko*." *Huntington Library Quarterly* 67.4 (2004): 573–605. Print.

[La Calprenède, Gauthier de Costes, Sieur de]. *Cassandra*. [1644–50]. Trans. Sir Charles Cotterell. London, 1661. Print.

LaCombe, Michael A. "Warner, Thomas (*c.*1630–1674)." *Oxford Dictionary of National Biography*. Oxford UP, 2004. Web. 11 Apr. 2010.

———. "Willoughby, Francis, Fifth Baron Willoughby of Parham." *Oxford Dictionary of National Biography*. Oxford UP, 2004. Web. 17 July 2010.

Lamarra, Annamaria, and Bernard Dhuicq. *Aphra Behn: In/and Our Time*. Proc. of the Aphra Behn Europe Symposium, Naples, 7–9 July 2005. Paris: d'En Face, 2008. Print.

Laqueur, Thomas. *Making Sex: Body and Gender from the Greeks to Freud*. Cambridge: Harvard UP, 1990. Print.

The Lawes Resolutions of Womens Rights; or, The Lawes Provision for Woemen. London, 1632. Facsim. ed. New York: Garland, 1978. Print.

Lennox, Charlotte. *The Female Quixote; or, The Adventures of Arabella*. Ed. Margaret Dalziel. Introd. Margaret Anne Doody. Oxford: Oxford UP, 1989. Print. Oxford World's Classics.

Lerner, Gerda. *The Creation of Patriarchy*. New York: Oxford UP, 1996. Print.

Lilley, Kate. Introduction. Cavendish, Blazing World ix–xxxii.

Lindemann, Mary. *Medicine and Society in Early Modern Europe*. Cambridge: Cambridge UP, 1999. Print. New Approaches to European History.

Link, Frederick. *Aphra Behn*. New York: Twayne, 1968. Print.

Lipking, Joanna. "Confusing Matters." Todd, *Aphra Behn Studies* 259–81.

———. "The New World of Slavery." Behn, *Oroonoko; or, The Royal Slave* [Lipking] 75–89.

———. "'Others,' Slaves, and Colonists in *Oroonoko*." Hughes and Todd 166–87.

———. Preface. Behn, *Oroonoko; or, The Royal Slave* [Lipking] xi–xvi.

Locke, John. *An Essay concerning Humane Understanding in Four Books*. London, 1690. *EEBO*. Web. 13 Feb. 2010.

———. "Of the Conduct of the Understanding." *Posthumous Works of Mr. John Locke*. London, 1706. 1–137. *Google Books*. Web. 16 Jan. 2010.

———. *Second Treatise of Government*. 1690. Ed. C. B. Macpherson. Indianapolis: Hackett, 1980. Print.

Loomba, Ania, and Jonathan Burton, eds. *Race in Early Modern England: A Documentary Companion*. New York: Palgrave, 2007. Print.

Lusts Dominion; or, The Lascivious Queen: A Tragedie. London, 1657. Print.

Machiavelli, Niccolò. *The Art of War*. 1521. Trans. Ellis Farneworth. Ed. and introd. Neal Wood. Rev. ed. New York: Da Capo, 1990. Print.

Macpherson, C. B. *The Political Theory of Possessive Individualism, Hobbes to Locke*. Oxford: Clarendon, 1962. Print.

Marshall, P. J., ed. *The Oxford History of the British Empire: The Eighteenth Century*. New York: Oxford UP, 1998. Print.

Marvell, Andrew. "Bermudas." *Luminarium*. Luminarium.org, n.d. Web. 17 Aug. 2009.

Matsuoka, Mitsuharu. "Aphra Behn." *The Victorian Literary Studies Archive: Hyper-Concordance*. Graduate School of Langs. and Cultures, Nagoya U, n.d. Web. 26 Oct. 2009.

McHale, Brian. "Free Indirect Discourse: A Survey of Recent Accounts." *PTL: A Journal for Descriptive Poetics and Theory* 3 (1978): 249–87. Print.

McKeon, Michael. *The Origins of the English Novel, 1600–1740*. Baltimore: Johns Hopkins UP, 1987. Print.

Melville, Herman. *Typee*. Ed. Arthur Stedman. New York, 1892. *Project Gutenberg*. Web. 17 Aug. 2009. N. pag.

Metzger, Lore. Introduction. Behn, *Oroonoko* [Metzger] ix–xv.

Milton, John. *Complete Poems and Major Prose*. Ed. Merritt Y. Hughes. 1957. Cambridge: Hackett, 2003. Print.

———. Introduction. Milton, *Complete Poems* 173–210.

———. *Paradise Lost*. Milton, *Complete Poems* 173–469.

Montagu, Mary Wortley. "The Reasons That Induced Dr. S. to Write a Poem Called *The Lady's Dressing Room*." Damrosch et al. 1C: 2350–52.

———. From *The Turkish Embassy Letters*. 1717. Damrosch et al. 1C: 2544–48.

Montrose, Louis. "The Work of Gender in the Discourse of Discovery." *New World Encounters*. Ed. Stephen Greenblatt. Berkeley: U of California P, 1993. 177–217. Print.

More, Thomas. *Utopia*. Greenblatt and Abrams 1: 521–90.

Morrison, Toni. *Beloved*. New York: Knopf, 1987. Print.

———. "Black Matters." *Playing in the Dark: Whiteness and the Literary Imagination*. Cambridge: Harvard UP, 1992. 3–28. Print.

Munns, Jessica. "Reviving *Oroonoko* 'in the Scene': From Thomas Southerne to 'Biyi Bandele." Iwanisziw, *Troping* 174–93.

Nelson, Holly Faith, and Sharon Alker. "Memory, Monuments, and Melancholic Genius in Margaret Cavendish's *Bell in Campo*." *Eighteenth-Century Fiction* 21.1 (2008): 13–35. Print.

Newell, Stephanie. "'Paracolonial' Networks: Some Speculations on Local Readerships in Colonial West Africa." *Interventions* 3.3 (2001): 336–54. Print.

Newman, Gerald. *The Rise of English Nationalism: A Cultural History, 1740–1830*. Rev. ed. New York: St. Martin's, 1997. Print.

Nixon, Cheryl L. "Accounting for the Self: Teaching *Robinson Crusoe* at a Business School." *Approaches to Teaching Defoe's* Robinson Crusoe. Ed. Maximillian E. Novak and Carl Fisher. New York: MLA, 2005. 207–15. Print.

Novak, Maximillian E., and David Stuart Rodes. Introduction. Southerne, *Oroonoko* [Novak and Rodes] xiii–xlii.

Nussbaum, Felicity. "Black Women: Why Imoinda Turns White." *The Limits of the Human: Fictions of Anomaly, Race, and Gender in the Long Eighteenth Century*. Cambridge: Cambridge UP, 2003. 151–88. Print.

Nutton, Vivian. "The Fatal Embrace: Galen and the History of Ancient Medicine." *Science in Context* 18.1 (2005): 111–21. Web. 17 Feb. 2010.

"Oblige." *The Oxford English Dictionary*. 2nd ed. 1989. Print.

O'Donnell, Mary Ann. *Aphra Behn: An Annotated Bibliography of Primary and Secondary Sources*. 1986. 2nd ed. Aldershot: Ashgate, 2004. Print.

———."Aphra Behn: The Documentary Record." Hughes and Todd 1–11.

———. "Chronology." Hughes and Todd xi–xxii.

———. "Myth and Mythmaking in the Works of Aphra Behn." O'Donnell, Dhuicq, and Leduc 101–10.

O'Donnell, Mary Ann, and Bernard Dhuicq, eds. *Aphra Behn (1640-1689): Le modele européen*. Entrevaux: Bilingua GA, 2005. Print. Proc. of conf., Sorbonne, 7–9 July 2003.

O'Donnell, Mary Ann, Bernard Dhuicq, and Guyonne Leduc, eds. *Aphra Behn (1640–1689): Identity, Alterity, Ambiguity*. Paris: L'Harmattan, 2000. Print.

Ogilby, John. *Africa*. London, 1670. *EEBO*. Web. 26 Oct. 2009.

Orlando: Women's Writing in the British Isles from the Beginnings to the Present. Ed. Susan Brown, Patricia Clements, and Isobel Grundy. Cambridge UP, n.d. Web. 26 Oct. 2009.

Ortiz, Joseph M. "Arms and the Woman: Narrative, Imperialism, and Virgilian Memoria in Aphra Behn's *Oroonoko*." *Studies in the Novel* 34.2 (2002): 119–40. *Literature Online*. Web. 2 June 2009.

Owens, W. R., and Lizbeth Goodman, eds. *Shakespeare, Aphra Behn and the Canon*. London: Routledge, 1996. Print.

Pacheco, Anita. "Royalism and Honor in Aphra Behn's *Oroonoko*." *SEL* 34 (1994): 491–503. Print.

Paulson, Ronald. "Dryden and the Energies of Satire." *The Cambridge Companion to John Dryden*. Ed. Steven N. Zwicker. Cambridge: Cambridge UP, 2004. 37–58. Print.

Pearson, Jacqueline. "Gender and Narrative in the Fiction of Aphra Behn." *Review of English Studies* ns 42.165 (1991): 40–56; 42.166 (1991): 179–90. Print.

Penn, William. *A Letter from William Penn . . . to the Committee of the Free Society of Traders of That Province, Residing in London*. [London], 1683. Print.

[Phillips, Edward.] *The New World of Words; or, A General English Dictionary*. 4th ed. London, 1678. *EEBO*. Web. 23 Jan. 2010.

Pitts, Joseph. *A Faithful Account of the Religion and Manners of the Mahometans . . . with an Account of the Author's Being Taken Captive; the Turks' Cruelty to Him; and of His Escape*. London, 1731. *ECCO*. Web. 11 May 2010.

Platt, Harrison Gray, Jr. "Astrea and Celadon: An Untouched Portrait of Aphra Behn." *PMLA* 49.2 (1934): 544–59. Print.

Pope, Alexander. "Epistle II: To a Lady: Of the Characteristics of Women." Black et al. 479–84.

———. *The Rape of the Lock*. Damrosch et al. 1C: 2471–91.

Pratt, Mary Louise. *Imperial Eyes: Travel Writing and Transculturation*. London: Routledge, 1992. Print.

Price, Jacob M. "The Imperial Economy, 1700–1776." Marshall 78–104.

"Prostrate." *The Oxford English Dictionary*. 2nd ed. 1989. Print.

"Prostration." *The Oxford English Dictionary*. 2nd ed. 1989. Print.

Pulsipher, Jenny Hale. "*The Widow Ranter* and Royalist Culture in Colonial Virginia." *Early American Literature* 39.1 (2004): 41–66. Print.

Purchas, Samuel. *Purchas His Pilgrimage*. London, 1613. Print.

Purkiss, Diane. *Literature, Gender and Politics during the English Civil War*. Cambridge: Cambridge UP, 2005. Print.

Rahim, Avril. *National Labour Law Profile: Trinidad and Tobago*. Intl. Labour Org., 17 June 2011. Web. 4 Aug. 2013.

Raleigh, Walter. *The Discovery of . . . Guiana*. London, 1596. *Project Gutenberg*. Web. 17 Aug. 2009.

Ramchand, Kenneth. *Introduction to the Study of West Indian Literature*. Sunbury-on-Thames: Nelson Caribbean, 1976. Print.

Ramusio, Giovanni Battista. *Navigazione e viaggi*. Ed. Marica Milanesi. 6 vols. Turin: Einaudi, 1978–88. Print.

Ray, John. Preface. *The Ornithology of Francis Willughby*. London, 1678. *EEBO*. Web. 20 Jan. 2010.

Rediker, Marcus. *The Slave Ship: A Human History*. New York: Penguin, 2007. Print.

Reinhardt, Catherine A. *Claims to Memory: Beyond Slavery and Emancipation in the French Caribbean*. New York: Berghahn, 2006. Print.

Reiss, Timothy. *The Discourse of Modernism*. Ithaca: Cornell UP, 1982. Print.

Report. *Public Advertiser* 6 Jan. 1787: 4. Print.

Richardson, John. "Modern Warfare in Early-Eighteenth-Century Poetry." *SEL* 45.3 (2005): 557–77. Web. 2 June 2009.

Rimmon-Kenan, Shlomith. *Narrative Fiction: Contemporary Poetics*. 2nd ed. London: Routledge, 2002. Print.

Rinaldo, Peter M. *Marrying the Natives: Love and Interracial Marriage*. Briarcliff Manor: DorPete, 1996. Print.

Rivero, Albert J. "Aphra Behn's *Oroonoko* and the 'Blank Spaces' of Colonial Fiction." *SEL* 39.3 (1999): 443–62. Print.

Roach, Joseph. *Cities of the Dead: Circum-atlantic Performance*. New York: Columbia UP, 1996. Print.

Robinson, Mary. "The Negro Girl." 1796. *The Poetical Works of the Late Mrs. Mary Robinson*. London: Jones, 1824. 124. *Women Writers Online*. Web. 15 Aug. 2010.

———. "To the Poet Coleridge." 1800. Damrosch et al. 2A: 604–06.

Rochefort, Charles de. *The History of Barbados, St. Christophers, Mevis, St. Vincents, Antego, Martinico, Monserrat, and the Rest of the Caribby-Islands*. Trans. J. Davies of Kidwelly. London, 1666. Print.

Rochester, John Wilmot, earl of. "The Imperfect Enjoyment." 1680. Damrosch et al. 1C: 2205–07.

Rogers, Katharine M. "Fact and Fiction in Aphra Behn's *Oroonoko*." *Studies in the Novel* 20.1 (1988): 1–5. Print.

Rose, Mary Beth. *Gender and Heroism in Early Modern English Literature*. Chicago: U of Chicago P, 2002. Print.

Rosenthal, Laura J. "Owning Oroonoko: Behn, Southerne, and the Contingencies of Property." *Renaissance Drama* 23 (1992): 25–38. Print.

———. "Owning Oroonoko: Behn, Southerne, and the Contingencies of Property." Iwanisziw, *Troping* 83–107.

Ross, Shannon. "*The Widdow Ranter*: Old World, New World—Exploring an Era's Authority Paradigms." O'Donnell, Dhuicq, and Leduc 81–90.

Rossetti, Christina. "Goblin Market." 1862. Damrosch et al. 2B: 1650–63.

Rowlandson, Mary. *The Sovereignty and Goodness of God, together with the Faithfulness of His Promises Displayed: Being a Narrative of the Captivity and Restoration of Mrs. Mary Rowlandson and Related Documents.* 1682. Ed. Neal Salisbury. Boston: Bedford, 1997. Print.

Rowson, Susanna Haswell. *Charlotte Temple.* 1794. Ed. Cathy N. Davidson. New York: Oxford UP, 1986. Print.

Rublack, Ulinka. "Fluxes: The Early Modern Body and the Emotions." Trans. Pamela Selwyn. *History Workshop Journal* 53 (2002): 1–16. Web. 17 Feb. 2010.

Salzman, Paul. Introduction. Behn, Oroonoko *and Other Writing* ix–xxiv.

Sanderson, Robert. "Sermon VII: Greenwich, July 1638." *The Works of Robert Sanderson, D. D., Sometime Bishop of Lincoln*. Vol. 1. Oxford: Oxford UP, 1854. 174–96. Print.

Sansay, Leonora. Secret History; or, The Horrors of St. Domingo *and* Laura. 1808. Ed. Michael J. Drexler. Peterborough: Broadview, 2007. Print.

Saunders, J. B. deC. M., and Charles D. O'Malley. *The Illustrations from the Works of Andreas Vesalius of Brussels*. 1950. New York: Dover, 1973. Print.

Sawday, Jonathan. *The Body Emblazoned: Dissection and the Human Body in Renaissance Culture*. London: Routledge, 1995. Print.

Schiebinger, Londa. *Nature's Body: Gender in the Making of Modern Science*. Boston: Beacon, 1993. Print.

Segal, Ronald. *The Black Diaspora: Five Centuries of the Black Experience outside Africa*. New York: Farrar, 1995. Print.

Seymour, Frances. The Story of Inkle and Yarico *and* An Epistle from Yarico to Inkle, after He Had Left Her in Slavery. 1738. Krise 141–46.

Shakespeare, William. *Othello. The Complete Works.* Ed. Alfred Harbage. New York: Viking, 1969. 1018–59. Print.

———. *Othello*. Ed. Michael Neill. Oxford: Clarendon, 2006. Print.

———. Sonnet 127. Greenblatt and Abrams B: 1073.

———. Sonnet 130. Greenblatt and Abrams B: 1074.

———. *Titus Andronicus*. Ed. Thomas L. Berger and Barbara Mowat. New York: Oxford UP, 2003. Print.

Shapin, Steven. *A Social History of Truth: Civility and Science in Seventeenth-Century England*. Chicago: U of Chicago P, 1994. Print.

Sheridan, Richard B. "The Formation of Caribbean Plantation Society, 1689–1748." Marshall 394–415.

Sidney, Philip. Sonnet 9. *Astrophil and Stella*. Greenblatt and Abrams B: 977–78.

Skinner, Gillian. *Sensibility and Economics in the Novel, 1740–1800: The Price of the Tear*. New York: St. Martin's, 1999. Print.

Smith, Adam. *Lectures on Jurisprudence*. Ed. Ronald Meek, David Daiches Raphael, and Peter Stein. Oxford: Oxford UP, 1978. Print.

Smith, Barbara Herrnstein. *Contingencies of Value: Alternative Perspectives for Critical Theory*. Cambridge: Harvard UP, 1988. Print.

Smith, Charlotte. "The Sea-View." 1800. Damrosch et al. 2A: 86.

———. "Written in the Church-Yard at Middleton in Sussex." 1800. Damrosch et al. 2A: 85.

Smith, Nigel. *Literature and Revolution in England, 1640–1660*. New Haven: Yale UP, 1994. Print.

Southerne, Thomas. *Oroonoko*. Ed. Maximillian E. Novak and David Stuart Rodes. Lincoln: U of Nebraska P, 1976. Print. Regents Restoration Drama Ser.

———. *Oroonoko*. D. Hughes, *Versions* 191–278.

"The Speech of Moses Bon Sàam." 1735. Krise 101–07.

"A Speech Made by a Black of Guardeloupe." 1709. Krise 93–100.

Spencer, Jane. *Aphra Behn's Afterlife*. Oxford: Oxford UP, 2000. Print.

———. *The Rise of the Woman Novelist: From Aphra Behn to Jane Austen*. Oxford: Blackwell, 1986. Print.

Spengemann, William C. "The Earliest American Novel: Aphra Behn's *Oroonoko*." *Nineteenth-Century Fiction* 38.4 (1984): 384–414. Print.

Spenser, Edmund. *Epithalamion*. Greenblatt and Abrams B: 907–16.

———. Sonnet 64. Greenblatt and Abrams B: 904–05.

Spillers, Hortense J. "Mama's Baby, Papa's Maybe: An American Grammar Book." *Diacritics* 17.2 (1987): 65–81. Print.

Sprat, Thomas. *The History of the Royal-Society of London, for the Improving of Natural Knowledge*. London, 1667. *EEBO*. Web. 23 Jan. 2010.

Spurr, David. *The Rhetoric of Empire: Colonial Discourse in Journalism, Travel Writing, and Imperial Administration*. Durham: Duke UP, 1993. Print.

Stapleton, M. L. *Admired and Understood: The Poetry of Aphra Behn*. Newark: U of Delaware P, 2004. Print.

Starr, G. A. "Aphra Behn and the Genealogy of the Man of Feeling." *Modern Philology* 87.4 (1990): 362–72. Print.

Staves, Susan. *A Literary History of Women's Writing in Britain, 1660–1789*. Cambridge: Cambridge UP, 2006. Print.

Steadman, John M. "The Idea of Satan as the Hero of *Paradise Lost*." *Proceedings of the American Philosophical Society* 120.4 (1976): 253–94. Web. 27 May 2009.

Stedman, John Gabriel. *Narrative of a Five Years' Expedition against the Revolted Negroes of Surinam*. 1796. 2nd ed. London: J. Johnston, 1813. *Internet Archive*. Web. 29 Aug. 2013.

———. *Narrative of a Five Years Expedition against the Revolted Negroes of Surinam: Transcribed for the First Time from the Original 1790 Manuscript*. Ed. Richard Price and Sally Price. Baltimore: Johns Hopkins UP, 1988. Print.

Steele, Richard. "*Spectator* 11." Damrosch et al. 1C: 2333–35.

Stewart, Jeffrey C. Introduction. *Narrative of Sojourner Truth*. New York: Oxford UP, 1991. xxxiii. *Google Books*. Web. 1 May 2010. Schomburg Lib. of Nineteenth-Century Black Women Writers.

Strachey, William. *A True Reportory of the Wreck and Redemption of Sir Thomas Gates*. 1610. *The Bedford Companion to Shakespeare: An Introduction with Documents*. Ed. Russ McDonald. 2nd ed. Boston: Bedford–St. Martin's, 2001. 180–82. Print.

Sugg, Richard. *Murder after Death: Literature and Anatomy in Early Modern England*. Ithaca: Cornell UP, 2007. Print.

"Survey." *The Oxford English Dictionary*. 2nd ed. 1989. Print.

Sussman, Charlotte. "The Other Problem with Women: Reproduction and Slave Culture in Aphra Behn's *Oroonoko*." Behn, *Oroonoko; or, The Royal Slave* [Lipking] 246–56.

Swift, Jonathan. *Gulliver's Travels*. 1726. Greenblatt and Abrams B: 2323–462.

———. "The Lady's Dressing Room." 1732. Damrosch et al. 1C: 2346–49.

———. "A Modest Proposal." Damrosch et al. 1C: 2431–37.

———. "Part 4." *Gulliver's Travels*. Damrosch et al. 1C: 2371–426.

Sypher, Wylie. *Guinea's Captive Kings: British Anti-slavery Literature in the Eighteenth Century*. 1942. New York: Octagon, 1969. Print.

Thomas, Hugh. *The Slave Trade: The Story of the Atlantic Slave Trade, 1440–1870*. New York: Simon, 1997. Print.

Thomas, Nicholas. *Entangled Objects: Exchange, Material Culture, and Colonialism in the Pacific*. Cambridge: Harvard UP, 1991. Print.

Todd, Janet, ed. *Aphra Behn*. New York: St. Martin's, 1999. Print. New Casebooks.

———, ed. *Aphra Behn Studies*. Cambridge: Cambridge UP, 1996. Print.

———. "Behn, Aphra (1640?–1689)." *Oxford Dictionary of National Biography*. Oxford UP, 2004. Web. 6 July 2010.

———. *The Critical Fortunes of Aphra Behn*. Columbia: Camden, 1998. Print.

———. *Gender, Art, and Death*. New York: Continuum, 1993. Print.

———. *The Secret Life of Aphra Behn*. London: Deutsch; New Brunswick: Rutgers UP, 1996. Print.

[Tryon, Thomas]. *Friendly Advice to the Gentlemen-Planters of the East and West Indies*. [London], 1684. Krise 51–76.

Twagilimana, Aimable. *Race and Gender in the Making of an African American Literary Tradition*. New York: Garland, 1997. Print.

Valiant, Sharon. "Maria Sibylla Merian: Recovering an Eighteenth-Century Legend." *Eighteenth-Century Studies* 3 (1993): 467–79. Print.

Vespucci, Amerigo. *Mundus Novus: Letters from a New World: Amerigo Vespucci's Discovery of America*. Trans. David Jacobson. Ed. Luciano Formisano. New York: Marsilio, 1992. Print.

Walcott, Derek. "A Frowsty Fragrance." Rev. of *Caribbeana*, by Thomas Krise. *New York Review of Books* 15 June 2000: 57+. Print.

Warren, George. *An Impartial Description of Surinam upon the Continent of Guiana in America*. London, 1667. *Google Books*. Web. 17 Aug. 2009.

Wheeler, Roxann. *The Complexion of Race: Categories of Difference in Eighteenth-Century British Culture*. Philadelphia: U of Pennsylvania P, 2000. Print.

———. "Racial Legacies: The Speaking Countenance and the Character Sketch in the Novel." *A Companion to the Eighteenth-Century English Novel and Culture*. Ed. Paula R. Backscheider and Catherine Ingrassia. Malden: Blackwell, 2005. 419–40. Print.

White, Ed. "Captaine Smith, Colonial Novelist." *American Literature* 75.3 (2003): 487–513. Print.

Widmayer, Anne F. "The Politics of Adapting Behn's *Oroonoko*." *Comparative Drama* 37.2 (2003): 189–223. Print.

Williams, Eric. *Capitalism and Slavery*. Richmond: Byrd, 1944. Print.

Williams, Roger. *A Key into the Language of America*. 1643. Ed. John J. Teunissen and Evelyn J. Hinz. Detroit: Wayne State UP, 1973. Print.

Winkfield, Unca Eliza, pseud. *The Female American; or, The Adventures of Unca Eliza Winkfield*. 1767. Ed. Michelle Burnham. Peterborough: Broadview, 2001. Print.

Wiseman, Susan J. *Aphra Behn*. 2nd ed. Tavistock: Northcote; British Council, 2007. Print. Writers and Their Works.

Wollstonecraft, Mary. *Vindication of the Rights of Woman*. 1792. Damrosch et al. 2A: 288–310.

Woodcock, George. *The Incomparable Aphra*. London: Boardman, 1948. Print. Rpt. as *Aphra Behn: The English Sappho*. 1989.

Woolf, Virginia. *Mrs. Dalloway*. 1925. Damrosch et al. 2C: 2338–437.

———. *A Room of One's Own*. 1929. New York: Harcourt, 1989. Print.

Wordsworth, Dorothy. "From the *Grasmere Journals*, 1800–02." Damrosch et al. 2A: 538–44.

Wordsworth, William. "Composed upon Westminster's Bridge, September 3, 1802." Damrosch et al. 2A: 436.

———. "Lines Written a Few Miles above Tintern Abbey." 1798. Damrosch et al. 2A: 390–94.

Wycherley, William. *The Country Wife*. *The Plays of William Wycherley*. Ed. Peter Holland. Cambridge: Cambridge UP, 1981. 227–341. Print.

Yeats, William Butler. "Easter 1916." 1924. Damrosch et al. 2C: 2181–83.

———. "Leda and the Swan." 1916. Damrosch et al. 2C: 2194–95.

Zimbardo, Rose A. *At Zero Point: Discourse, Culture, and Satire in Restoration England*. Lexington: UP of Kentucky, 1998. Print.

Zook, Melinda. "Contextualizing Aphra Behn: Plays, Politics, and Party, 1679–1689." *Women Writers and the Early Modern British Political Tradition*. Ed. Hilda Smith. Cambridge: Cambridge UP, 1998. 75–93. Print.

INDEX

Modern Language Association of America

Approaches to Teaching World Literature

Achebe's Things Fall Apart. Ed. Bernth Lindfors. 1991.
Arthurian Tradition. Ed. Maureen Fries and Jeanie Watson. 1992.
Atwood's The Handmaid's Tale *and Other Works*. Ed. Sharon R. Wilson, Thomas B. Friedman, and Shannon Hengen. 1996.
Austen's Emma. Ed. Marcia McClintock Folsom. 2004.
Austen's Pride and Prejudice. Ed. Marcia McClintock Folsom. 1993.
Balzac's Old Goriot. Ed. Michal Peled Ginsburg. 2000.
Baudelaire's Flowers of Evil. Ed. Laurence M. Porter. 2000.
Beckett's Waiting for Godot. Ed. June Schlueter and Enoch Brater. 1991.
Behn's Oroonoko. Ed. Cynthia Richards and Mary Ann O'Donnell. 2014.
Beowulf. Ed. Jess B. Bessinger, Jr., and Robert F. Yeager. 1984.
Blake's Songs of Innocence and of Experience. Ed. Robert F. Gleckner and Mark L. Greenberg. 1989.
Boccaccio's Decameron. Ed. James H. McGregor. 2000.
British Women Poets of the Romantic Period. Ed. Stephen C. Behrendt and Harriet Kramer Linkin. 1997.
Charlotte Brontë's Jane Eyre. Ed. Diane Long Hoeveler and Beth Lau. 1993.
Emily Brontë's Wuthering Heights. Ed. Sue Lonoff and Terri A. Hasseler. 2006.
Byron's Poetry. Ed. Frederick W. Shilstone. 1991.
Works of Italo Calvino. Ed. Franco Ricci. 2013.
Camus's The Plague. Ed. Steven G. Kellman. 1985.
Writings of Bartolomé de Las Casas. Ed. Santa Arias and Eyda M. Merediz. 2008.
Cather's My Ántonia. Ed. Susan J. Rosowski. 1989.
Cervantes' Don Quixote. Ed. Richard Bjornson. 1984.
Chaucer's Canterbury Tales. Ed. Joseph Gibaldi. 1980.
Chaucer's Troilus and Criseyde *and the Shorter Poems*. Ed. Tison Pugh and Angela Jane Weisl. 2006.
Chopin's The Awakening. Ed. Bernard Koloski. 1988.
Coleridge's Poetry and Prose. Ed. Richard E. Matlak. 1991.
Collodi's Pinocchio *and Its Adaptations*. Ed. Michael Sherberg. 2006.
Conrad's "Heart of Darkness" and "The Secret Sharer." Ed. Hunt Hawkins and Brian W. Shaffer. 2002.
Dante's Divine Comedy. Ed. Carole Slade. 1982.
Defoe's Robinson Crusoe. Ed. Maximillian E. Novak and Carl Fisher. 2005.
DeLillo's White Noise. Ed. Tim Engles and John N. Duvall. 2006.
Dickens's Bleak House. Ed. John O. Jordan and Gordon Bigelow. 2009.
Dickens's David Copperfield. Ed. Richard J. Dunn. 1984.
Dickinson's Poetry. Ed. Robin Riley Fast and Christine Mack Gordon. 1989.
Narrative of the Life of Frederick Douglass. Ed. James C. Hall. 1999.

Works of John Dryden. Ed. Jayne Lewis and Lisa Zunshine. 2013.
Duras's Ourika. Ed. Mary Ellen Birkett and Christopher Rivers. 2009.
Early Modern Spanish Drama. Ed. Laura R. Bass and Margaret R. Greer. 2006.
Eliot's Middlemarch. Ed. Kathleen Blake. 1990.
Eliot's Poetry and Plays. Ed. Jewel Spears Brooker. 1988.
Shorter Elizabethan Poetry. Ed. Patrick Cheney and Anne Lake Prescott. 2000.
Ellison's Invisible Man. Ed. Susan Resneck Parr and Pancho Savery. 1989.
English Renaissance Drama. Ed. Karen Bamford and Alexander Leggatt. 2002.
Works of Louise Erdrich. Ed. Gregg Sarris, Connie A. Jacobs, and James R. Giles. 2004.
Dramas of Euripides. Ed. Robin Mitchell-Boyask. 2002.
Faulkner's As I Lay Dying. Ed. Patrick O'Donnell and Lynda Zwinger. 2011.
Faulkner's The Sound and the Fury. Ed. Stephen Hahn and Arthur F. Kinney. 1996.
Fitzgerald's The Great Gatsby. Ed. Jackson R. Bryer and Nancy P. VanArsdale. 2009.
Flaubert's Madame Bovary. Ed. Laurence M. Porter and Eugene F. Gray. 1995.
García Márquez's One Hundred Years of Solitude. Ed. María Elena de Valdés and Mario J. Valdés. 1990.
Gilman's "The Yellow Wall-Paper" and Herland. Ed. Denise D. Knight and Cynthia J. Davis. 2003.
Goethe's Faust. Ed. Douglas J. McMillan. 1987.
Gothic Fiction: The British and American Traditions. Ed. Diane Long Hoeveler and Tamar Heller. 2003.
Poetry of John Gower. Ed. R. F. Yeager and Brian W. Gastle. 2011.
Grass's The Tin Drum. Ed. Monika Shafi. 2008.
H.D.'s Poetry and Prose. Ed. Annette Debo and Lara Vetter. 2011.
Hebrew Bible as Literature in Translation. Ed. Barry N. Olshen and Yael S. Feldman. 1989.
Homer's Iliad *and* Odyssey. Ed. Kostas Myrsiades. 1987.
Hurston's Their Eyes Were Watching God *and Other Works*. Ed. John Lowe. 2009.
Ibsen's A Doll House. Ed. Yvonne Shafer. 1985.
Henry James's Daisy Miller *and* The Turn of the Screw. Ed. Kimberly C. Reed and Peter G. Beidler. 2005.
Works of Samuel Johnson. Ed. David R. Anderson and Gwin J. Kolb. 1993.
Joyce's Ulysses. Ed. Kathleen McCormick and Erwin R. Steinberg. 1993.
Works of Sor Juana Inés de la Cruz. Ed. Emilie L. Bergmann and Stacey Schlau. 2007.
Kafka's Short Fiction. Ed. Richard T. Gray. 1995.
Keats's Poetry. Ed. Walter H. Evert and Jack W. Rhodes. 1991.
Kingston's The Woman Warrior. Ed. Shirley Geok-lin Lim. 1991.
Lafayette's The Princess of Clèves. Ed. Faith E. Beasley and Katharine Ann Jensen. 1998.
Works of D. H. Lawrence. Ed. M. Elizabeth Sargent and Garry Watson. 2001.
Lazarillo de Tormes *and the Picaresque Tradition*. Ed. Anne J. Cruz. 2009.

Lessing's The Golden Notebook. Ed. Carey Kaplan and Ellen Cronan Rose. 1989.
Works of Naguib Mahfouz. Ed. Waïl S. Hassan and Susan Muaddi Darraj. 2011.
Mann's Death in Venice *and Other Short Fiction*. Ed. Jeffrey B. Berlin. 1992.
Marguerite de Navarre's Heptameron. Ed. Colette H. Winn. 2007.
Works of Carmen Martín Gaite. Ed. Joan L. Brown. 2013.
Medieval English Drama. Ed. Richard K. Emmerson. 1990.
Melville's Moby-Dick. Ed. Martin Bickman. 1985.
Metaphysical Poets. Ed. Sidney Gottlieb. 1990.
Miller's Death of a Salesman. Ed. Matthew C. Roudané. 1995.
Milton's Paradise Lost. First edition. Ed. Galbraith M. Crump. 1986.
Milton's Paradise Lost. Second edition. Ed. Peter C. Herman. 2012.
Milton's Shorter Poetry and Prose. Ed. Peter C. Herman. 2007.
Molière's Tartuffe *and Other Plays*. Ed. James F. Gaines and Michael S. Koppisch. 1995.
Momaday's The Way to Rainy Mountain. Ed. Kenneth M. Roemer. 1988.
Montaigne's Essays. Ed. Patrick Henry. 1994.
Novels of Toni Morrison. Ed. Nellie Y. McKay and Kathryn Earle. 1997.
Murasaki Shikibu's The Tale of Genji. Ed. Edward Kamens. 1993.
Nabokov's Lolita. Ed. Zoran Kuzmanovich and Galya Diment. 2008.
Works of Ngũgĩ wa Thiong'o. Ed. Oliver Lovesey. 2012.
Works of Tim O'Brien. Ed. Alex Vernon and Catherine Calloway. 2010.
Works of Ovid and the Ovidian Tradition. Ed. Barbara Weiden Boyd and Cora Fox. 2010.
Poe's Prose and Poetry. Ed. Jeffrey Andrew Weinstock and Tony Magistrale. 2008.
Pope's Poetry. Ed. Wallace Jackson and R. Paul Yoder. 1993.
Proust's Fiction and Criticism. Ed. Elyane Dezon-Jones and Inge Crosman Wimmers. 2003.
Puig's Kiss of the Spider Woman. Ed. Daniel Balderston and Francine Masiello. 2007.
Pynchon's The Crying of Lot 49 *and Other Works.* Ed. Thomas H. Schaub. 2008.
Works of François Rabelais. Ed. Todd W. Reeser and Floyd Gray. 2011.
Novels of Samuel Richardson. Ed. Lisa Zunshine and Jocelyn Harris. 2006.
Rousseau's Confessions *and* Reveries of the Solitary Walker. Ed. John C. O'Neal and Ourida Mostefai. 2003.
Scott's Waverley Novels. Ed. Evan Gottlieb and Ian Duncan. 2009.
Shakespeare's Hamlet. Ed. Bernice W. Kliman. 2001.
Shakespeare's King Lear. Ed. Robert H. Ray. 1986.
Shakespeare's Othello. Ed. Peter Erickson and Maurice Hunt. 2005.
Shakespeare's Romeo and Juliet. Ed. Maurice Hunt. 2000.
Shakespeare's The Taming of the Shrew. Ed. Margaret Dupuis and Grace Tiffany. 2013.
Shakespeare's The Tempest *and Other Late Romances.* Ed. Maurice Hunt. 1992.
Shelley's Frankenstein. Ed. Stephen C. Behrendt. 1990.

Shelley's Poetry. Ed. Spencer Hall. 1990.

Sir Gawain and the Green Knight. Ed. Miriam Youngerman Miller and Jane Chance. 1986.

Song of Roland. Ed. William W. Kibler and Leslie Zarker Morgan. 2006.

Spenser's Faerie Queene. Ed. David Lee Miller and Alexander Dunlop. 1994.

Stendhal's The Red and the Black. Ed. Dean de la Motte and Stirling Haig. 1999.

Sterne's Tristram Shandy. Ed. Melvyn New. 1989.

Works of Robert Louis Stevenson. Ed. Caroline McCracken-Flesher. 2013.

The Story of the Stone (Dream of the Red Chamber). Ed. Andrew Schonebaum and Tina Lu. 2012.

Stowe's Uncle Tom's Cabin. Ed. Elizabeth Ammons and Susan Belasco. 2000.

Swift's Gulliver's Travels. Ed. Edward J. Rielly. 1988.

Teresa of Ávila and the Spanish Mystics. Ed. Alison Weber. 2009.

Thoreau's Walden *and Other Works*. Ed. Richard J. Schneider. 1996.

Tolstoy's Anna Karenina. Ed. Liza Knapp and Amy Mandelker. 2003.

Vergil's Aeneid. Ed. William S. Anderson and Lorina N. Quartarone. 2002.

Voltaire's Candide. Ed. Renée Waldinger. 1987.

Whitman's Leaves of Grass. Ed. Donald D. Kummings. 1990.

Wiesel's Night. Ed. Alan Rosen. 2007.

Works of Oscar Wilde. Ed. Philip E. Smith II. 2008.

Woolf's Mrs. Dalloway. Ed. Eileen Barrett and Ruth O. Saxton. 2009.

Woolf's To the Lighthouse. Ed. Beth Rigel Daugherty and Mary Beth Pringle. 2001.

Wordsworth's Poetry. Ed. Spencer Hall, with Jonathan Ramsey. 1986.

Wright's Native Son. Ed. James A. Miller. 1997.